The Soul Delusion

The Soul Delusion

David P. Barash, Ph. D.
Professor of Psychology Emeritus,
University of Washington

BLOOMSBURY ACADEMIC
NEW YORK · LONDON · OXFORD · NEW DELHI · SYDNEY

BLOOMSBURY ACADEMIC
Bloomsbury Publishing Inc
1359 Broadway, New York, NY 10018, USA
50 Bedford Square, London, WC1B 3DP, UK
29 Earlsfort Terrace, Dublin 2, Ireland

BLOOMSBURY, BLOOMSBURY ACADEMIC and the Diana logo are trademarks
of Bloomsbury Publishing Plc

First published in the United States of America 2026

Copyright © David P. Barash, 2026

Cover design: Diana Nuhn
Cover image © iStock/francescoch

All rights reserved. No part of this publication may be reproduced or transmitted in any form or by any means, electronic or mechanical, including photocopying, recording, or any information storage or retrieval system, without prior permission in writing from the publishers.

Bloomsbury Publishing Inc does not have any control over, or responsibility for, any third-party websites referred to or in this book. All internet addresses given in this book were correct at the time of going to press. The author and publisher regret any inconvenience caused if addresses have changed or sites have ceased to exist, but can accept no responsibility for any such changes.

Library of Congress Cataloging-in-Publication Data Available

ISBN: HB: 979-8-8818-0568-5
ePDF: 979-8-7651-6451-8
eBook: 979-8-8818-0569-2

Typeset by Deanta Global Publishing Services, Chennai, India
Printed and bound in the United States of America

To find out more about our authors and books visit www.bloomsbury.com
and sign up for our newsletters.

"Well! I've often seen a cat without a grin," thought Alice, "but a grin without a cat! It's the most curious thing I ever saw in my life!"
— LEWIS CARROLL, *ALICE IN WONDERLAND* (1865)

I wish to propose for the reader's favorable consideration a doctrine which may, I fear, appear wildly paradoxical and subversive. The doctrine in question is this: that it is undesirable to believe in a proposition when there is no ground whatever for supposing it true.
— BERTRAND RUSSELL, "ON THE VALUE OF SCEPTICISM" (1928)

Contents

1. Grappling with the Grin 1
2. What Is It? 11
3. Escaping Death: The Cosmic Carrot 25
4. The Cosmic Stick: Hell 47
5. The Golden Helmet of Centrality 73
6. Dueling with Dualism 93
7. Purported Proofs and Practical Problems 133
8. Soul-Free! 155

Notes 187
Bibliography (Actually, Suggested Further Reading) 199
Index 205
About the Author 210

1

Grappling with the Grin

"I have put my heart and soul into this book."

Don't believe it. Although I have a heart, I do not have a soul. And neither do you, dear reader. Few ideas are as widespread and as deeply held, but as I hope to show, few are as unsupported, ridiculous, and, on balance, harmful. In the universe of under-examined crackpot ideas, the soul is due for a takedown.

This is a serious book—critics might call it a polemic—about one of humanity's silliest ideas. The word "soul" often means something that is deeply held as part of one's self-definition. No problem here. My beef is with its theological meaning: a disembodied cat's grin that nonetheless manages to inhabit the body and is immaterial, the seat of consciousness, God-given, immortal, that somehow influences one's behavior and is also influenced by it so that it goes either to heaven or to hell (or maybe purgatory) when you die. When considering a topic under discussion—or, more often, dispute—a frequent conciliatory trope is that it is "something about which rational people can disagree." Not in this case. The existence of a soul in its theistic sense as an ineffable divine core of humanity is something that rational people can and should discard, just as adults reject the existence of Santa Claus, and, increasingly, the Devil.

I believe this in the depths of my nonexistent soul.

The Soul Delusion is intended as an intellectual wake-up call, encouraging people to think critically about something widely taken for granted. It will assert that the emperor has no clothes and no soul. We'll start (Chapter 2) with a quick overview of what has been meant by the soul, a brief historical survey along with some cross-cultural commonalities (and significant local variations) but focusing on the perspectives of the Abrahamic religions, especially Christianity. Next come four chapters that critically examine why the soul exerts such appeal to so many. We explore the cosmic carrot of immortality; that is, the promise that their souls offer human beings escape from their greatest fear, namely death (Chapter 3). In assessing the soul's enticement, we then consider how and why it has been taken up by organized religion, which employs immortality's scary side, the cosmic stick, namely fear of hell. And so, Chapter 4 continues our exploration of (mostly Christian) eschatology by reviewing the threat of eternal damnation, whereby believers are manipulated into obedience, and, often as not, also terrified that they will be condemned to unending misery. In such cases, the Cheshire Cat's grin is more of a snarl, useful for organized religion, not despite its frightening aspect, but because of it (Figure 1.1).

The third component of the soul's four-pronged appeal is its egotistic satisfaction. It's not just a cliché but a genuine fact that each of us is small and the world, very big. Moreover, everyone yearns to be validated as not just unique but important. This makes it especially gratifying to know that

Figure 1.1 *Alice encounters the Cheshire Cat. Here, the Cat is intact and his grin isn't menacing. Source: Original illustration by John Tenniel, 1865; colorized in 1911.*

despite how insignificant we are in the Great Scheme of Things, each of us carries our own special, spiritually sanctioned guarantee of God's concern, our personalized quixotic Golden Helmet of Mambrino. And so, in Chapter 5, we look into the delusive allure of personal centrality.

Among the attractions of soul-power, we then confront an issue of long-standing philosophical concern: its role as a stand-in for consciousness and the human mind. We know ourselves to be made of physical matter, and yet we also have subjective experiences that seem incompatible with our flesh-based bodily selves. The resulting "dualism" has sought to reconcile these two seemingly disparate facts by positing that mind and matter are separate, although they somehow meet in our lived experience. Dualism doesn't logically necessitate a soul, but it does require some kind of immaterial, incomprehensible influence that is pretty darn close to a version of spirituality and that transcends or ignores science. Accordingly, Chapter 6 duels with the delusion that is dualism, concluding that it is almost as nonsensical as the soul and certainly not a solution to what has been called "the hard problem of consciousness."

Faith has been described (okay, criticized) as belief without evidence. Faithful soul-believers have on occasion tried to point to—or generate—supporting evidence. Chapter 7 evaluates that evidence and, unsurprisingly, finds it not only unconvincing but no evidence at all. At the same time, there is no way to demonstrate that the soul *doesn't* exist, which raises this question: Who bears responsibility for proving an assertion, especially one that goes counter to science as well as everyday experience? The penultimate chapter also points out that if we take souls seriously, some challenging and maybe even insurmountable problems arise. Finally, Chapter 8 considers the implications of not having a soul and—more to the point—acknowledging it.

For some, it may be novel and dispiriting to consider their soullessness, something too true to be good, leading to a dark night of the no-soul. But if Socrates was correct and the unexamined life isn't worth living, what about the soul, which has long been at least as unexamined as most people's lives? Whether or not we are ensouled, isn't it worthwhile to critically examine the notion? All the more so because the soul has increasingly become something of an intellectual embarrassment, even for many traditional believers, a kind of madwoman in the attic that isn't much discussed in polite company. Or if it is, its illogic and contradictions are rarely interrogated.

Socrates was condemned to death in part because his constant questioning, his unending recourse to logic and argumentation, was downright annoying. The phrase "know thyself," sometimes attributed to Socrates, actually predated him, having been carved above the Temple of Apollo. This Delphic pronouncement, for all its wisdom, can be downright onerous if taken seriously. I'm no Socrates; perhaps the only thing he has in common with this book is that it, too, will be seen as annoying. Maybe even dangerous. So be it. We can also agree that any harm it causes will be minor. Very few soul-believers—if any—will change their minds in the unlikely event that they read it. To those already soul-skeptical and perhaps looking for arguments to support your position, I hope you won't be disappointed.

As for the few who might be moved to join the ranks of the soul-deniers, will they be consumed with self-loathing, disgusted with themselves, or with each other once deprived of their belief? T. S. Eliot warned that humankind cannot bear too much reality. I disagree, even though there are aspects of reality that are genuinely painful. It is precisely because reality is so important and on occasion distasteful that we'd better stop denying it and start honestly facing our world, perhaps beginning with ourselves. Facing reality doesn't have to be dispiriting (as you'll see in chapter 8), despite those who will doubtless feel bereft if they confront their soullessness. They may regret losing the promise of heaven but probably won't miss the terrors of hell. I hope, moreover, to show that by prioritizing real, material, time-limited life over an immaterial fantasy, recognizing one's soullessness offers the prospect of acknowledging and improving things in the genuine here-and-now, with a newfound appreciation of the present moment.

We live in our own precious, private, subjective experiences, each of us immersed in hopes, fears, thoughts, memories, desires, urges, regrets, expectations, and a vast kaleidoscope of perceptions, from the smell of roses, the taste of chocolate, to the almost-infinite array of sights and sounds that make up each complex and one-of-a-kind existence. For some people, especially those religiously inclined, this ineffable selfhood is tantamount to, or at least evidence for a divine soul. But it needn't be. In fact, it isn't. Rather, it is testimony to the fact that each of us has a *mind*, a biological product of our complex nervous system and something that is wonderful and fascinating, and also susceptible to scientific inquiry, without bringing in anything supernatural. Our minds also have no implications for heaven or hell—except that there is nothing in us that points to either of these destinations. In short, there aren't two worlds, the natural and the supernatural. There's only one, and for better and worse, it isn't the latter.

Marianne Moore wrote that poetry embodies "imaginary gardens with real toads in them." She could as well have been writing about the soul, imaginary (albeit not quite a garden) and infected with real toads[1]: fear of hell, delusions about personal immortality and the source of our minds, permission to ill-treat animals, support for antiabortion policies, and, most of all, a bold-faced, reality-denying lie. Christian and Islamic traditions in particular argue that our soul urges us upward, toward God and goodness, while simultaneously imagining it as a heavy anchor that drags us down, an ineluctable consequence of our sinful, disobedient past.

It is not my goal to dance on the grave of the soul (well, actually it is). A more realistic hope is to penetrate some of the smug, unquestioned certainty that surrounds this topic. It won't be easy. It has been said that the Devil's best trick was convincing people, especially in modern times, that he doesn't exist. Maybe the soul's best trick has been convincing many people that it does. More likely, we've been really good at convincing ourselves, mostly because there are many aspects of the religious soul that meet—rather, pander to—certain psychological needs. In the chapters to come, we'll examine some of them. We'll also look at the liberation that comes with being soul-free.

Ecclesiastes writes, wisely, that "In much wisdom there is much vexation, and he who increases knowledge increases sorrow." In *The Soul Delusion*, I'm hoping to offer a bit of knowledge and maybe even a hint of wisdom. The bottom line for some, however, may also be an increase in sorrow. Along with it, however, perhaps a decrease in unexamined credulity. The ecologist Warren Hays wasn't shy about critiquing the latter, employing a little-used but potentially useful word, "stupefacient":

Stupefacients are officially defined as something producing a stupor, but the word could more usefully be expanded to include anything inhibiting clear thought: mind-altering chemicals, mental illness, plain old-fashioned stupidity, refusal or inability to look deeply into things. Other stupefacients would include impulsivity, social conformity, hedonic distraction, stubbornness. And, not least, belief in god and his henchman and fellow traveler, the soul, which carry with them their own burden (or benefit) of mental inhibitions and are themselves inspired by some of these factors, notably conformity to social practice along with the various factors that make us susceptible to accepting that we "must" have a soul, all the more so if we don't bother to think about it.[2]

Anyone seeking insight should bother to think about all sorts of things. They shouldn't be reluctant to "look deeply into their soul," to investigate whatever lies in their mind—conscious or not—that impacts behavior. But don't expect to find any immaterial or supernatural underpinnings. What you will find is that the soul, and the whole belief structure erected around it, is a human construct. You could "sell you soul," which says nothing about a transaction with the Devil, but a lot about a possible decision to betray some deep-seated human ethical principles—seated, that is, in your conscious or unconscious life, but either way in your physically real nervous system. And if you are so fortunate as to find your soulmate, it will be in this life, not anywhere else, despite what various stupefacients might have you believe.

Although I have the soul directly in my sights, I shall often take aim at the supernatural as well, about which Joseph Conrad observed:

> I am too firm in my consciousness of the marvelous to be ever fascinated by the mere supernatural which (take it any way you like) is but a manufactured article, the fabrication of minds insensitive to the intimate delicacies of our relation to the dead and to the living, in their countless multitudes; a desecration of our tenderest memories; an outrage on our dignity.[3]

Throughout this book, I'll write soul without quotation marks, although I'd prefer to set it off with scare quotes each time, because the "soul has long been thought . . . " or even "the soul supposedly . . . " suggests that it is real. I'll avoid doing so, however, because it would become tedious. But please, when you see that ridiculous word, add a pinch of pixie dust and put in your own imagined quotation marks, because let's face it: Considered objectively, the theological soul is a bizarre concept, at odds with everything we know about how the world works. Moreover, even though the idea occasionally offers some consolation, we'll see that it is also hugely problematic, not only logically and scientifically but also downright hurtful.

Time to lay my cards on the table (bare my soul?). You probably intuit that I'm an atheist, a word that warrants two designations: soft and hard. Soft atheists do not believe in any of the gods currently on offer. Hard atheists go one step further, not merely disbelieving in a particular proposed deity but maintaining more affirmatively that there is no such dude, anywhere, anyhow. Richard Dawkins pointed out that even traditional monotheists are atheists in that there are thousands of different gods in the human-generated pantheon, of which even the most devout (especially them!) deny the existence of all but their chosen one. Atheists, hard and soft, simply go the devout one step further and disbelieve in that one too.

Alas, there is currently no word analogous to "atheism" that applies to the soul. The English word "psyche" comes from the Greek, *psukhē*, which means "breath," "life," or "soul." So, here is a neologism: apsychism,[4] meaning disbelief in the soul, with such disbelievers therefore being apsychists. Moreover, apsychists, like atheists, come in soft and hard versions: Soft apsychists don't believe in the existence of a soul; while hard apsychists don't merely not-believe, they actively maintain that there is no such thing.[5]

I'm not just a hard apsychist but also a dyed-in-the-wool materialist, not someone who values a Rolex watch more than knowing what time it is, but who is convinced that the universe consists of matter and energy, and nothing more. No supernatural substances or powers, no divine entities who take a personal interest in what we wear, eat, read, see, think, what words we speak, with whom and how we have sex, and who might choose to suspend natural principles in response to the right kind of prayers—but who, curiously enough, are reported to have done so only in the absence of any reliable documentation, usually very long ago—and who send our souls to heaven or to hell.

The Soul Delusion is a paean to scientific materialism, the principle that all events follow from the action of matter and energy, even if some of the precise workings have yet to be pinned down by science, and even if much of that matter and energy—for example, the "dark" forms—is currently up for grabs, along with understanding what the hell quantum physics is all about. But the *fact* of neurobiology underlying consciousness, along with the permanence of death, just like the correctness of physics, is not up for grabs. Arguments favoring the soul are obliged, instead, to deny scientific materialism, mostly because of religious insistence, plus, as we'll see, a kind of subjective plausibility, psychological pressure, and a heavy dose of wishful thinking.

"It is a common sentence," wrote George Eliot in her novel, *Daniel Deronda*, "that knowledge is power; but who hath duly considered or set forth the power of ignorance?" There is something even more powerful than ignorance, namely delusion, defined by psychiatry's *Diagnostic and Statistical Manual 5* as a "false fixed belief that is not amenable to change in light of conflicting evidence."[6] Welcome to the soul delusion—the phenomenon and the book.

No reputable scientist searches for the soul's material cause, just as none search for invisible trolls hiding under bridges, because scientists don't bother studying nonsensical notions that are immune to serious inquiry. When, albeit rarely, the soul-struck seek to buttress soul-hood with empirical evidence, negative findings are simply bypassed as irrelevant because, of course, the soul isn't fundamentally material after all. It's not of this world, so it can't be disproved. "The brighter the light," according to Carl Jung, "the darker the shadow." In *The Soul Delusion*, I try to shine a light, however bright. If I succeed, perhaps it will only induce some readers to burrow deeper into the darkness of their delusive belief. If so, then soul be it.

It might appear to atheist[7] readers that in critiquing the soul this book is seeking to deflate something that already has no air inside, that it pushes against an open door only to grapple futilely with a grin that lacks a cat. Maybe so, but if nothing else, I also hope to provide a useful resource for the steadily increasing demographic of atheists, agnostics, and "nones." My message—that the soul is a fiction—comports with science, even as it departs from much conventional thinking, or rather, from what many people claim to believe, often without thinking about it at all. Time to do so.

In the early 1990s, political scientist James Overton looked into what constitutes acceptable discourse surrounding a given topic. His focus was the range of policy options that politicians could realistically propose and expect to be taken seriously. Subsequently, the concept has been generalized to the Overton Window, identifying what is likely to be taken seriously, hence open to discussion without placing its proponents beyond the pale. When it comes to debunking the soul, that Overton Window is currently rather narrow, although not closed altogether. This book is an effort to widen it.

But we should be under no illusions as to success. Consider that evolution by natural selection is among the most intellectually coherent and empirically supported findings of modern science, and yet, in the United States, significantly more people hold to the biblical version of creation. Nonetheless, it might be easier for them to give up on creationism than on the existence of their souls, because for most people evolution is a story of what happened in the distant past, whereas their souls ostensibly exist in the here-and-now. Even though fundamentalists may bristle at the implication that they have "descended from monkeys," evolutionary theory generally carries fewer implications for their personal identity than does their soul. Some believers have squared their religious faith with "revealed" biology by satisfying themselves that evolution is the way God specially created human beings, along with the rest of the living world. For them, natural selection is acceptable (it fits, barely, inside their Overton Window) as a kind of divine tool, wielded on behalf of all life, but not necessarily with consequences for themselves. Belief in one's soul, by contrast, is intensely personal, something not readily abandoned, logic and evidence be damned.

A peculiar trait among most believers in the paranormal playbook—in the soul, but also angels, astral projection, astrology,[8] aura massage, breatharianism (look it up), clairvoyance, conjuration (ditto), creationism, crystal power, demons, djinns, ESP, exorcism, fairies, fortune-telling, goblins, haunted houses, hobgoblins, occultation, Ouija boards, palm reading, precognition, predestination, psychokinesis, pyramid power, reincarnation, seances, second sight, telepathy, and all the rest—is their insistence that whenever scientific materialism has not definitively pinned down all possible loose ends about a phenomenon or an idiosyncratic report, however unlikely and unverified, they are fully justified, even somehow obliged, to attribute it to supernatural forces instead of simply acknowledging, as do essentially all scientists, that We Simply Don't Know. Yet. Science's embrace of thus-far-unsolved problems as grist for the materialist research mill is consistent with Occam's Razor, which urges us not to add unnecessary explanatory entities. Invoking the supernatural is worse than unnecessary because it isn't an explanation, but an evasion.

Nonetheless, I don't expect that this book will induce many readers to question their assumptions about the reality of the soul, or, even less likely, to embrace their own soullessness (although Chapter 8 tries). For anyone open-minded and/or on the fence, please read on. You have nothing to lose but your souls. Which is to say, you have nothing to lose.

2

What Is It?

If apsychists[1] don't believe in the soul, what is it that they don't believe in? Here goes.

Within the Abrahamic big three—Judaism, Christianity, and Islam—Jewish doctrine is the most reticent about the soul. "As to the blissful state of the soul in the world to come," wrote the influential Jewish philosopher Moses Maimonides (twelfth century CE), "There is no way on earth in which we can comprehend or know it."[2] (Presumably we'll come to know it somewhere or somehow else.) This agnostic attitude is consistent with Judaism's lack of focus on an afterlife generally, and on heaven and hell in particular. The Hebrew Bible's "Sheol," the realm of the dead, is neither heaven nor hell but the absence of anything: "For the living know that they shall die: but the dead know not any thing, neither have they any more a reward; for the memory of them is forgotten" (Eccl. 9:5). Nonetheless, and as ever when it comes to most religious views of the soul, Judaism is heterogeneous. The Hebrew word for soul is *nefesh* or *neshamah*, which means "breath." In biblical Judaism, allusion to the soul is nearly always metaphoric rather than literal, except, paradoxically, right off the bat when God creates humanity: "And the Lord God formed man of the dust of the ground, and breathed into his nostrils the breath of life; and man became a living creature" (Gen. 2:7).

Especially in Hasidic circles and the mystical branch of Judaism known as Kabbala, the soul is taken at least somewhat seriously as the God-given self that animates each body. Moreover, each soul is or should be guided by the

Torah, the first five books of Moses, with the quality of each being a function of how closely it follows Judaic law and, therefore, how closely it adheres to God.

It is sometimes said that if you get three Jews in a room, you'll have a dozen opinions, and beliefs about the soul are no exception. Thus, although there are many Jewish interpretations of what happens after death, the dominant (although not the only) perspective is that immortality is not in the cards: "God said, 'My breath will not govern man forever, since he is flesh'" (Gen. 6:3). On the other hand, some Jewish traditions recognize a sort of afterlife, although it is safe to conclude that neither heaven nor hell figure prominently. Followers of Kabbala maintain, however, that the soul contains 613 distinct spiritual channels, each connected to its own specified part of human anatomy, and each must be purified either before death or—somehow—after. In any event, there is nothing in the Hebrew Bible and almost nothing in the extensive rabbinical commentary known as the Talmud that calls for posthumous punishment so prominent in Christian and Islamic theology.

It's not that formal Jewish doctrine is avowedly apsychist. Rather, biblical Judaism largely bypasses the question. One of those rare occasions when the soul is hinted at, although not specifically referenced, occurs in the Book of Daniel, the last addition to the Hebrew Bible: "And they that be wise shall shine as the brightness of the firmament; and they that turn many to righteousness will be as the stars for ever and ever" (Dan. 12:3). Even here, the majority interpretation favors metaphor ("*as* the stars") rather than a claim of literal immortality.[3]

Seeing the soul as the "breath of life" parallels many other traditions that conceive soul-stuff as the secret sauce that enlivens brute matter, although this doesn't necessarily sit well with immortality, given that one agreed-upon characteristic of living things is that they die! The majority idea, however, at least in Christianity and Islam, is that after conveying life to otherwise inert mortal bodies, the soul keeps on carrying on, typically reuniting with its body somehow, sometime, somewhere after death.

By contrast to Judaism's largely agnostic attitude, Christianity and Islam are "all in" when it comes to the soul, notably as a chip off the Old Divine Block, conceived as immaterial, immortal, and subject to an afterlife in which it is either saved or damned. In later chapters, we'll see that immateriality and immortality are, as it were, soulmates, cut from the same mythic cloth. We'll also see (Chapter 6) that the soul is invoked—sometimes explicitly, sometimes not—as part of dualist philosophy that seeks to explain mind and consciousness as other than something that matter does, that is, the work of neurons organized as brains.

Before we take a quick dive into other concepts of the soul, let's take an even quicker look at its material alter egos, at least as developed in the early Western thought tradition. The pre-Socratic philosopher Democritus was the first to propose that everything was composed of infinitesimal particles called "atoms," which came in different varieties, colliding and combining in different ways, thus forming the real world as we know it. For Democritus, the most influential early materialist, there was nothing but atoms and the void: "Atoms and the vacuum are the beginning of the universe; and everything else exists only in opinion."[4] It is probably just coincidence that in addition to a kind of atomic theory, Democritus dreamed up the multiverse, which finds its own parallels in modern physics. In any event, Socrates hated these ideas because they conflicted with his preference for immaterial, immortal Forms, closely allied to the soul.

Epicurus was the next prominent prescientific materialist, followed later by Lucretius, who, in his immodestly titled work, *On the Nature of Things*, further developed the claim that the world was made only of physical stuff. Although he made room for a kind of materially based soul, Lucretius also argued that all things come from other things, so even his version of the soul consisted of atoms that generate consciousness and other atoms that produce sensation, all of which dissipate at death, "like smoke." Such material interpretations of reality were unpopular during the ancient, medieval, and early modern periods, overshadowed by religious belief and often violently suppressed. Versions persisted nonetheless, as with Thomas Hobbes, who, in his masterpiece, *Leviathan* (1651), wrote that "Life is but a motion of limbs, for what is the heart, but a spring; and the nerves, but so many strings; and the joints, but so many wheels, giving motion to the whole body."

Similar material (aka "physicalist") perspectives eventually gave rise to Enlightenment rationality and the emerging scientific revolution, with its insistence that the world is exclusively material and that, moreover, physical events arise exclusively from other physical events, and not from immaterial—that is, supernatural—causes. Which brings us back to the soul.

Prior to around the year 1700 (just before the Enlightenment, broadly identified), soul and mind were used interchangeably. In fact, many of the great early modern scientists such as Robert Boyle (chemistry), Isaac Newton (physics), and William Harvey (biology) were devout Christians who, even as they studied the material nature of the physical world, readily accepted—at least, publicly—the existence of the human soul as something apart from organic nature. At the same time, there arose undercurrents of association between mind and matter, the previously heretical notion that thoughts are somehow produced by bodies, notably in the work of physician-philosopher John Locke, who suggested it, oh so gently. This began to undercut strict reliance on the biblical soul as sole source of mental experience. Mental illness in particular began to be seen as brain-based disease, rather than possession by the Devil. Along with this tentative opening of the mind-brain Overton Window, there came advances not only in medicine but also in social tolerance, owing to acceptance that there are different brains, hence different minds for different people, rather than one "correct" soul implanted by God, with deviations due only to sin or demonic possession.

Nonetheless, the soul persisted, as it does even today.

As with all theology, there is significant diversity within Christianity—between Protestant, Catholic, and Orthodox conceptions—and also within each version, just as Protestantism, for example, ranges from evangelical fundamentalism to the more relaxed and philosophical approaches of modern-day Quakers and Unitarians. Although all Christian traditions continue to espouse the existence of a human soul, there is considerable doctrinal diversity, for example whether these souls are inherently sinful, how they can be saved (e.g., by good works or through faith alone), what happens to those souls that haven't embraced God and Jesus (either because of benighted resistance or because they died before having a chance to save themselves, or were never exposed to missionary outreach), whether souls will be reunited with their bodies and, if so, at what point after death and what will be the state of those bodies, when and how souls are instantiated into a person And a whole lot more.

Nonetheless, despite the abundant disputes and unanswered questions, there is no doubt that Christian perspectives embrace the human soul. Animals, not so much. Although formal doctrine is conflicted when it comes to whether animals have souls, the majority opinion is that they don't. Pope Pius IX was definite about this, adding that they lack consciousness; he even opposed the establishment of an Italian branch of the Society for the Prevention of Cruelty to Animals. On the other hand, there is an unconfirmed claim that when he met a boy who was grieving over the death of his dog, Pope Paul VI comforted him with the following: "One day, we will see our animals again in the eternity of Christ. Paradise is open to all God's creatures."[5] Pope Benedict, by contrast, was unambiguous that it isn't, because "they" are clearly sans souls. That's currently the official line.

It is widely assumed that the idea of a human soul independent of the body came from the Bible, but in fact, it seems more due to Augustine, whose Platonism (separating body from soul) was promptly incorporated into traditional Christian belief. In the *Phaedo*, Plato adduces various arguments, none of them traditionally "religious," for the existence of the soul and for its immortality. Channeling his teacher, Socrates, Plato equated mind and soul, claiming that both are immaterial because Forms (e.g., justice, beauty, mathematics) are immaterial and the soul can only perceive something if it is similarly composed. If, as Alfred North Whitehead suggested, all Western philosophy is a footnote to Plato, then Plato precedes Descartes as the founder of dualism (see Chapter 6).

For Plato, however, the soul itself was tripartite, made of appetitive, spirited, and rational components. Of these, the appetitive—located in the gut—controlled our appetites, including sex and hunger. The spirited, located in the heart, handled bodily and mental energy while also mediating between lowly appetite and the highest: the rational, which inhabits the head. Plato employed a metaphor in which the rational soul was a charioteer forever struggling to control two troublesome horses, one appetitive and one spirited.

The three-pronged Platonic soul lives imprisoned within its associated body, ever trying to escape and join its natural home, the world of Forms, when that body dies. Most of the time, however, it gets stuck in yet another body and thus finds itself reincarnated against its will, analogous to its Hindu fate. Some scholars suggest that such convergence indicates that there was contact between ancient Greece and India.

Plato's student Aristotle also taught that there were three kinds of souls, but he was less concerned with dividing up the human experience than with situating people among other living things. According to Aristotle's *De Anima*, the "vegetative soul" was shared with all animals and even plants. It governed survival, growth, and reproduction. Next in the hierarchy is the "sensitive soul," limited to humans and animals, and overseeing movement and sensation. Finally comes the "rational soul," unique to humans and no other critters; it underpins intelligent thought. Aristotle differed from Plato in that he denied reincarnation, but as to the soul's immortality, his views are ambiguous.

Then there's Aquinas, especially his 1253 book, *On Being and Essence*—being being body and essence being soul. We can say that for Aquinas and much of Christian thought after him, the existentialists' credo ("existence precedes essence") is reversed because essence (soul) precedes existence (body). By contrast, here is the foremost twentieth-century existentialist, Jean-Paul Sartre: "If one considers an article of manufacture, as, for example, a book or a paper knife, one sees that it has been made by an artisan who had a conception of it. . . . Man first of all exists, encounters himself, surges up in the world—and defines himself afterwards."[6]

Christian doctrine maintains the opposite: that essence (i.e., our soul) precedes existence, and is overwhelmingly more important, being a gift from God. Christian theology tends to devalue the body as mere dross, a kind of unavoidable collateral damage mandated by our being part of the mortal, material world compared to the soul, which emanates from God and is our connection to the divine.

Aquinas accepted Aristotle's tripartite soul, with the proviso that the part reserved for human beings—the rational component—was immortal. For Aquinas, the soul cannot be localized into just one body part (heart, liver, brain) but is *tota in toto corpore*, present everywhere in the body, from which it cannot be separated except in death. At this point, Christian doctrine diverges. Martin Luther maintained that the soul dies with the body, remaining insensate until the resurrection of the dead. John Calvin claimed that it retained consciousness after the death of its body. Some Protestant traditions currently believe that when a body dies, its soul is promptly judged and sent either to heaven or hell, a doctrine shared by the Catholic and Eastern Orthodox churches. Others maintain that even immortality isn't guaranteed and is decided by divine dictat depending on whether the person has accepted Jesus in their mortal life. Calvinist tradition maintains that the soul's ultimate fate is determined by God alone, independent of whatever actions the body may undertake. To believe otherwise is sacrilege, claiming that mere human beings can coerce God.

Islam, by contrast, appears to have a more-or-less unitary perspective on the soul. In the Qur'an, it is referred to as *nafs* (life breath) and *rūḥ* (spirit). Similar to Jewish doctrine, the Qur'an mostly concludes that humanity can't fathom it: "If they ask you [Mohammed], say 'The soul is of the affair of my Lord. And mankind has not been given of knowledge, except a little'" (Sura 17:85). According to the hadith (sayings of Mohammed), this "little" includes that each fetus gets its soul 120 days after conception, by which time it has become a "lump of flesh," whereupon Allah sends an angel to breathe life into it. Once again, we get a connection between soul and life, specifically life as respiration. After breathing a life-giving soul into the fetus, an angel identifies the future of each: its subsequent livelihood, the nature of its mortal deeds, how and when its body will die, and whether the soul will then be blessed or damned.

The Qur'an is especially clear that a disobedient soul is in for big trouble:

When the sun shall be darkened,
When the stars shall be thrown down,
When the mountains shall be set moving,
When the pregnant camels shall be neglected,
When the savage beasts shall be mustered,
When the seas shall be set boiling, . . .
When hell shall be set blazing,
When paradise shall be brought nigh,
Then shall a soul know what it has produced. (Sura 81:1–14)

Traditional belief among most Christians, Muslims, and at least some Jews is that upon death of the body one's soul persists in a separate world. Most of the ancient Greeks believed similarly, although afterlife for them was boringly low-key, involving sad, vague "shades" who—consistent with the English understanding of that word—flit about in an ill-lit, understated existence. Something like this was also the case among the ancient Egyptians, but only for those whose bodies are preserved as mummies, because the body was thought to be essential for the soul to persevere.

Many, although not all, current religions maintain that the soul continues after its body's demise, being rehoused anew. This is, loosely speaking, the general view among Hindus, Jains, Sikhs, many Hasidic Jews, and most Druse Muslims.

If the ubiquity of a belief speaks to its verity, then the soul must be real, even though viewed historically and across different social groups, it is immensely variable. Gandhi wrote that "all religions are true," which sounds delightfully ecumenical, but is less than satisfying when applied to the soul. Nonetheless, some patterns are nearly universal. Souls almost always reside inside their associated bodies and are defined as immaterial, in contrast to their fleshy housing. Immortality is another close, but not quite invariant characteristic. Also widespread, but not immutable, is the ability to travel independent of their bodies, sometimes after death but also during sleep. Dreams are widely seen as demonstrating not only that the soul is real, but that it occupies its own unique plane of reality. Whatever that means.

The Hindu soul resembles its Christian and Islamic counterpart when it comes to immateriality and immortality, but with two major differences. For one, the soul (*atman*, or "self") is conceived as merely a local, personalized part of the greater world-soul (*brahman*, closer to Western "God"), so each soul—yours, mine, everyone's—has always existed, extending back into the infinite past. Second, the Hindu soul is subject to regular reincarnations following the death of its body, including excursions into different kinds of animals, depending on its accumulated *karma*. Acquire bad *karma* and you might end up a cockroach in the next life. The final desired liberation from this process of repetitive birth and rebirth—oversimplified as *nirvana*—somewhat resembles the Western concept of heaven, although conceived as a respite from the cycle of birth-and-rebirth rather than as an abode of eternal delight.

On a practical level, the Hindu soul is a three-edged sword. Combined with *karma*, it has a prosocial moral dimension, inducing people to behave well. But it also justifies inequity and the caste system: People in bad situations are there because they deserve it, due to their own bad behavior in past lives. Finally, it has paved the way for mass murder.[7] The *Bhagavad Gita* is revered as the central kernel of Hindu devotion. In it, the god Krishna argues with the warrior Arjuna, who had resisted fighting in a civil war that would involve killing many of his relatives. Krishna convinces Arjuna to put aside his qualms and partake in the slaughter, because "For the soul there is neither birth nor death at any time. He is unborn, eternal, ever-existing, and primeval. . . . He is not slain when the body is slain." So, because you can only kill the body and not the soul, confidence in reincarnation and in the transience of current lives means that killing is not such a big deal.

The soul-belief of Jains, by contrast, reaches an alternative extreme, embracing life-affirming consequences of reincarnation. Jainism unequivocally condemns killing other living things—any of which, after all, might be one's deceased great-grandparents. Devout Jains, if they can afford it, commission servants to walk in front of them and sweep the path, to avoid stepping on any small organisms. Often, Jains will automatically brush a chair with their hand before sitting down.

There is a small but surprisingly influential coterie of people in the modern Western world who claim to recall their past lives. Not surprisingly, however, they were never cockroaches. Inevitably they had been an Egyptian Pharaoh, or Napoleon, or for the blasphemously psychotic, Jesus or Mohammed, whereas "realistically," if their souls had occupied other bodies in the past, the overwhelming statistical likelihood is that they were some poor wretch who labored to build their boss's pyramids or maybe one among Napoleon's hundreds of thousands of human cannon-fodder who froze to death while retreating from Moscow.

Shinto tradition seems to distinguish the souls of living and dead persons, but the details are unclear and disputed. For Sikhs, "God is in the soul and the soul is in god," and according to Daoists, everyone possesses ten distinct souls, seven yin and three yang.

Buddhism embraces something like the soul, but in ways that differ from its ancestral Hindu tradition and that can be especially difficult for Westerners to grasp. The Buddhist conception of the soul, *anatman*—different from the Hindu *atman*—denies that it has any independent existence, insisting on the connectedness of all things and therefore disputing the presence of any separate, independent self, including soul-selves.

A frequent metaphor among Buddhists is a flame that is passed from one candle (the body) to the next. Upon death, the body is left behind, but the soul/flame gets rehoused in a new one. But like a flame, it has no separate existence. Rather, it flickers within its inhabited person and repeats the process when transmitted from one body to another. Unlike Hindus, Buddhists do not subscribe to the existence of a permanent, unchanging soul that gets transmigrated upon death from one abode to its next (they deny the persistence of *anything*), so the flame is not seen as a continuing entity. There is, however, belief in a kind of *karma* whereby one's past *actions* persist and thereby influence each current instantiation. So, the Buddhist soul-flame is somehow freighted with an individualized stamp, a kind of cosmic VIN number, something that, although not a separately existing, autonomous self-driving vehicle, is more than a mere life spark.

As with all religious belief systems, there is heterogeneity within Buddhism. When trekking in the Himalayas, one is advised to follow the Sherpa advice to pause every third day, "to let your soul catch up with your body." One needn't be a Buddhist or traveling at extreme elevation to appreciate this wisdom, one of many cases in which soul-sauce provides palatable mental seasoning to nonbelievers as well as the devout: Consider such cheerful chestnuts as soulmate, soul food, soul music, and *Chicken Soup for the Soul*.[8]

Beyond its evocation in the world's most prominent religions and its widespread invocation as a metaphor for anything deeply personal, the soul has long existed in the cross-cultural imaginings of most human social groups. Here is a quick fly-by.

Some Inuit groups maintain that everyone has at least two varieties of soul: one connected with breathing while the other accompanies each physical body as a kind of shadow. A recent review of indigenous soul-concepts explained that

Four souls are distinguished by the Cherokee. The "soul of consciousness" denotes an individual's consciousness and is located in the head or throat. The remaining three souls are the "hepatic soul" located in the liver, the "visceral soul" located in the flesh and associated with blood, and the "osseous soul," which resides in the bones and is associated with sperm. The Cherokee model of consciousness considers an individual's consciousness to have the characteristics of a soul, which expects consciousness to be a spiritual essence of the human body.[9]

Among the Oglala Sioux:

Individual mind and consciousness are believed to emerge at the moment when a fundamental force called the "Great Mystery" breathes the spirit into a human body. So, the subject's body is suggested to be potentiated by a spirit, and this act causes the emergence of mind and consciousness. However, after the death of a subject, the spirit is believed to be freed from the body and transformed into a kind of non-localized state. This non-local state is described as "being everywhere and pervading all nature." In this case, the process of disembodiment of mind and consciousness is considered to cause dissolution and non-local existence.[10]

The human imagination has concocted a dizzying kaleidoscope of soul-systems, of which the above are just two accounts, chosen almost at random from Native American traditions. Moreover, as recorded by legions of ethnographers, the diversity of soul-stories and expectations is not just limited to their human carapace. The soul has been conceived cross-culturally as not merely analogous to, but, depending on local practices, actually contained within birds, butterflies, mice, snakes, even fish and plants, as well as manifested by shadows, ghosts, dreams, fire, clouds, certain physical objects such as shooting stars and rivers, conceived as single or multiple, being ethically good, bad, or indifferent, located in the heart, liver, bones, breath, and brain.[11]

Historical—and presumably prehistoric—conceptions are equally wide-ranging. In 2008, University of Chicago archaeologists found an 800-lb stone structure (technically, a "stele") in modern-day Turkey that has been dated to the eighth century BCE.[12] Three thousand years ago, a man named Kuttamuwa had this burial monument inscribed with the request that his descendants celebrate not only his mortal life but also his postmortem "prolonged life," noting that his soul will continue to flourish inside the stone. It may be difficult even for modern soul-enthusiasts to imagine being happily encased within solid rock, but this fate evidently appealed to Kuttamuwa (Figure 2.1).

Ignoring for the time being that such conceptions have been notoriously diverse, does their ubiquity and historical persistence suggest that some version—or, somehow, all of them—is correct? Actually, no. Lots of ideas are ubiquitous and persistent, many of them based on intuition but nonetheless incorrect, such as the intuitive sense that the Earth is flat, that the Sun goes around the Earth, that hard objects really are solid even though science tells us unequivocally that they are mostly empty space, that living things have always been pretty much as they currently are, although we know that they evolved.

Given the stubborn persistence of soul-belief in the face of zero supporting evidence, there must be some powerful reasons for its ubiquity. Although the soul is diversely conceived and represents different things to different people, there are, as we have noted, some common threads, especially in the major Western religious traditions that will be the primary concern of this book: It

Figure 2.1 *Kuttamuwa stele (stone tablet), within which Mr. Kuttamuwa's soul is enclosed—or so he once believed, and maybe still does. Source: Captured by Dosseman at the Gaziantep Archaeology Museum, September 17, 2019.*

is immaterial, immortal, and God-given; it needs saving; it is associated with each human body yet also capable of independent existence (especially after death); and it is closely allied to consciousness.

We turn next to various aspects of the soul's allure, recognizing that as with Justice Potter Stewart's famous account of pornography—"I may not be able to define it, but I know it when I see it"—the soul is slippery. Even though it cannot be seen (or smelled, touched, heard, or tasted), the soul-certain agree that it is important, and that they know it when they imagine it.

3

Escaping Death
The Cosmic Carrot

With the exception of some martyrs, even sincere believers in a divine afterlife do what they can to keep from dying. "It's the last thing I'm planning to do," quipped Groucho Marx.

Fear of death makes immortality devoutly to be wished; hence, it's a key part of the soul's appeal and not just for the devout. Writing more than three centuries ago, Thomas Hobbes observed that "Fear of things invisible is the natural seed of that which every one in himself calleth religion."[1] With an eye to avoiding death, there is also the *hope* of things invisible, which many people in themselves calleth their immortal soul.

In most religious traditions, it is impossible to imagine a soul that isn't immortal. After all, a consistent defining feature is that whatever else it is—how it arises, when it arises, where it resides, where it goes after the body's death, whether it is corruptible or for sale to the Devil—the soul promises eternal life. "You can kill my body but not my soul." And of course, no one would yearn for immortality if it were not for death and the near-universal desperation to avoid it or at least transcend it by having some part of us persist afterward. Somehow. Somewhere. Sometime. Bottom line: Whether or not Souls R Us, they are a Get Out of Death Free Card. When we pass Go and cast off our mortal coil, we don't collect $200, but we get to enjoy our own personal Monopoly of death-defying eternal life.

Sigmund Freud had plenty to say about this (as he did about so many things). In *The Future of an Illusion*, he took a gimlet-eyed look at religion, concluding that the religious impulse was an attempt to revisit the comfort and security provided to young children by their parents. (Someone—I haven't ascertained who—once observed that whereas Nietzsche claimed that God is dead,[2] Freud claimed that God is Dad.) The English word "illusion" typically refers to a mirage, something misleading, often tempting but untrue. Freud used the word somewhat differently, as a belief held because we *want* it to be true. He defined illusions this way: "We call a belief an illusion when wish-fulfillment is a prominent factor in its motivation, and in doing so we disregard its relation to reality."[3] This doesn't mean that illusions must be false; they could turn out to be true. The key is that they meet two criteria: We *want* them to be true, and if that wanting is sufficiently strong, our belief in them is impervious to evidence. When it comes to meeting these two standards, avoiding death takes the cake. And the soul provides the icing.

"The life imposed on us is too hard to bear," wrote Freud, "it brings too much pain, too many disappointments, too many insoluble problems. If we are to endure it, we cannot do without palliative measures."[4] Insofar as life is hard to bear—unavoidably bringing pain, disappointments, and insoluble problems—you ain't seen nuthin' compared to death and the pain, disappointment, and problems that come with contemplating, never mind facing it. No surprise, therefore, that when it comes to Freud's palliative measures, belief in an immortal soul is so enduring that it seems immortal itself.

"Try to imagine to yourself," urged the Spanish philosopher Miguel de Unamuno,[5] "when you are wide awake, the condition of your soul when you are in a deep sleep; try to fill your consciousness with the representation of no-consciousness, and you will see the impossibility of it. The effort to comprehend it causes the most tormenting dizziness. We cannot conceive ourselves as not existing."

If, as usually understood, illusions are false perceptions (think "optical illusions")—then to be *dis*illusioned, freed from error, should be a good thing. And yet, consistent with Freud's suggestion, "disillusionment" has a negative connotation, indicating disappointment rather than satisfaction at having gotten over an illusion and experienced a helpful dose of reality. If, on the other hand, an illusion is something that we believe because it makes us feel good regardless of its truth value, then being disillusioned is indeed painful because we've been deprived of a belief for which we yearn. This chapter delves into fear of death and how an immortal soul assuages that fear by nourishing the user-friendly illusion that we can escape Unamuno's "tormenting dizziness" by not having to imagine our unimaginable nonexistence.

We are aware of our mortality; no sane person denies they will die someday. Although it is sometimes claimed that death-awareness can lead to heightened life-appreciation, most people appreciate their lives just fine without keeping their eventual demise front-and-center. It is unusual for one's living to be enhanced by contemplating one's dying. Most people don't do it, likely reflecting a solid dose of underlying psychological wisdom. In the most famous chapter ("Snow") in Thomas Mann's towering novel, *The Magic Mountain*, the main character barely survives a blizzard, gaining this insight: "For the sake of goodness and love, man shall grant death no dominion over his thoughts." And yet, whatever we choose to grant or withhold, fear of death lurks in the human unconscious, where nearly always its impact isn't benevolent.

In the oldest of all extant stories, *The Epic of Gilgamesh*, written in Sumerian around 2100 BCE, the eponymous hero becomes obsessed with overcoming death after the demise of his best buddy, a former wild-man named Enkidu. Gilgamesh, inconsolable, clings to his friend's body for several days before, in an account perhaps intentionally comic, a maggot crawls out of the corpse's nose. It takes a larval fly to get our boy to accept the reality of death—especially his own, which is now painfully front and center. Feverishly pursuing immortality, Gilgamesh travels widely and eventually meets Utnapishtim (don't we all?), who gives him several tasks, none of which Gil is able to accomplish. Eventually, he too dies.

Ernest Becker, an anthropologist heavily influenced by psychoanalysis, was especially attuned to the paradox that every person is

> out of nature and hopelessly in it; he is dual, up in the stars and yet housed in a heart-pumping, breath-gasping body that once belonged to a fish and still carries the gill-marks to prove it. His body is a material fleshy casing that is alien to him in many ways—the strangest and most repugnant way

being that it aches and bleeds and will decay and die. Man is literally split in two: he has an awareness of his own splendid uniqueness in that he sticks out of nature with a towering majesty, and yet he goes back into the ground a few feet in order to blindly and dumbly rot and disappear forever. It is a terrifying dilemma to be in and to have to live with.[6]

Immortality helps us resolve this painful dilemma by adding an afterlife—taken literally, but not too literally, because our imagination of an "afterlife" doesn't really embrace after our life. Inability to imagine death is a predictable result of our constricted mental powers, because we can only know what it is to be alive, not dead. And so, on those uncomfortable, blessedly uncommon occasions when we contemplate our own death, we do so by extending our lived experience—imagining, say, blackness or quiet or lack of physical sensation—not unlike how most sci-fi depictions of extraterrestrials, as with the bar scene in the first *Star Wars* movie, typically repurpose anatomy that we encounter in Earthbound creatures: arms, legs, heads, eyes, albeit with different dimensions and, sometimes, different arrangements. Even the motivations of our fictional extraterrestrials tend to be familiar to our earthbound selves: nearly always versions of fear, anger, sadness, greed, and the like. Although souls are supposed to be incorporeal and independent of our all-too-familiar, often sinful selves, visions of life in heaven may be sparkly, but never radically different from our prior lives: singing in a heavenly choir, sitting by a celestial throne, looking down from the clouds at earthly goings-on.

Even to contemplate something that seems less quotidian, namely utter blackness or silence, is to imagine *something* with which we are already familiar, namely our experiences—our *only* experiences, those that take place during our lives. As the seventeenth-century poet Thomas Browne observed, "The long habit of living indisposeth us for dying."[7] (It might be consoling that once we have died, we won't know that it has happened.) This indisposition is not only due to the widespread horror of contemplating a nothingness that will last forever but also because, as Unamumo observed, we literally cannot imagine that nothingness. On the other hand, if we possess an immortal soul, then some version of our consciousness will last forever, and we can transport our mental experiences into a familiar future.

Details vary, but death-based anxiety persists cross-culturally. In the *Dhammapada*, a collection of the Buddha's most cherished sayings, we read that "Like a fish that is thrown on dry land, taken from his home in the waters, the mind strives and struggles to get free from the power of death."[8] People everywhere worry and wonder about what will eventually happen to them and to their loved ones. I have witnessed "sky burials" in Tibet and northern Nepal, in which the corpse is laid out on a high, flat plateau, its body ritually sliced open and offered to vultures, while mourners chant encouragement to the deceased's soul, which is thought to take flight along with the newly-nourished birds, thence to proceed, after taking its obligatory tour in the upper air, to relocate itself in other bodies, whether human or not. When I asked one of the celebrants what would happen to the soul of the dear-departed if these procedures were not followed, the response was that it would remain trapped forever within the decaying body, where it would be seriously unhappy.[9] Despite being eternally entrapped, it would manage to exact revenge upon those who let it down. (Another English-speaking Tibetan said with a wry smile that she thought the only problem would be some underfed vultures. But hers is very much a minority view.)

Unsurprisingly, and despite the reassuring, death-defying role of the soul, *memento mori* are more often painful than pleasant. This pain should be eased by believing that someone deceased, along with those still alive, will know eternal life, including the anticipated pleasure of encountering one another in "a better place." It would also be a better emotional place, because once you are dead yet in some sense alive insofar as you find yourself able to experience God-knows-what—not to mention God himself—you're no longer worried about dying. "You only live once"? Maybe so, but there's good news: You can only die once. (Hindus excepted.)

Nonetheless, despite all the life-after-death "gospel"—a word derived from the Old English "good news"—after death the deceased's spirit often becomes frightening, as in the expectation that anyone whose sky burial is ignored or inadequately carried out will revenge themselves on the living. Ghosts aren't just scary; they often represent conscience, or revenge, past wrongdoing come back to haunt the living and remind them that misbehavior has its comeuppance. Souls, in this sense, aren't merely our better natures; frequently, they're grudge-keepers, bailiffs operating in what Michael Shermer calls the "cosmic courthouse." Wrongdoers who somehow get away with postponing their punishment until they die eventually get theirs when St. Peter gives them a one-way ticket to hell. (This is one of the rare gratifying consequences of hell, which gets it due in the next chapter.)

Ghosts aren't always terrifying, however. On occasion, because dead souls are usually so frightening, they are defanged by being made the butt of humor (viz, the movie *Ghostbusters*). In general, however, ghosts bad, souls good. Both are inseparable from fear of death and the hope that mortality can somehow be avoided or at least repackaged into eternal life. A haunted house is scary; a soul-haunted body is, or can be, reassuring.

Part of being a believing Christian or Muslim is that—assuming you have lived a sufficiently pious life and that God concurs—the "saved" will go to heaven, which is to say, their souls will do so. Bodies are more problematic. The Christian belief that Jesus is their savior comes from two seamlessly connected assumptions: that we have a soul—the entity to be saved—and that Jesus will provide it with immortality: "For God so loved the world that he gave his only begotten Son, that whosoever believeth him shall not perish but have eternal life" (Jn 3:16).

It is therefore paradoxical that even sincere believers typically mourn rather than celebrate the death of their beloveds. Are they heaven-denying hypocrites or do they simply feel selfish regret that they are deprived, albeit temporarily, of the departed's company in this life? Or is there a part that recognizes the unlikelihood that anyone survives death? Ouija boards, seances, and the claims of organized religion aside, wishful thinking and the misrepresentation of extreme terror aside as well, no one has ever returned from the dead. The potential data set is huge: Billions of people have died. Common sense argues that at least a few return trips (beyond the best-known, faith-based Christian tale) would have been validated. Moreover, there is also our shared experience of being embodied creatures. "The fact of having been born," as philosopher George Santayana pointed out, "is a bad augury for immortality."[10]

There is yet another bad augury for immortality, the simple fact that everything around us—including our own bodies—changes over time and eventually falls apart. The center doesn't hold, except, we are asked to believe, our divinely granted central self. We are surrounded by overt manifestations of the Second Law of Thermodynamics, namely that entropy increases in every closed system. This immutable phenomenon is troublesomely apparent regardless of one's background in theoretical physics. "Things fall apart," as W. B. Yeats pointed out in his poem, "The Second Coming." Messiness happens, disorder occurs, any organized system—whether living or nonliving—runs downhill unless outside energy is added. Nothing that we encounter lasts forever, with the outcome especially impactful upon living things because they are highly organized, and when they become disorganized, they die. Accordingly, even if people tend to be intuitive dualists, readily imagining a separation between mind and body (see Chapter 6), *anything* going on forever is a very Big Ask. But ask it we do. And the answer is one of the oldest and least examined of all cock-and-bull stories.

After a certain age, children seem to develop an intuitive aversion to death, especially when they learn that a beloved pet or family member is gone and won't be available to them ever again. Well, not quite "ever again," because in many households some variant of the immortality myth is proclaimed and adherence expected: Rover has gone to a better place, or Grandpa will meet you some day (presumably in heaven). Intended in most cases to assuage the grief of separation, such pronouncements cohere with many families' religious tradition, establishing an expectation that death isn't final, which, in turn, requires that something—especially something associated with a human being—survives into an afterlife, despite the lack of evidence of anything else doing so. The expectation is gratifying, although only rarely does the promise of eventual postmortem reunion cause believers to welcome their own demise.

Instead, awareness of death is nearly always shoved aside as we pursue our daily lives. Most human beings are appalled by anything that might kill them, even aside from anxiety about terminal pain and suffering. The announcement by Poe's raven—"Nevermore!"—isn't just mournful, but horrifying in its finality. Rather than "concentrating his mind wonderfully," as suggested by Samuel Johnson in the eighteenth century, awareness of one's demise is more often terrifying, which makes the ameliorating effect of soul-belief yet more welcome, even if it hardly ever goes far enough.

For believing Christians, the most important "good news" is that just as Jesus rose from the dead, they too will ultimately achieve a consummation devoutly wished: not death à la Hamlet, but to defeat death à la John Donne ("Death be not proud . . .") so that their souls, if not their bodies, achieve immortality.

> One short sleep past, we wake eternally
> And death shall be no more; Death, thou shalt die.

Fat chance. Nor does it seem that many people share Donne's taunting confidence that they will—what?—outlive death. In her poem "Dirge Without Music," Edna St. Vincent Millay expressed the majority opinion:

> Down, down, down into the darkness of the grave
> Gently they go, the beautiful, the tender, the kind;
> Quietly they go, the intelligent, the witty, the brave.
> I know. But I do not approve. And I am not resigned.

Speaking for the near-ubiquitous lack of resignation in the face of death, Yeats compared animal[11] and human attitudes toward mortality in his poem titled—of all things!—"Death."

> Nor dread nor hope attend
> A dying animal;
> A man awaits his end
> Dreading and hoping all . . .

In his poem, "Aubade," Philip Larkin lamented

> The sure extinction that we travel to . . .
> nothing more terrible, nothing more true.
> Most things may never happen: this one will . . .

Perhaps the most anguished *cri de coeur* comes from the Romanian born Nobel Prize-winning writer Elias Canetti, who long identified himself as death's "mortal enemy" and who never, till the day he died, was resigned to it. In *The Book Against Death*, Canetti recognizes that being "against death" is a hopeless cause:

> What will become of all that has piled up within you, so much, so much, an enormous stock of memories and habits, deferred questions, frozen answers, thoughts, emotions, tender feelings, hardships, everything there, everything there, what will become of it all the moment life extinguishes within you? The disproportionate size of this stockpile—and all of it for nothing?[12]

Regardless of whether we are resigned and whether it is for nothing or something, death has reasons to be proud, for, *contra* Mr. Donne, it is indeed mighty, and, for most people, dreadful. Hence the paradox that even those who deny its importance and profess confidence that it isn't really their personal termination go to great lengths to delay it. "I don't want to be immortal through my work," wrote Woody Allen. "I want to be immortal by not dying. I don't want to live on in the hearts of my countrymen; I want to live on in my apartment."[13]

There is abundant evidence that Paleolithic humans, Neanderthal as well as *Homo sapiens*, buried their dead in stylized postures, often with objects presumably intended to equip them for their afterlives.[14] The idea of some sort of soul-stuff surviving bodily death has been well documented among ancient Egyptians, attested by detailed drawings that show spirits departing their bodies and heading for their next venue. Elaborate funerary customs endowed the departed bigwig with whatever he or she needed for a satisfying existence in the nonlife to come: not just a mummified body to preserve its physical structure but also clothing, jewelry, weapons, food, even an equally deceased and possibly deified cat or two. It appears that thousands of years ago, belief in an afterlife—including the assumption that posthumous existence isn't all that different from its everyday version—wasn't much different from what most modern religions currently teach. (That Freudian illusion has had a long life.)

Given that faith in some sort of immortal hereafter that resembles the here-and-now is found in societies around the world, such expectations qualify as what anthropologists call a "cross-cultural universal," something deeply rooted in human nature, or at least, in shared human experience. (More to the point, shared hope.) This, despite the fact that no people, nowhere, have ever encountered ghosts that came back to testify "After I died, I really appreciated having my battle axe handy, and my favorite flowers to sniff," or maybe "I wish I had been better equipped," or "Thanks for worshipping my memory after I died." More likely, elaborate funerary rituals and the widespread practice of burying the deceased with useful implements and companions betokens a shared human encounter with others' death and the anxiety it provokes about their own. "I'd like to have my favorite soup bowl in my afterlife, so I bet that Uncle Harry would, too."

Here is a cold dose of reality. Damage to even a small part of the brain causes all sorts of mental disruption (see Chapters 6 and 7). Depending on the part of the brain impacted, people may lose the ability to think coherently, to see, to hear, to speak, to move different parts of their body. And yet, we are supposed to believe that when we die and the whole brain is destroyed, all our mental faculties remain as normal?

As research psychologist Julien Musolino points out:

> Your memory, your ability to talk, and your personality can be wiped out by brain damage. People who suffer from asomatognosia will assure you that part of their body, say their left arm, does not belong to them. In anosognosia, patients are convinced that a paralyzed limb is perfectly functional. The Capgras delusion is a condition in which patients sincerely believe that their loved ones have been replaced by impostors. Individuals who suffer from Fregoli syndrome hold the delusional belief that they are persecuted by a person who can take the appearance of different people. All these conditions result from damage to different areas of the brain. The allegedly indestructible soul is very fragile indeed. In light of such evidence, how can anyone believe that the mind will continue to function when the entire brain has given up?[15]

And yet, many people continue to believe it. No one asks what happens to kidney function when the body dies. We all know: It stops, because kidney function—like liver function, respiratory function, and the like—is a process, not a *thing* separate from the organs that make it happen. As John Dewey put it, mind is a verb not a noun. And yet, it is common to ask what happens to the soul when the body dies, even though we know—in our brains and therefore in our minds—that what we call soul is a function of that delicate and altogether mortal brain, just as respiration is a function of the lungs.

"If we are to believe that a person survives death," wrote Bertrand Russell,

> we must believe that the memories and habits which constitute the person will continue to be exhibited in a new set of occurrences. No one can prove that this will not happen. But it is easy to see that it is very unlikely. Our memories and habits are bound up with the structure of the brain, in much the same way in which a river is connected with the riverbed. The water in the river is always changing, but it keeps to the same course because previous rains have worn a channel. In like manner, previous events have worn a channel in the brain, and our thoughts flow along this channel. This is the cause of memory and mental habits. But the brain, as a structure, is dissolved at death, and memory therefore may be expected to be also dissolved. There is no more reason to think otherwise than to expect a river to persist in its old course after an earthquake has raised a mountain where a valley used to be.[16]

Sorry, Uncle Harry.

In view of the importance so widely associated with "surviving death"—an oxymoron if ever there was one—it's notable how little detail accompanies expectation of where that survival would take place (heaven is a bit vague as a geographic destination), or how our souls would spend time once there, not to mention the fraught question of which body would those souls occupy, given that we all experience different ones as we mature and age.

The American reading public looks the other way when it comes to Mark Twain's vigorous opposition to late nineteenth-century US imperial expansion, and—even more troubling to many—his unbridled atheism, preferring his humor and nonthreatening novels. But Samuel Clemens was unapologetic about his politics and, notably, his angry atheism, expressed in his sometimes-suppressed book, *Letters from the Earth*, in which he noted that the Christian vision of heaven often includes singing eternally in an angelic choir, a peculiar yearning for people who in their Earthly life would never attend such events, much less want to sing in them. In Twain's sardonic masterpiece, the Devil takes pride in having included the tsetse fly, purveyor of African sleeping sickness, among the passengers in Noah's Ark.

Even with faith in a heavenly afterlife, other mundane problems arise. Some Christians believe that only the soul, not the body, is immortal. The most popular doctrine, however, maintains that soul and body will be reunited after death, although nitty-gritty details have long been debated, including the exact age and condition of the body to be resurrected. In *The City of God*, Augustine laid out many of the complexities, seeking to clarify things and in the process raising some heretofore unappreciated difficulties. Augustine asked, for example, what would become of the flesh that had been consumed by a cannibal and incorporated into the diner's body. Who gets that meat next time around?

Also, if soul and body are to be reunited, what version of the latter will it be? Presumably not an infant (unless the resurrected one died as such) and unlikely to be one's mortal coil in feeble old age. Some Christian thought converges on age thirty-three, thought to be the body's most perfect attainment because Jesus is said to have been that age when he died. Getting your body back may not be that simple, however. In his masterful book, *Heavens on Earth*, Michael Shermer recounts:

> When the Saturday Night Live comedian Julia Sweeney was told by Mormon missionary boys that in heaven her body would be returned to its original state of health, she wondered 'What if you had a nose job . . . and you liked it? Do you have to get your old nose back?' After she explained to

her interlocutors that she had her cancerous uterus removed and they told her she would get it again, she told them "I don't want it back!"[17]

As Shermer points out, there is also ethnocentric bias when it comes to imagining heaven. This shouldn't be surprising, given that such biases are little noticed; that's what ethnocentricity is all about. But the reality of culture-limited blinders undermines confidence in the exclusive accuracy of any one account of the afterlife, except for those convinced that their view, and only theirs, is correct. The Vikings looked forward to a Valhalla that encompassed riotous drinking in great mead halls and presumably bashing one's enemies between draughts. Islamic heaven features milk and honey, abundant dates (of both sorts) and flowing streams of clear water—just what a desert dwelling people would crave. The equivalent of Hindu heaven involves cessation of repetitive births and rebirths; i.e., stepping off the earthly rat race. One soul's heaven isn't always heavenly for another. Ditto for one culture's. Here is Michael Shermer once again:

> The nineteenth-century ethnologist Élie Reclus described the resistance Christian missionaries faced when attempting to convert Inuits with the promise of a Christian-like Heaven. Inuit: "And the seals? You say nothing about the seals. Have you no seals in your heaven?" Missionaries: "Seals? Certainly not. We have angels and archangels, 12 apostles and 24 elders, we have . . . ." Inuit: "That's enough. Your heaven has no seals, and a heaven without seals is not for us!"[18]

By the same token, it seems likely that some people, even those brought up in a Western monotheistic tradition, might not delight in the prospect of spending eternity singing psalms in praise of a Lord God. The late, great Christopher Hitchens—whose book *God Is Not Great* really is great—had this analogy for dying: You have been attending a party when suddenly someone taps you on the shoulder and tells you that you must leave, but the party will go on without you. How terrible! Hitchens then added a kind of consolation. Would this be worse than the Christian heaven, in which the party will go on forever, and you'll never be able to leave? "Eternity is very long," Woody Allen is said to have noted, "especially toward the end."

If devout Christians grant a soul to Muslims and Hindus (and some do), mainstream believers might also be willing to grant them their own preferred version of heaven, although such tolerance has rarely been documented. It also seems unlikely that devout Muslims or Hindus believe that devotees of other faiths will go to whatever afterlives they happen to prefer.

For all the heterogeneous opinions about how and if souls and bodies will be reunited, not to mention the details of their immediate heavenly surroundings, there has been very little debate over the spiritual state of souls once they've been transported. But unlike the physical body, the soul—being immaterial and immortal—isn't subject to change, and yet, the doctrine of original sin maintains that our souls are unavoidably fallen and in need of redemption. So, we all have work to do. Theologians often claim, as well, that the soul can be debased or otherwise lost. Also, on occasion, purified and thereby redeemed. That's where the Catholic doctrine of purgatory comes in: a divine laundromat that washes the soul, preparing it for eternal, stainless bliss.

There is an influential Calvinist perspective in which we cannot assure ourselves a place in heaven, no matter what we do. Good works and devotion to God are admirable and probably worth a shot, but don't fool yourself, they don't guarantee heaven. You can try to save your soul, but face it, mere mortal: It's not up to you. You can't grease your way into heaven on your own. This would be twisting His Divine Arm. The decision of who is saved and who is damned is up to God; his behavior matters, not yours. For some believers, the uncertainty was—and still is—excruciating. In 1678, John Bunyan wrote the following in *Pilgrim's Progress*, a Christian allegory that was long second in influence only to Dante's *Divine Comedy*: "How can you tell if you are elected? . . . My thoughts were like masterless hell-hounds; my soul like a broken vessel, driven into the winds, and tossed sometimes headlong into despair."

Nonetheless, the view within mainstream Christianity is that heaven is not just something bestowed upon us by God's whim, but is also earned, in large measure as a function of our actions in this world. We can obtain grace and save our souls if we are sufficiently devout and resist the Devil, who is portrayed in the Christian Bible as the Great Tempter who tried unsuccessfully, three times, to turn Jesus from his divine purpose. (Oscar Wilde, by contrast, quipped that he could resist anything except temptation.)

In the Western tradition, the ultimate cautionary tale of someone who didn't resist temptation is Faust, who sells his soul to the Devil and, as a result, he—rather, his compromised soul—gets dragged to hell.[19] It's easy to blame Faust for making such a bad deal. And yet, deal-making isn't foreign to the devout, who endeavor to sell their soul to God in a nonmonetary transaction,

Figure 3.1 *Faust signing away his soul; Faust on the right, a cool-looking Mephistopheles on the left.Source: Painting by E. Delacroix, 1827–8.*

by which they ascend to heaven. For both the Faustian and the devout, it's an exchange: a soul for power (Faust) or for eternal bliss (the devout). Either way, one's soul is evidently a marketable commodity (Figure 3.1).

Mel Blanc was the voice of dozens of beloved cartoon characters, including Bugs Bunny, Daffy Duck, Porky Pig, and Tweety Bird. On his tombstone is inscribed his most famous concluding phrase: "That's all folks!" although Mr. Blanc's voice isn't usually heard in this particular context. Unless they're suffering intractable pain and often even then, or committed to martyrdom, nearly all "folks" yearn to avoid their final sign-off, eager to believe that "that" won't be "all." If wishes were horses, goes the saying, then beggars would ride. If wishes created immortality, then maybe we'd all believe in souls. Wishes don't do that, but wishful thinking thrives, especially when it offers surcease from pain and fear.

No surprise that we readily adopt beliefs and behavior that soften pain. A searing example comes from George Orwell's *1984*. At the novel's end, Winston Smith is being tortured by O'Brien, a flunky of the despotic Big Brother. Earlier, Winston had insisted on a basic truth: Two plus two equals four. But under torture, he recants and accepts that two plus two equals five. He loves Big Brother, and the agony stops.

What stops the torture of facing death? Easy: When a Bigger Brother offers the promise of everlasting life.

> "The time is coming when all who are in the grave will hear God's voice and come forth from their graves" (Jn 5:28).
>
> "I am the resurrection and the life. The one who believes in me will live, even though they die" (Jn 11:25).
>
> "For this corruptible must put on incorruption, and this mortal must put on immortality. So, when this corruptible has put on incorruption, and this mortal has put on immortality, then shall be brought to pass the saying that is written: 'Death is swallowed up in victory'" (1 Cor. 15:53-54).
>
> "Death shall be no more, neither shall there be mourning, nor crying, nor pain anymore, for the former things have passed away" (Rev. 21:4).

Big Promises are alluring, especially when they offer solutions to a Big Worry, and death is humanity's biggest. Unfulfilled promises, however, quickly wear thin, and the one involving eternal life after death is the biggest unfulfilled promise of all. We've noted that considering the billions of people who have died in prehistoric and historic time, there is not a single case—not one—of anyone's soul living on, anywhere or in any manner, afterward. Case closed? Of course not. For believers, the promise of eternal life is fulfilled over and over, every time a saved soul dies. It's just that we can't witness or prove it. And to demand empirical evidence simply confirms, oh closed-minded skeptic, your limited understanding when it comes to spiritual matters. So, just shut up and have faith.

Moreover, there is incontrovertible evidence, witnessed by John. It's right here, in Holy Scripture! What more could anyone want?

> I saw the souls of those who had been beheaded because of their testimony for Jesus and because of the word of God. They had not worshipped the beast or his image and had not received his mark on their foreheads or their hands. They came to life and reigned with Christ for a thousand years. (Rev. 20:4-6)

The promise of immortality looms large in nearly all religious traditions, although as we have seen, less so in Judaism, with Ecclesiastes downright dismissive: "Surely, they all have one breath; man has no advantage over animals, for all is vanity. All go to one place: all are from the dust, and all return to dust" (3:19) And for good measure, "The living know that they will die; but the dead know nothing" (9:5).

It doesn't appear that believing in eternal life is a prerequisite for believing in a god. In theory, it should be possible to acknowledge a supernatural, all-powerful deity who created the world, including ourselves, and who urges us to accept his/her/their/its teaching and demands, and who permits us to enjoy his/her/their/its gifts, but who says nothing about an afterlife. Or who may even assert that when we die, we're kaput. Hence, there's no reason that an apsychist must be an atheist, or that a god-believer must be a soul-believer. Given there is no logical or even theological connection between believing in a god and getting a money-back guarantee that the believer will live forever, the promise of overcoming death has likely been thrown in to sweeten the deal. If so, it's brilliant marketing because death looms so large and so balefully in the human imagination.

Here is the much-loved nighttime prayer, widely recited as a consolation no less than a request: "Now I lay me down to sleep. I pray the Lord my soul to keep. If I should die before I wake, I pray the Lord my soul to take." This imploration has probably helped provide many people with a good night's sleep. And if the prayerful person indeed dies before awakening, no one knows the outcome.

This chapter relies heavily on the supposition that death—whether arriving while one is asleep or, more frighteningly, awake—is a significant motivator of soul-belief. But here's a conceptual sidebar. It's at least possible that belief in the soul's immortality is a *cause* of death anxiety rather than a result, insofar as fear of eternal punishment may well be greater than fear of death itself. If you believe you have a soul, and if you subscribe to either Christian or Muslim doctrine, then you're also expected to believe that your soul is potentially subject to damnation. Alternatively: no soul, no damnation and thus less death-anxiety. Hence, both Epicurus and Lucretius, who didn't worry about hell and who didn't look ahead to any kind of afterlife, were also notably less worried about death. (Or so they claimed.)

In any event, any effort to assess the allure of soul-belief must acknowledge the power of wishful thinking, not the power to make things come true, but the power that such beliefs exert over otherwise rational people. Take the mundane example of buying a lottery ticket, which has been described as a tax on the stupid—or, more sympathetically, on those in the grip of wishful thinking. Let's grant that it could be psychologically beneficial to spend a few dollars now and then on a crazy bet that you know is statistically guaranteed to fail but is compensated by the pleasure of imagining that maybe, just maybe, you'll win a fortune. Such pleasant imagining, although known to be hopeless, might occasionally be worth a few bucks, just for its short-lived entertainment value. The nighttime prayer doesn't seem to have done anyone any harm. But what about someone who is so convinced that they *really are* going to win the lottery that they destroy the family budget buying innumerable tickets in pursuit of their forlorn wish?

Wishful thinking runs deep, even in the healthiest human psyche. In *The Future of an Illusion*, Freud pointed out that

> the benevolent rule of a divine Providence allays our fear of the dangers of life; the establishment of a moral world-order ensures the fulfilment of the demands of justice, which have so often remained unfulfilled in human civilization; and the prolongation of earthly existence in a future life provides the local and temporal framework in which these wish-fulfillments shall take place.

Dreams (about which Herr Freud had a lot to say!) are sometimes more pleasant than reality, but they're dreams, after all. A Buddhist parable notes that it's one thing to point at the moon, quite another to mistake one's finger for it. Believing that dreams can literally create reality has itself become a kind of reality for many people; for some, a very lucrative one. Case in point: *The Secret*, first a 2006 feature film and then a book that sold more than thirty million copies. Its key claim is the "law of attraction," that we attract or become what we think about. We produce outcomes by believing in them. In many situations, a positive attitude doubtless contributes to a positive outcome, so there is much to be said for positive thinking, but nothing whatever for the claim that positivity and wishful thinking by themselves can change objective reality. Believing that you can lose weight may encourage you to diet and eventually drop some pounds, but the belief itself won't do the trick, and believing you can fly won't make you sprout wings.

"The essence of faith," wrote the philosopher Ludwig Feuerbach, "is the idea that that which man wishes actually is: he wishes to be immortal, therefore he is immortal; he wishes for the existence of a being who can do everything which is impossible to Nature and reason, therefore such a being exists."[20]

Then there is the placebo effect, which is real and neither wishful thinking nor faith-based. If you take a medicine believing that it will convey some benefit to your body, in roughly 30 percent of the time, it works. This is not because you have summoned some sort of mystical attraction whereby expectations magically become manifest, but rather because of how the human autonomic nervous system functions, including a likely role of psychological conditioning and our elaborate immune system. It would be nice if eternal life were a kind of placebo effect, a "secret" waiting only for us to believe (i.e., to have faith in our immortal souls) in order for us to escape death and cavort forevermore in heaven.

Placebo doesn't fix a broken bone or cure appendicitis, but in other cases it generates real improvement, especially in subjective symptoms involving chronic and even acute pain. In fact, recent research has found that you don't even have to believe in placebo for its effect to show up; what works is the attention and focus provided by visiting a doctor—even when the doctor acknowledges that the sugar pills being prescribed are in fact placebos![21] The promise of immortality could be a potent placebo, surrounded as it is with the rituals of religious devotion, ceremonies whose solemnity and thus, impact, exceed that of a doctor's office. It's not that belief in one's immortal soul generates actual immortality. It's enough that it generates a soothing belief in it.

For our purposes, the key point—the real secret—isn't the nonsensical belief that belief, by itself, makes objective things happen, but that so many people are vulnerable to believing that belief, all alone, is efficacious in impacting the real world. It's a vulnerability that increases in proportion as the credulous want it to be true. And, boy, do people want immortality. In his treatise, *Novum Organum* (1620), Francis Bacon, one of the conceptual architects of modern science, wrote that: "What a man would like to be true, he preferentially believes. . . . . . Numberless are the ways and sometimes imperceptible, in which the affections color and infect the understanding."

Not surprisingly, if the wanting is sufficiently strong, all that coloring and infecting armors the relevant belief with a Kevlar capacity to not only survive failure to confirm, but to outmuscle contradictory evidence. Psychologists call it "confirmation bias," when people ignore evidence that goes against their preexisting insistence, while latching onto and if need be, twisting any thread, however slender, that bolsters their presupposition. The first serious research into confirmation bias—published in a book titled *When Prophecy Fails*[22]—examined how doomsday cult members dealt with the failure of their prediction that the world would end on a specific date. Although some lost their faith, most clung to their prior insistence, as though their lives or the aftermath of their deaths depended on it. Some nineteenth-century millennial cults responded to the failure of the world to end on the predicted date by claiming that their faith in the event prevented it from happening.

Confirmation bias goes back a long way. In his account of the Peloponnesian War, written 2,500 years ago, the Greek historian Thucydides noted, "It is a habit of mankind to entrust to careless hope what they long for, and to use sovereign reason to thrust aside what they do not fancy." It's a notable paradox that we use "sovereign reason" to defend what we carelessly hope for. Among those prospects that humankind does not fancy, death looms uniquely large, while the illusion of an immortal soul helps believers to thrust that worry aside. In the process, many people take the longed-for heavenly bait so readily that they miss the hell-hook that it hides. That's next.

4

The Cosmic Stick Hell

People believe in souls mostly because they want to, but sometimes they're coerced into it, not for their benefit but that of organized religion. We've just looked at a leading cause of soul-belief, namely the yearning to transcend mortality. The present chapter inverts the personal perspective and considers how the soul has provided a stick for religious institutions to extort compliance by menacing their followers with eternal punishment. From the viewpoint of mainstream Christianity and Islam, the soul as a delusion isn't the point; what matters is that combined with the threat of hell, it's useful.

One might think that fear of losing one's life would be bad enough, but mainstream religious organizations have been especially cruel and made things worse by adding additional terrors about a punishing afterlife. There have long been other threats in the armamentarium of organized religion: ostracism, banishment, excommunication, inquisitions, not to mention torture and death. But the eternal cosmic stick is the only weapon that threatens to exact its punishment beyond this life.

"Nice soul you've got there. A shame if it ends up in hell." Whether from mob boss or God boss, a little fear goes a long way, and a lot goes even farther, making hell an example of intelligent but malignant design.

"He sees you when you're sleeping. He knows when you're awake. He knows if you've been bad or good, so be good for goodness sake!" Make that for your soul's sake. Traditionally, the worst that comes from not being good is a lump of coal in your Christmas stocking, a threat that once loomed large for many children, but for adults, not so much. Thanks to hell, however, Christians and Muslims, young and old alike, can look forward (if that's the right phrase) to eternal torment.

The Hindu and to a lesser extent Buddhist concepts of *karma* apply here as well, although with resonance that is a smidgeon less terrifying: Be good and your soul will end up in a happy, admirable body, or perhaps even get off the karmic merry-go-round and achieve Nirvana. Be bad, and you (i.e., your atman, spirit, life-flame, or soul) will find itself stuck inside a cockroach or a snake. There's much less attention to the consequences of how the newly inhabited cockroach or snake comports itself, although presumably a good cockroach could accumulate positive *karma* and be rewarded in its next incarnation, perhaps coming back as a butterfly. And vice versa—although it's difficult to imagine a misbehaving butterfly.

We don't know how the deeper selves of present-day cockroaches and snakes feel about their current situation, although the Indian guru Meher Baba maintained that it was okay—in fact, admirable—to kill snakes and to swat flies and mosquitoes, because the sad souls stuck inside don't like their current incarnations and would be grateful to try their luck in the next body.

In the Christian and Islamic traditions, it is entirely possible that holding hell over the head of malefactors results in behavior that is more prosocial than would otherwise be the case, leading many to claim that without God and the threats that he imposes, morality would be defunct. (Cue Ivan Karamazov and Chapter 8.) If so, then the soul serves many masters in addition to satisfying a need for immortality, insofar as it—rather, *believing* in it, as with Santa Claus— induces people to be good, at least in part by providing a kind of role model, representing the better angel of their nature, their best self.

But the hard-working, multitasking soul is more than just scrumptious bait. It provides a handle whereby the world's most influential religions induce people to do their bidding, not merely to avoid disappointing God but to keep eternal damnation at bay. Even though Jewish tradition downplays hell, the Hebrew Bible offers many cases of retribution *in this world*, announced with apparent satisfaction as divinely appropriate comeuppance for disobedience. Here is a sample.

For the sin of disobedience, Adam and Eve were expelled from Eden (Gen. 3:14-24), while the serpent was stuck with having to crawl on its belly (a kind of punishment meted out to modern zoologists as well, who have thereby been deprived of learning how that creature got around previously: Flying, like an arrow? Bouncing on its tail, like a pogo stick?); the Noahic Flood was imposed upon a sinful planet (Gen. 6:7); the people of Sodom and Gomorrah were obliterated because of their indiscretions, chiefly sexual (Gen. 19:23-29); ditto for Onan because of, as one might expect, onanism (Gen. 38:6-10); plagues were visited upon the Egyptians because they ignored the entreaties of Moses (Exod. 7-14); different plagues scourged the Israelites for worshipping the Golden Calf (Exod. 32); and Uzzah—admittedly, a lesser-known malefactor—was struck dead for having touched the Ark of the Covenant (Sam. 6:1-7). The Old Testament God is short-tempered and inclined to prompt, violent, and often lethal anger, but to his credit, perhaps, the punishments he dished out occurred in the here and now. The New Testament God also isn't shy when it comes to real-time disasters, nearly always describing them as condign punishment. But things get more serious when it comes to the afterlife.

Among the Christian Bible's statements of God's retributive inclinations, we read: "Whoever believes in the Son has eternal life; whoever does not obey the Son shall not see life, but the wrath of God remains on him" (Jn 3:36); "For the wrath of God is revealed from heaven against all ungodliness and unrighteousness of men, who by their unrighteousness suppress the truth" (Rom. 1:18); and "Let no one deceive you with empty words, for because of these things the wrath of God comes upon the sons of disobedience" (Eph. 5:6).

The idea that God's wrath can be discerned in natural disasters, from epidemics to floods, hurricanes, and the like is denied in some quarters, but is nonetheless widespread, especially among fundamentalists and evangelicals. The Lisbon Earthquake and tsunami of 1755 killed roughly one-third of that city's population. It also caused tremors among Enlightenment thinkers, including Rousseau and Kant, and it stimulated Voltaire to write his satiric novel *Candide*, which made fun of Gottfried Leibniz's contention that "all is for the best in this best of all possible worlds."

Televangelist Pat Robertson proclaimed that the devastating 2010 earthquake in Haiti was divine punishment for Haitians having made a "pact with the devil" when they overthrew their French slave-holding overlords two centuries earlier. A week after the 9/11 attacks, when appearing on *The 700 Club*, a television show hosted by Robertson, Rev. Jerry Falwell thundered:

> The abortionists have got to bear some burden for this because God will not be mocked. And when we destroy 40 million little innocent babies, we make God mad. I really believe that the pagans, and the abortionists, and the feminists, and the gays and the lesbians who are actively trying to make that an alternative lifestyle, the ACLU, People for the American Way, all of them who have tried to secularize America, I point the finger in their face and say, "You helped this happen."[1]

To this, Mr. Robertson added, "I totally concur, and the problem is we have adopted that agenda at the highest levels of our government." In mid-March 2020, one month into the devastation caused by the coronavirus, Ralph Drollinger of Capitol Ministries, and a senior "faith adviser" to the Trump Administration, announced that America was "experiencing the consequential wrath of God."[2] Christian fundamentalists aren't alone in such "thinking." According to some ultra-orthodox Jewish teaching, the Holocaust happened because God was angry with European Jewry for having invented reform Judaism.

These assertions of God's real-time wrath, however controversial, are mild compared with damnation and eternal torment. It is not uncommon to invoke hell in a nonthreatening mode, just for the helluvit. But when intended literally and taken seriously, as they have been for most of the past two thousand years, notably in the Christian and Islamic worlds, such threats are serious indeed.

This chapter will visit, sometimes in gory detail, a few of the torments believed to await sinners within a variety of religious traditions, especially Christianity. They reflect a widespread fascination with the imagined grotesque, evidently shared by much of humanity, including more than a few devout believers. But no matter how temping it may be to lose oneself in hell-horror or to revel in schadenfreude, please don't lose sight of the significance of all this misery, not just as a cultural creation but as a stunning manifestation of the powerful imagery long associated with the torments in store for errant souls after their bodies die. It is impossible to overstate the psychological impact of these threats, especially when drummed into the head of children. (More on this at the end of the current chapter.)

Whether expressed in ancient Egyptian belief, or emerging full-blown out of Dante's fertile (and, to some extent, febrile) imagination, or via official church doctrine, the agony of the damned takes on real consequence because it is based on some important, often-unspoken assumptions. Notably, damnation after death presumes that souls are real. There could be no suffering in hell without some sort of something that persists after death and is available to be tortured. Moreover, those truly lost souls must be encumbered with responsibility for sins committed by their bodies—and presumably, sanctioned by those souls—when alive. By extension, if only the poor souls/bodies hadn't transgressed, they wouldn't be in such hot water . . . or unending flames, boiling oil, in the grip of ravenous beasts, and so on. As we tour the horrors of eternal damnation, don't lose sight of the conceptual realities hiding in plain sight: no sinning, no eternal torment. No souls to have sinned, nothing to punish postmortem. In short, when it comes to hell, the soul is a necessary, sufficient, and convenient handle whereby religious authorities terrify and manipulate their followers.

Given the well-established negative correlation between bookishness and religious commitment, it is possible that a large proportion of those reading *The Soul Delusion* will doubt the depth and ubiquity of belief in hell. But a 2021 Pew Research Center report[3] found that 62 percent of all US adults believe that hell exists (heaven, 73 percent). Looking just at Christians, the proportions were 79 percent for hell, and 92 percent for heaven. So, heaven wins—but hell isn't far behind, with the proportion of Catholics and Protestants being pretty much the same. Among Protestants, however, there's a big difference depending on denomination: Although 74 percent of Catholics believe in hell, nearly 90 percent of Protestants in the evangelical and historically Black churches do so compared with 69 percent of mainline Protestants. A different survey in 2016 found that roughly the same percentage of Americans believed in the Devil (61 percent) as in hell (64 percent), while more than 80 percent of "highly religious" and "somewhat religious" Americans maintain that hell is a "real place" inhabited by real souls.[4] Really. These numbers haven't changed very much. According to the Pew Foundation 2023–2024 "Religious Landscape Study," reported in 2025, 86 percent of U.S. respondents "believe people have a soul or spirit in addition to their physical body," and 70 percent "believe in an afterlife (heaven, hell or both)." Compared with earlier such surveys, belief in hell has declined a bit in modern times but that's no reason to discount its prominence in the past as well as the present.

None of these surveys asked respondents if they felt especially frightened about hell or inappropriately manipulated by their religions, although it seems a good bet that many would respond Yes to the former question and No to the latter. In any event, we must conclude that if belief makes something so (e.g., see Chapter 3), then hell is real. At least for most Americans.

It can be argued that proclaiming an unpleasant afterlife for sinners is merely intended to encourage pious and socially acceptable behavior in *this* life, the theological equivalent of offering a gold star to a toddler who pees in the potty. This seems too optimistic, however. The influential late nineteenth-century French writer and poet Leon Bloy referred to the oxymoronic "good news of damnation," maintaining that only the fear of perpetual hellfire can motivate moral behavior. Such encouragement could be worthwhile if it results in more prosocial behavior, despite whatever personal anguish it may occasion. And indeed, cross-cultural research has found that belief in divine punishment is correlated with lower national crime rates.[5]

But there is a line, however fine, between providing a gentle spur to gentle behavior and sharpening that spur into a laceration. It is one thing to demand, as in Pink Floyd's *The Wall*, "You can't have your pudding if you don't eat your meat"—that is, no heaven if you aren't good—quite another to threaten a child with a beating, never mind brandishing the prospect of unending torture. In short, when does encouragement and training morph into abuse? Sure enough, research reported under the descriptive title "The Emotional Toll of Hell" found that whatever its positive effects at the societal level, belief in hell is associated with reduced individual happiness and life satisfaction.[6] And so, although hell makes people more likely to follow prescribed norms out of fear that otherwise there will literally be hell to pay, it also makes them unhappy. Behaviorists say the same about the use of punishment generally in getting a child to toe the line: Children might obey but be sullen and unhappy about doing so, and more likely to misbehave when out of immediate parental oversight.

Henri Thiry, Baron d'Holbach, was a major figure in the French Enlightenment. In *The System of Nature* (1770), he wrote that a priest had subjected Holbach's dying wife to a lecture about how she would suffer in hell unless she accepted Jesus as her hope and savior. It's not clear how the terrified woman responded, but Holbach became convinced that the Christian perspective[7] on the afterlife was not only likely to be factually wrong but made people frightened and miserable: "Far from holding forth consolation to mortals," he wrote, "far from cultivating man's reason, far from teaching him to yield under the hands of necessity, religion strives to render death still more bitter to him, to make its yoke sit heavy, to fill up its retinue with a multitude of hideous phantoms, and to render its approach terrible."[8]

Some believers might prefer confidence that a righteous god will punish sinners here on Earth to claims about hell and its terrors to come. Nonetheless, religious admonitions have traditionally focused on the prospect of misery after death rather than comeuppance during life, mostly because it is all too apparent that bad people often do well in this life while good people frequently suffer, with no sign that justice ultimately triumphs during their lifetimes. Hence, it can be helpful to think that sinners and other evildoers will eventually "get theirs," while the righteous will receive their just rewards. Claims of a punishing afterlife satisfy a widespread need to balance the scales of justice, to make the universe fair when our mortal life isn't. Thus, a readily evoked sense of justice demands—"Hell, yes!"—that the likes of Hitler, Stalin, Mao, Pol Pot, and, for many these days, Putin, get their proper payback, if not in this life, then in whatever comes after.

Some of that justice is more benevolent than the fire-and-brimstone that waits for slippery sinners who somehow ducked their earthly punishment. Also promised is reward in heaven for those who toe the line, who not only fear God and do good works, but who also don't make trouble and who accept their lot in life, an acceptance powered by assurance that by doing so their souls will be rewarded in the next. When Karl Marx criticized religion as the opiate of the masses, he was confronting precisely this issue: that organized religion anesthetizes its followers, urging them to accept their situation, however unfair, with the promise that social passivity will lead to ultimate rewards in the hereafter.

"The Preacher and the Slave," a song written in 1911 by union organizer Joe Hill, made fun of that promise in a parody of the gospel song "In the Sweet Bye and Bye," sung to the same melody. Hill's version begins by satirizing religion's claim that eternity will reward those who remain pliant in the present, regardless of their current misery (it also introduced the phrase "pie in the sky"):

> *Long-haired preachers come out every night*
> *To tell you what's wrong and what's right.*
> *But when asked how about something to eat*
> *They will answer in voices so sweet:*
> *"You will eat, bye and bye*
> *In that glorious land above the sky.*
> *Work and pray, live on hay.*
> *You'll get pie in the sky when you die."*
> *That's a lie.*

The song goes on to critique the claim that heaven will not only reward souls that imbibe religion's reassuring opiate, but that hell will punish those who try to better their situation, warning potential troublemakers not to aim so high as to disrupt the status quo:

> *If you fight hard for children and wife,*
> *Try to get something good in this life,*
> *You're a sinner and bad man, they tell.*
> *When you die you will sure go to hell.*

It's easy to see Marx's point, that is, how difficult it is to resist the dangling of heavenly rewards and how socially hurtful is the heavenly temptation. As a promised eternal desert, pie can be terminally tempting, even more so when combined with its flip side, the threat of unending postmortem torment. Compared to pie-in-the-sky promises, unending punishment is more attention-grabbing and, in many cases, more effective. As a way of manipulating the living, its power has long been recognized. We might invert Marx's critique and suggest that religion does double duty, not only as opiate but also as amphetamine of the masses, insofar as the yearning to avoid hell for one's self while enthusiastically inflicting it on one's enemies helped to engender the religious energy that resulted in mass murder and genocidal war (see Chapter 8).

We may never know how it was that so many religions settled on the threat of a punishing afterlife as a way of scaring people into obedience, but one interesting possibility has been suggested by Ara Norenzayan, a social psychologist at the University of British Columbia. In his book, *Big Gods*,[9] Norenzayan traces the development of human societies from small hunter gatherer bands to large urban civilizations, pointing out that when groups are small, everyone can know and watch everyone else, making antisocial behavior less likely. But that is no longer the case as societies become big and anonymous, which is where Big Gods come in. By establishing an expectation that there are deities (usually, but not necessarily, just One), that are omniscient, omnipresent, and omnipotent, group members are more likely to stay on the straight-and-narrow. After all, they are being watched and judged, wherever they are and whatever they do, and are ultimately subject to punishment if they misbehave. Equally important, they are inclined to assume that others who subscribe to the same belief system will do the same. The result is not only a more pliant population but a more internally cooperative one.

This could help explain how social cooperation evolved in large-scale societies that might otherwise be unwieldy because of people's temptation to go it alone and defy social rules when they aren't being watched by a moralizing and punishing Eye in the Sky. Moreover, the proposed payoff might provide incentive for promoting the notion that each group member has their own soul, a personal handle by which a malefactor can be grabbed by the group's Big God and tossed into an eternity of damnation.

Voltaire anticipated the Big God hypothesis. His sardonic *Philosophical Dictionary* includes the following reply to someone who had the effrontery to question the existence of hell: "I no more believe in the eternity of hell than yourself; but recollect that it may be no bad thing, perhaps, for your servant, your tailor, and your lawyer to believe in it." The narrator goes on to observe the following:

> To those philosophers who in their writings deny a hell, I will say: "Gentlemen, we do not pass our days with Cicero, Atticus, Marcus Aurelius, Epictetus. In a word, gentlemen, all men are not philosophers. We are obliged to hold intercourse and transact business and mix up in life with knaves possessing little or no reflection, with a vast number of persons addicted to brutality, intoxication, and rapine. You may, if you please, preach to them that the soul of man is mortal." As for myself, I shall be sure to thunder in their ears that if they rob me they will inevitably be damned.[10]

Voltaire's personal feelings were clear, however, as when he asked, "Were the time ever to arrive in which no citizen of London believed in a hell, what would be adopted? What restraint upon wickedness would exist?" To which he answered, "The feeling of honor, the restraint of the laws, that of the Deity Himself, whose will it is that mankind shall be just, whether there be a hell or not." His is an optimistic expectation,[11] but one that most of the world's religious traditions have not embraced. Even many nonbelievers have touted the benefits of religion as a mechanism of social hygiene, allegedly keeping in check some of humanity's more unpleasant impulses. In fairness, we should also recall the tradition whereby threatening hellfire and brimstone is appropriate to the salvific responsibility of religious leadership, according to which the intent is not so much to impose social responsibility in this life upon those who would otherwise misbehave, but to restrain potential sinners for their own benefit: to save them from hellfire and brimstone.

Let's turn now to a drive-by survey of hell.

Among the classical Greeks and Romans, hell was neither a place of punishment nor a restraint upon wickedness, notwithstanding occasional individual torments reserved for a small number of specific wrongdoers. For the sin of revealing Olympian secrets and trying to fool the gods into eating his own son (a perverse sacrifice he sought to make), Tantalus was condemned to stand forever in water that retreated when he tried to drink and within sight of fruit that withdrew when he tried to eat. (His hell was being "tantalized.") Prometheus was punished for having granted human beings the gift of fire by having his liver daily torn out by an eagle, after which it regrew for a repeat performance. Sisyphus, a notorious trickster, had to spend eternity pushing a heavy rock uphill only to have it roll back down.

For the most part, however, hell for the ancient Greeks and Romans was simply the abode of the dead where all mortals end up, regardless of their merits or demerits. Living heroes could visit there under special circumstances, hang out and converse with the "shades" of the deceased and then return; for example, Odysseus in the *Odyssey* and Aeneas in the *Aeneid*, who met Achilles, Agamemnon, and Tiresias. In most of the world's better-known current religious traditions, by contrast, fear of death has been augmented by additional fears: that the afterlife has particular horrors in store for the souls of those who transgressed in life.

For the ancient Egyptians, one traveled after death through different regions of the *Duat*, which was more a place of judgment than of punishment, although those who failed the former were subject to the latter, notably being chomped and then swallowed by *Ammit*, the designated devourer of souls. *Ammit* was suitably intimidating, with the rear end of a hippo, the upper body of a lion, and the head and jaws of a crocodile. One could avoid being eaten by *Ammit*, however, by successfully passing the "weighing of the heart," during which *Osiris*—Lord of the Underworld and Judge of the Dead—assessed each corpse's heart, comparing it with the "feather of *Maat*," a stand-in for fairness and truth. Those whose hearts were heavier than the feather (which presumably was rather light, and thus a challenging threshold) were in big trouble (Figure 4.1).

In a related telling, one might escape this outcome by uttering a series of denials, such as "I have not cheated," "I have not blasphemed," and so forth. It is unclear how worrisome early Egyptians found either version of this postmortem evaluation, because there does not appear to be any recorded claim that anyone ever ended up a meal for Ms. *Ammit*.

Similarities to the West's conception of hell can be found in the majority of other religious traditions, complete with explicit threats that associate torture

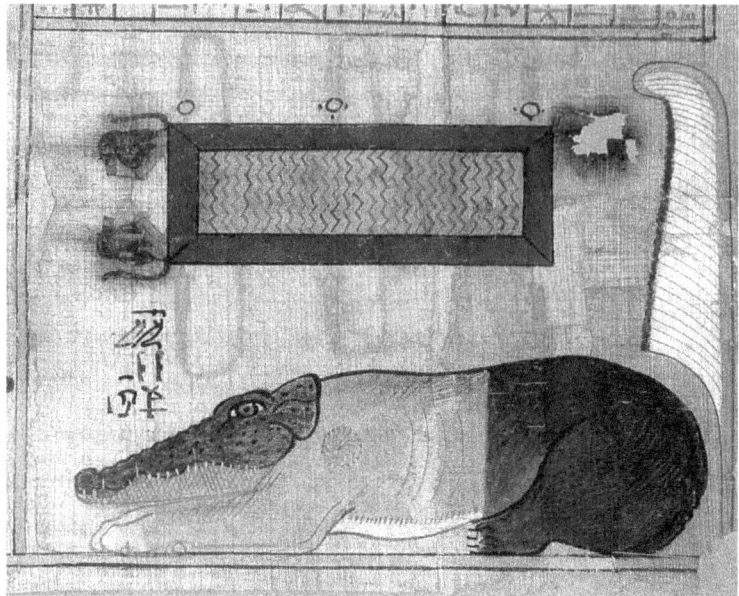

Figure 4.1 *Amit, waiting to devour a soul that failed the Weighing of the Heart, as depicted in an illustration from the Egyptian Book of the Dead. Source: Detail from the Book of the Dead of Nebqed, Eighteenth Dynasty of Egypt (c. 1550–1300 BC).*

with failure to live up to designated rules and expectations. Some versions of Buddhism and Daoism competed by literally multiplying their visions of hell in a kind of posthumous poker. At one point, the Buddhists wagered 8 different levels of hell, to which the Daoists responded with 10, after which the Buddhists countered with 8 cold ones and 8 hot ones, and the bidding went on, mostly in the double digits, until the Buddhists jumped to 84,000, whereupon the Daoists folded.

One version of Burmese Buddhism had (and for some devotees still has) 40,040 different hells, each associated with its own misbehavior, such as one for not returning borrowed books and another for throwing shards of pottery over a wall. It isn't clear how this diverse array of punishing domains, with different outcomes reserved for different malefactors, coheres with the Buddhist denial that souls have any independent existence. On the other hand, it's problematic to generalize about any of the world's sacred traditions; consider, for example, the differences within Christianity alone, between Roman Catholicism and, say, Unitarianism or Quakerism. But with that caveat, here is a generalization:

Insofar as, on occasion, some Eastern religions consigned offenders to a prolonged stay in hell rather than punishment via a nasty reincarnation, these sentences usually specified a duration short of eternity. Albeit not all that much short: One story in Tibetan Buddhism posits a great cube of sesame seeds one hundred miles on a side, from which a small bird removes one seed every thousand years; when the seeds are all gone, the sinner gets a kind of parole to try living their life again.

Better known in the West, of course, is the Hindu warning that misbehavior generates bad *karma*, which in turn can lead to a regrettable rebirth, albeit not quite as loathsome and certainly not as lengthy as the eternal damnation that failed Christians and Muslims are expected to endure. Like corporal punishment of misbehaving children, the threat of hell is somewhat out of fashion these days, but it has enjoyed (if that is the right term) a long run as a fear-inducer, persisting in the hot, painful imagination of millions of psychologically traumatized people.

Many thinkers preceded Voltaire in disputing that moral behavior depends on the promulgation of threats (hell) versus the promise of rewards (heaven). Plato's Socrates maintained that such virtues as justice and moral probity were "goods" unto themselves. In one of Plato's more challenging dialogs, the *Euthyphro*, Socrates raised but didn't answer the vexed question whether certain behavior is good because the gods demand it or if they demand it because it is good. Aristotle's *Nicomachean Ethics* explored the origin and maintenance of justice, morality, and happiness without once venturing into discussion of eternal rewards (heaven) or unending punishments (hell). In many African folk traditions, hell has been more a regrettable situation than a place of physical torment, less a location than a state of being ignored by one's descendants.

The Jewish perspective is closer to this conception of hell as a kind of nothingness than as understood in the Christian or Islamic world. It contains many descriptions of God's power, evidently intended to erase any doubts as to the advisability of complying with divine commands, but with no explicit mention of hell as found in the other two major monotheistic traditions. The Hebrew Bible does, however, identify a realm called *sheol*: a circumstance of oblivion and nonspecific darkness. Translated into Greek, it became *hades*, but there are conflicting views among Jewish scholars about whether *sheol* should be seen as a place of punishment or merely a situation experienced by all dead souls, regardless of their virtue or iniquity. On the other hand, some ancient rabbinical teaching purportedly claimed that a kind of heaven existed within which the fortunate inhabitants would spend eternity studying Torah,[12] while hell, by contrast, would be so dark and heavy that its victims couldn't even open the Holy Books.

In contrast to the views of ancient Egyptians, Eastern traditions, and those of the Hebrew Bible, the Christian perception of hell is quite explicit and dire. As horrifying as is the Hebrew Bible with its depictions of God-inspired rape, murder, infanticide, and genocide, at least the suffering of victims ends at their deaths. But with the New Testament and the arrival of the allegedly meek, mild, and loving Christ, we get an explicit extension of suffering into eternity. "Do not be afraid of those who kill the body but cannot kill the soul. Rather, be afraid of the One who can destroy both soul and body in hell" (Mt. 10:28). Jesus subsequently goes on to leaven the "good news" of the gospels with dire warnings about a place of darkness where "the worm dies not, the fire is not quenched, and there shall be weeping and gnashing of teeth" (Mt. 9:48).

Pre-Christian followers of Molloch allegedly sacrificed their victims in the sinister valley of Gehenna, a place considered so real that Jesus repeatedly threatened his own followers with punishments that were similar, or worse: "If you say, 'You fool,' you will be liable to the hell [i.e., *Gehenna*] of fire," he declared in one of the less humanistically appealing parts of the Sermon on the Mount (Mt. 5:22). And the synoptic gospels attribute many comparable warnings to the Savior:

> It is better for you to lose one of your members, than for your whole body to be thrown into hell (Mt. 5:29).
>
> If your eye causes you to stumble, tear it out and throw it away; it is better for you to enter life with one eye than to have two eyes and to be thrown into the hell of fire. (Mt. 18:9)

> If your hand causes you to stumble, cut it off; it is better for you to enter life maimed than to have two hands and to go to hell, to the unquenchable fire. (Mk 9:43)
>
> But I will warn you whom to fear: fear him who, after he has killed, has the authority to cast into hell. (Lk. 12:5)

The third-century treatise *Apocalypse of Paul* contains much material beloved of hell-mongers. It purports to be an eye-witness account of torments, what Harvard's Stephen Greenblatt calls a "ghastly travelogue" that includes but is not limited to rivers of fire, insatiable worms, swirling sulfur and pitch, stench, and sharp stones raining like hail on the unprotected bodies of the damned.[13]

> There are adulterers strung up by their eyebrows and hair; sodomites covered in blood and filth; girls who lost their virginity without their parents' knowledge shackled in flaming chains; women who had abortions impaled on flaming spits. There are virtuous pagans who "gave alms and yet did not recognize the Lord God" and who are therefore blinded and placed forever in a deep pit. Demons—here called the "angels of Tartarus"—carry out special tortures designed for particular sins. For example, this befell a "lector" (a reader of the lessons in church services) who did not follow God's commandments: An angel in charge of his torments arrived with a long flaming knife, with which he sliced the lips of this man and his tongue as well.

Not to be outdone, the Islamic conception of hell (*Jahannam*), deriving from the Qur'an, contains seven different levels of misery, each successively more intense and intolerable, and each correlated with the severity of the misbehavior being punished. *Jahannam* is well stocked with boiling water and especially fire (sometimes *Jahannam* is translated as "blazing" or "roaring fire"), along with the tree of *Zagunnum*, which has germinated from the transgressions committed by each malefactor and is thus tailored individually to each suitably suffering soul. Sinners are forced to consume the fruit of this tree, which gnaws interminably at their insides. Islamic scholars are divided over whether the trip to *Jahannam* is one-way or if, eventually—and depending on the misdeeds in question—inhabitants are finally paroled to heaven.

The early church father, Tertullian, who wrote extensively about hell in the second century after Jesus, maintained that after death, the pious would get to delight in witnessing forever the suffering of the damned—among whom Tertullian included essentially anyone who disagreed with him. A twelfth-century text, the *Vision of Tundale*, enjoyed great currency in its day, not least (one suspects) because of its explicitly horrifying images of the suffering of the damned, a kind of extreme schadenfreude à la Tertullian. For just one example, here is the comeuppance undergone by nuns and especially monks, priests, bishops, archbishops, cardinals, and even popes who violated their vows of celibacy: "The genitals of the men and the women were like serpents, which eagerly mangled the lower parts of their stomachs and pulled out their guts."[14]

In these accounts of the suffering of the damned, transgressors' bodies are dead and gone, leaving only immaterial souls behind. And so, paradoxically, the torments of the flesh are somehow inflicted not upon flesh but upon souls. Evidently you don't need to have a body to suffer agony, although all descriptions—verbal or pictorial—of the suffering of the damned show bodies in torment, perhaps because there is no way to depict souls without their habitation. In theory, nevertheless, when it comes to misery, a material body clearly isn't necessary; an immaterial soul does just fine.

Within Christianity, hell became especially prominent after the fifth century CE, its horrors becoming more strenuous as the early church faced more dissenters and heretics, a situation that began long before the famous protests of Martin Luther. Christian proselytizing occurred not only by the sword, or by pointing to the gospel of Jesus's eventual return, but also by threatening nonadherents with a hefty dose of unGospel Bad News, namely that they would eventually be damned to hell. Vigorous debate ensued over the fate of those poor souls who had not been saved by Christianity, specifically heathens who through no fault of their own died without having encountered Jesus's teachings. Augustine was particularly unrelenting in this regard, insisting that unbaptized babies, no less than unrepentant sinners, were doomed.

Some support for a more lenient Christian approach to those who predated Jesus comes from the "harrowing of hell," whereby Jesus is said to have descended into hell after his death and resurrection to liberate worthy souls, especially those who had preceded him in life. In a famous medieval painting by Benvenuto di Giovanni, this included Adam and Eve. The word "harrowing" derives from an Old English word for "plundering," and the main sources for the tale are the Gnostic Gospels and the Apocrypha rather than formal Christian theology. Today, what many people find harrowing is the description of what will befall them if they don't shape up and live according to the teaching of church or mosque.

In contrast to the somewhat more tolerant Constantinople-based Orthodox Church, the Roman Catholic Church particularly emphasized that punishment for mortal sins would be fixed and unyielding, with no recourse. Such rigidity was highly profitable for the medieval church, which maintained that repentance alone was inadequate to avoid hell. This opened the treasury door for the lucrative sale of indulgences. Prior to the Reformation, the Catholic Church made tons of money by threatening that anyone who committed a mortal sin would end up in hell. There was, however, one lucrative catch: The duration of punishment was reduced in proportion as the families of the damned paid for the malefactors to get time off, not for good behavior while alive (nearly always, those to be thus indulged were already dead) but rather for good and hefty payment by friends and family who cared about the fate of their loved ones' suffering souls. This practice was among those to which Martin Luther dissented with particular vehemence in his *Ninety-Five Theses*, issued in 1517. Of these, Thesis 82 was especially devastating. Luther asked.

> Why does not the pope liberate everyone from Purgatory for the sake of love (a most holy thing) and because of the supreme necessity of their souls? This would be morally the best of reasons. Meanwhile he redeems innumerable souls for money, a most perishable thing, with which to build St. Peter's church, a very minor purpose.

As part of the Counter-Reformation, in 1563 the Council of Trent finally responded to Luther's critique by decreeing that "all evil gains for the obtaining of [indulgences] be wholly abolished." This was formally certified by Pope Pius V four years later. The church's *volte face* reduced its income while also saving it considerable embarrassment, although at the cost of further immiserating the expectations of those who knew they had been guilty of mortal sins and would have to seek other means of expiation if their souls were to be spared the worst of what the afterlife had on tap for them. They could no longer count on their surviving relatives to bail them out, or at least to reduce their sentence by virtue of hard currency offered on their behalf. It isn't clear whether personal behavior improved as a result.

The horrors of a malign afterlife have been somewhat allayed in the post-Reformation Church by an insertion that has enjoyed theological traction as a kind of way station between heaven and hell: purgatory. According to current Catholic catechism, purgatory is "the state of those who die in God's friendship, assured of their eternal salvation, but who still have need of purification to enter into the happiness of heaven." (As ever, one must ask: "Who or what is doing that entering?") This ritual purification had long been conceived as somehow involving fire that—whether literally or figuratively—burns away the contamination of venial sin. As for mortal sin, forget it.

Among Catholics, purgatory is currently seen as less heated and more a site for extended soul-cleansing, while it continues to satisfy the need of those still alive to do something, typically via prayer, on behalf of their deceased loved ones, given that mere money no longer suffices and there is no reason to pray for those in heaven and ditto for those consigned irrevocably to hell. The word "purgatory" doesn't appear in the Bible and is rejected by Protestants who argue that salvation is achieved by grace alone. If you're damned, it's too damn bad.[15]

More than two centuries before the Protestant Reformation, popular focus on hell and its punishments had been intense, of which by far the most renowned and influential depiction was (and still is) Dante's magnificent poem, *The Divine Comedy*, which was composed when the sale of indulgences was in full flower. It is interesting that *Inferno*, with its exuberantly graphic depiction of the tortures of hell, has always been read more widely and enthusiastically than *Purgatorio* or *Paradiso*, the other two parts of Dante's masterpiece, although they are written with no less verve and brilliance.

Selective attention to painful, punishing situations is widespread and likely to be biologically adaptive because it induces us to focus on situations that are dangerous and might be life-threatening. (Think about traffic slowdowns at the scene of a car crash; what are people looking for, and why?) It's pleasant to envision happy people enjoying themselves, but, because such cheery imaginings are less consequential than life-threatening events, they are less riveting. Compare how few people look at the heavenly souls disporting themselves near water fountains in the first panel of Hieronymus Bosch's triptych, *The Garden of Earthly Delights*, with the attention given to the final, hellish part, in which a bestiary of nasty critters torture and mangle condemned souls (see Figure 4.2).

Maybe *Inferno*-infatuation is also testimony to a deep-seated fascination with the grotesque combined with a hefty dose of schadenfreude, along

Figure 4.2 *Hieronymus Bosch's three-part Garden of Earthly Delights (painted between 1490 and 1500). Heavenly pleasures are on the left, hellish torments on the right, and middling experiences are, suitably, in the middle. Source: Faithful photographic reproduction of the painting displayed in the Museo del Prado in Madrid.*

Figure 4.3 *Just one of the eternal torments reserved for sinners in Dante's Inferno. Source: Painting by Joseph Anton Koch, 1825–8.*

with genuine concern about what might be awaiting the sinful. It needs emphasizing that in its *ad hominem* specificity, *Inferno* mostly reveals the creative imagination of Dante Alighieri and his desire to get even with his Florentine enemies rather than any explicit teachings of the Roman Catholic Church (Figure 4.3).

In addition to the now-familiar torments of burning by fire, gnawing by ravenous beasts, and so forth, *Inferno* achieves power and even a sort of credibility as an extended warning because it often shows punishments fitting the crime—poetically, but also with gut-wrenching memorability. For example, the fate of adulterers, notably Paolo and Francesca, is to be blown about by torrential winds that reflect their uncontrolled illicit passion, while simultaneously keeping the couple near each other but forever apart. Also among the punished: equivocators who refused to take sides in the "Rebellion of the Angels" (derived from the biblical Book of Revelations) are condemned to run about, naked and continually stung by swarms of hornets and wasps, while unavailingly chasing an indistinct banner that represents their constant pursuit, when alive, of their own inconsequential self-interest.

Another cautionary tale presents the punishment of fortune-tellers, evidently considered serious malefactors in medieval times, who are forced to walk eternally straight ahead, but with their heads on backward. Then there are the politicians who accepted bribes, who find themselves stuck in a lake of boiling tar—full-body retribution for their sticky fingers—all the while harried by the Malebranche (literally, "evil claws"), which use those claws to rip their flesh if they try to get out of the scalding bath.[16] We also meet a sad collection of hypocrites forced to walk hopelessly along a narrow path, wearing seemingly lovely robes adorned with shining golden threads—resembling monk habits and thus appearing to be a reward for piousness—that are actually composed inside of unbearably heavy lead. They manifest hypocrisy made real, painful, and permanent.

The most appallingly suitable tortures are found deeper in *Inferno*'s bowels. The Sowers of Discord were guilty of ripping asunder that which should have been left intact; hence, they are dismembered by a ferocious demon, after which their lacerations heal, whereupon they are torn apart once again. Here we also find Mohammed, his body hacked open so that his guts spill out. Interestingly, his son-in-law, Ali, is similarly mutilated because he caused the schism between Shi'a and Sunni. Schismatics of any sort, even among heathens, are in Big Trouble. Those generating discord within a family are divided literally in their own bodies. Consigned to the deepest region of hell is the ultimate would-be schismatic, Satan, who is entombed waist-deep in ice and endowed with three horrible heads, the ones on each side chewing Brutus and Cassius, who are being punished for betraying Julius Caesar, while the middle one eternally masticates Judas, betrayer of Jesus. Satan's revolt against God was the ultimate treachery against the established order (whether secular or divine) and thus, the ultimate, irreconcilable sin.

Perhaps the most notable of all poetically just punishments is found at a slightly less stygian level, reserved for a pair of former inhabitants of the city-state of Pisa: Count Ugolino and Archbishop Ruggieri. These two had engaged in a sequence of mutual betrayals, so they are encased together in a frozen hole, each gnawing forever on the other's head. Admittedly, their maneuver would be anatomically challenging were they alive, but because these are souls and only sort-of bodies, they're capable of flesh-defying gymnastics. Again, note that none of Dante's fever-dream portrayals represent actual church doctrine, but, nonetheless, they have been immensely influential, not merely as literature, but as the stuff of personal nightmares.

Strange as it seems to secularists and even many believers, hell has often been conceived as a concrete physical place, a specificity entertained by some of humanity's greatest minds. As a twenty-four-year-old math genius, Galileo—widely revered as the preeminent founder of modern Western science—was approached by the Florentine Academy to calculate some of the quantitative details of hell, using Dante's poem as the underlying data. (*Inferno* enjoyed such a reputation in Galileo's day that many sophisticated scholars took it as literal truth.)

In 1588, Galileo presented his results in two lectures to his Florentine sponsors. Using proportional scaling from Dante's poem, he figured out that Satan was 1,180 meters (3,870 feet) tall, and, taking Dante's claim that Satan's navel was at the center of the Earth, Galileo determined the exact depth of hell and the thickness of its dome.[17] We'll never know if the great scientist believed all this, but it may be significant that what remains of him now is a bony finger—the middle one—from his right hand, on public display in Florence's science museum, where it points upward to the universe that he illuminated or perhaps issues a defiant obscene gesture toward the church that subsequently persecuted him for telling the truth about the solar system. Wisely, perhaps, he never tackled the soul.

It is one thing to acknowledge the lurid details by which hell is held forth as the ultimate punishment whereby the souls of sinners are made to suffer for their transgressions. But we don't know whether such remonstrances enjoyed anything like the credibility that led the Florentine Academy and possibly Galileo himself to take Dante's architectural surmises about hell as literal truth. After all, claims of souls in torment cannot be proved, and one might think, with Carl Sagan, that extraordinary claims require extraordinary evidence. On the other hand, they cannot be disproved. Unlike the exploits of Greek and Roman heroes, or the narrator in Dante's vast poem, no one has visited the underworld and returned to tell the tale.

Maybe hell's credibility doesn't matter, especially if it piggybacks on that of religion in general, in which only the credulous, pretty much by definition, deeply believe. Paraphrasing Louis Armstrong on those who ask for a definition of jazz, if you gotta ask, you won't understand the answer.

In any event, it's worth repeating that although belief in hell seems at low ebb in the modern world, the Devil and his punishing realm still retain adherents. Belief in the Devil has diminished of late, even for many deeply believing Christians, who, insofar as they claim that His Evilness actually exists, nonetheless find him an embarrassment, a bit like *Jane Eyre*'s madwoman in the attic. Or maybe his persistence and that of his realm is a case of what psychiatrist Randy Nesse calls the smoke-alarm principle. Here it is.

We accept the annoying occasional screams of a kitchen smoke alarm when we accidentally burn the toast because of benefit derived if there's a real fire. Analogously, even though it might just be the wind, our ancestors were likely predisposed to respond with tense alertness to a whispering in their Pleistocene grassland, because it could also be a leopard. Better safe than sorry. Better to believe in the legitimacy of hell's smoke alarm—even though it might be false—than to discover, after death and deprived of any recourse, that your personal house really is aflame. And your soul, beyond hope.

A metaphor is like a cookie: tasty, but if squeezed too hard, apt to crumble. (Please consider the above sentence a meta-metaphor: a metaphor about a metaphor, and don't squeeze it too hard.) The fear of eternal damnation isn't a well-intended but hypersensitive smoke alarm or anything like a biologically adaptive awareness of a lurking leopard's exhalations. Although some people may be induced to prosocial behavior by threats of eventual, eternal misery, it seems likely that many have also been consigned by those threats to lives of guilt, shame, and anxiety, not to mention unrelenting terror.

Detailed portrayal of the torments of hell have not been limited to Dante, whose imaginative genius is today read more as brilliant, entertaining literature than as an accurate recitation of sinners' afterlives. Christian preachers, Protestant no less than Catholic, have eagerly promoted their own blood-curdling accounts of hell's torments, portraying them not as metaphor but as something that genuinely awaits sinners, unbelievers and even those who merely backslide a bit in their devotion. Here is just a smidgeon from the immensely influential sermon "Sinners in the Hands of an Angry God," by eighteenth-century Congregationalist preacher, Jonathan Edwards, who helped stimulate what came to be known as "The Great Awakening" (but deserved to be labelled The Great Frightening): "The God that holds you over the pit of hell, much as one holds a spider or some loathsome insect over the fire, abhors you, and is dreadfully provoked; His wrath towards you burns like fire; He is of purer eyes than to bear to have you in His sight; you are ten thousand times more abominable in His eyes as the most hateful venomous serpent is in ours."

Similar threats to our soul-stuff are broadcast and taken seriously even today, notably dilated upon and intended to frighten children in particular with warnings that if they transgress they'll eventually suffer eternal tortures meted out by fiends. Such pronouncements deserve to be seen for what they are, nothing less than child abuse. It is especially easy to terrify, tyrannize, and bully children in this way, because it is biologically and socially adaptive for them to be credulous and highly receptive to what adults tell them. Their experience of the world is necessarily limited, and so, much of the information they need to acquire comes by listening and learning. Who better to provide it than parents and other respected adults? This is good to eat; that isn't. Here's how to make a spear, how to put together a Lego set, how to catch a fish, how to play the piano. What to worry about and what to ignore.

Youngsters are open vessels into which wisdom and information is poured, most of the time for their benefit. But not always.

This makes it particularly despicable to take advantage of their vulnerability. Iconic examples include "kinetic sermons," designed to get their listeners to fall on their knees and repent, to accept Jesus, to acknowledge their personal iniquity, whatever it takes to obtain for themselves a Get-Out-Of-Hell-Free card. Children aren't alone in being readily abused in this regard. Given that as Freud suggested in *The Future of an Illusion,* adults also look to God as a parent-substitute, they too are susceptible to hell-fear. But there is an especially perverse wisdom in the Jesuit motto "Give me the child until he is ten, and I will give you the man." Take a child and deform his psyche with terror and self-doubt, and there's a good chance that you'll have a terrified, self-doubting adult who is vulnerable to whatever the authorities demand.

In some parts of the American South, churches put on "Hell Houses" as part of Halloween. Unlike secular haunted houses designed solely for entertainment, Hell Houses feature local teenagers acting as sinners, with a different room devoted to a different transgression—premarital sex, abortion, drug use, blasphemy, homosexuality, and the like—each of which sends the perpetrators to (where else?) hell. Young children are paraded through to witness how, at the climax of each performance, Satan drags the malefactors, screaming, to eternal damnation. It is noteworthy that the local teenage performers often compete to partake in the "dirty dancing rooms," where they get to be lasciviously wicked with each other ... self-sacrificially acting against their inclinations, of course, and doing so merely to warn their younger colleagues about the consequences of sin.

Hell Houses aren't widespread. Most often, fundamentalists subject children to scary fire-and-brimstone preaching. Here is part of a kinetic sermon recalled by James Joyce as the young Stephen Dedalus in his autobiographical novel, *A Portrait of the Artist as a Young Man*[18]:

> The last and crowning torture of all the tortures of that awful place is the eternity of hell. Eternity! O, dread and dire word. Eternity! What mind of man

can understand it? And remember, it is an eternity of pain. Even though the pains of hell were not so terrible as they are, yet they would become infinite, as they are destined to last forever. But while they are everlasting they are at the same time, as you know, intolerably intense, unbearably extensive. To bear even the sting of an insect for all eternity would be a dreadful torment. What must it be, then, to bear the manifold tortures of hell forever? Forever! For all eternity! Not for a year or for an age but forever....

Ever to be in hell, never to be in heaven; ever to be shut off from the presence of God, never to enjoy the beatific vision; ever to be eaten with flames, gnawed by vermin, goaded with burning spikes, never to be free from those pains; ever to have the conscience upbraid one, the memory enrage, the mind filled with darkness and despair, never to escape; ever to curse and revile the foul demons who gloat fiendishly over the misery of their dupes, never to behold the shining raiment of the blessed spirits; ever to cry out of the abyss of fire to God for an instant, a single instant, of respite from such awful agony, never to receive, even for an instant, God's pardon; ever to suffer, never to enjoy; ever to be damned, never to be saved; ever, never; ever, never. O, what a dreadful punishment! An eternity of endless agony, of endless bodily and spiritual torment, without one ray of hope, without one moment of cessation, of agony limitless in intensity, of torment infinitely varied, of torture that sustains eternally that which it eternally devours, of anguish that everlastingly preys upon the spirit while it racks the flesh, an eternity, every instant of which is itself an eternity of woe.

Anyone who hasn't known the agony of having the torments of hell drummed into their young, impressionable head will find it difficult, perhaps impossible, to grasp the psychological consequences. But anyone seeking to understand, if only intellectually, how such threats have been used and how they have impacted their victims would do well to try. Robert Burton's seventeenth-century treatise *Anatomy of Melancholy* is a prescient account of what today is labeled depression. In it, Burton noted, "If there be a hell upon Earth, it is to be found in a melancholy man's heart."[19] One way to increase that melancholy and to bring him to heel is to bring hell upon Earth by threatening one's soul with a helluva bad time.

5

The Golden Helmet of Centrality

Once upon a time—actually, the late nineteenth century—there was a real Long John Silver. His name was William Ernest Henley, and, alas, he was not a pirate, but an English critic, editor, and poet. When he was twelve years old and suffering from tubercular arthritis, Henley had one leg amputated just below his knee. As an adult, he promoted work by the artist James Whistler, the sculptor Auguste Rodin, and became close friends with the novelist Robert Louis Stevenson, who partly based the pirate captain in *Treasure Island* on his peg-legged buddy. There was evidently something memorable about William Ernest Henley: His young daughter even provided the inspiration for Wendy, the heroine of J. M. Barrie's *Peter Pan*. An accomplished poet, Henley celebrated fortitude and inner strength, which he evidently had in abundance, most notably expressed in his best-known short masterpiece, "Invictus," which ends with the iconic lines, "I am the master of my fate/ I am the captain of my soul."

Henley's enthusiasm for his own perseverance speaks for itself. It also gestures toward a powerful aspect of the soul's appeal, the way it italicizes individuality and selfhood, and, on route, the importance and value of each person. In his poem, Henley's soul is not only "unconquerable" but also able to withstand the "bludgeonings of chance," leaving him "bloody but unbowed." Not only is he unconquered, he emerges triumphant, master of his fate and captain of his soul. All this fate-based mastery and naval captaincy speak to

Henley's resilience (and, by extension, that of others similarly endowed), as well as to the reader's centrality. Everyone is the center of their own existence, subject to pain and ill fortune, yet not only able to withstand and even triumph over these vicissitudes but also important enough to be a target of them.[1]

It's not solipsism, the notion that one's existence may be all that is. It's more like "centralism," the yearning that one's self is so important, so special, and so central to things that the world is organized around or at least orchestrated with an eye toward one's self: one's very own soul.

We all recognize that our private, particular souls, however unique and cherished, are not up to the task of standing in for all humanity. And so, in a small number of special cases, we're tempted to grant this role to certain charismatic figures. When in 1806 he saw Napoleon on horseback near the peak of his military success and widely acclaimed as representing populist yearnings, the philosopher Hegel described the erstwhile Little Corporal as "the soul of the world." Despite our own personal egotism and need for affirmation, most of us wouldn't go that far; we recognize that our Little Corporeal selves don't really embody or represent the world. Only a few qualify. But even if we don't make the grade in the immediate here-and-now, à la Napoleon, we can adopt a Hindu perspective and see ourselves as part of some kind of world-soul (*atman*), similar to the Christian and Muslim view of soul as God's gift to each of us, no matter how un-Napoleonic we know ourselves to be.

An iconic example is the 1946 movie, *It's a Wonderful Life*, directed by Frank Capra, and staring America's most consistently "everyman" actor, Jimmy Stewart, as George Bailey, a small-town everyman who has suffered many reverses and is on the verge of suicide. At the last minute, Bailey's guardian angel shows him what his town would have been like if he had never been born, whereupon Bailey/Stewart has a revelation: He is *really important*. This message—which Everyman America continues to adore and that has made this movie one of the country's most beloved—is that we all count.[2]

A theistic perspective is supposed to see God's handiwork everywhere: in mountains and molehills, hippos and humans, in the sky and the sea. This can be inspiring, but also more than a bit diffuse and subjectively diminishing because in most cases, neither our guardian angel nor a god-infused cosmic connection is readily apparent. Moreover, seeing God everywhere requires believers to share his love and concern widely, with all creation. That's a tough order, because like George Bailey, we yearn to be valued and taken seriously for what we know to be our own specialness, especially given that by contrast to the wide world, we can't avoid seeming small and insignificant. (Because, frankly, that's just what each of us is.) George Bailey learned that his was a wonderful life, based on a religiously infused, personalized perspective. But his epiphany was fiction.

We are vulnerable to many fictions, most of them embraced enthusiastically. Take, for example, the cognitive bias known as the Dunning-Kruger effect. It describes a widespread pattern whereby people are unable to accurately self-evaluate. Worse yet, part of that inability is that the less we know, the more we are inclined to overestimate ourselves. As a result, we tend to think that we know more than we really do, and that we are more skillful, moral, knowledgeable, better drivers, better lovers, better parents, better students, wiser, and stronger than we really are. Welcome to Lake Wobegon, where "all the children are above average." The truth is that most people are average. It's what "average" means. Ouch!

The Dunning-Kruger effect applies to the often disguised but nonetheless ubiquitous insistence on specialness. Alas, not only are we not more skillful, moral, knowledgable, wiser, stronger, and so on, but—brace yourself—we are not central to the cosmos.

In her masterpiece novel, *Middlemarch*, George Eliot used a homey metaphor to say something profound about centralism and human egotism:

> Your pier-glass or extensive surface of polished steel made to be rubbed by a housemaid, will be minutely and multitudinously scratched in all directions; but place now against it a lighted candle as a centre of illumination, and lo! the scratches will seem to arrange themselves in a fine series of concentric circles round that little sun. It is demonstrable that the scratches are going everywhere impartially, and it is only your candle which produces the flattering illusion of a concentric arrangement, its light falling with an exclusive optical selection. These things are a parable. The scratches are events, and the candle is the egotism of any person.

It is precisely this egotism that leads so many to imagine that they are special. What better way to italicize this than to conclude that you are endowed with a unique and imperishable soul, nothing less than God's divine gift to you? To *you* and no one else! God is very, very big, and has lots of things to do, so isn't it unspeakably wonderful that he should go out of his big and busy way to endow little *you* with a special indication of his unending love and esteem? As in Eliot's description, you are the center of illumination, with concentric circles going out from your oh-so-central sun.

Whether it is "unconquerable," as for Henley, could be debated by those worried that their soul just might be sent to hell, in which case it will have been conquered, permanently. But whatever your personal foibles, limitations and flaws, and wherever your soul might end up, the fact that you and you alone have received it directly from your Maker makes you a favored child, the center of your world—not just metaphorically, but actually.

If this seems ridiculously egocentric, it is.

In an essay titled "An Outline of Intellectual Rubbish: A Hilarious Catalogue of Organized and Individual Stupidity,"[3] Bertrand Russell argued that self-importance is a major source of our religious beliefs:

We believe, first and foremost, what makes us feel that we are fine fellows. Mr. Homo, if he has a good digestion and a sound income, thinks to himself how much more sensible he is than his neighbor so-and-so, who married a flighty wife and is always losing money. He thinks how superior his city is to the one 50 miles away: it has a bigger Chamber of Commerce and a more enterprising Rotary Club, and its mayor has never been in prison. He thinks how immeasurably his country surpasses all others. If he is an Englishman, he thinks of Shakespeare and Milton, or of Newton and Darwin, or of Nelson and Wellington, according to his temperament. If he is a Frenchman, he congratulates himself on the fact that for centuries France has led the world in culture, fashions, and cookery. If he is a Russian, he reflects that he belongs to the only nation which is truly international. If he is a Yugoslav, he boasts of his nation's pigs; if a native of the Principality of Monaco, he boasts of leading the world in the matter of gambling.

But these are not the only matters on which he has to congratulate himself. For is he not an individual of the species *homo sapiens*? Alone among animals he has an immortal soul, and is rational; he knows the difference between good and evil, and has learnt the multiplication table. Did not God make him in His own image? And was not everything created for man's convenience? The sun was made to light the day, and the moon to light the night. . . . The whole of theology, in regard to hell no less than to heaven, takes it for granted that Man is what is of most importance in the Universe of created beings. Since all theologians are men, this postulate has met with little opposition.

Ironically, another aspect of egocentrism reveals itself when we assume that something so important to ourselves as our soul must be equally real for other people, a larger version of the assumption that because you might like hot peppers, everyone else does. And so, we readily attribute a soul to others, at least those who look and think like us. It is a widespread European tradition to automatically say "God bless you" after someone sneezes. Little examined today, this verbal ritual developed in antiquity when it was thought that people sneezed out their souls, after which demons might enter the temporarily unsouled body. Invoking God's blessing deterred any fiendish trespasser. Granting a soul to others and trying to protect those we care about, including even when they sneeze, does not diminish the uniqueness of one's very own cherished possession, the centerpiece of each person's life that makes everyone a master and a captain.

Seen from outside, every religion looks homogeneous, but they never are. Within any belief tradition, only a small minority are deeply involved with doctrinal arcana such as the difference between transubstantiation (a Catholic belief), and consubstantiation (Protestant), or between salvation via works (Catholic) and via faith alone (Lutheran). It's a good bet, however, that even churchgoers who don't participate deeply in the details of theological hermeneutics are strongly committed to this shared teaching: They possess a soul. Unlike the question of whether spiritual authority is vested in the Vatican or in the Bible alone, and whether praying to saints is efficacious, having a special, personal soul touches everyone personally.

It is deeply flattering to be told that part of you is a personal gift from God, even more so given that the Devil is desperate to get it *from* you, while religion—acting as God's representative—is equally eager to save it *for* you. How empowering to be told that you possess something uniquely your own, and, moreover, that it is of such inestimable value, no matter your station in life, that these spiritual superheroes battle over it. And how democratically delightful that this non-thing thing, being immaterial, is not only possessed equally by everyone, rich or poor, old or young, believer or not, but because it is immaterial and therefore disconnected to things of this world (including one's wealth or social status), no one can refute the assertion that you have one, no matter how seemingly inconspicuous or lowly you might be. You may not be the "soul of the world," but it's your soul, inhabiting your world.

There is some reason to believe that in the early Christian church, everlasting life after death was available only for a select few. Being among the faithful was necessary for eternal salvation, but not sufficient. To be irrevocably saved, one also had to be a high-ranking male theologian. Gradually, however, the gates to eternal bliss were opened to all, so long as they met certain preconditions, notably committing their souls to Jesus. Democratizing access to heaven was undoubtedly a sound PR move, whereby everyone was confirmed in their centralism, offered the prospect of receiving what everyone, in their heart of hearts, soul of souls, knows to be their due.

This yearning to see oneself as not just valuable but central to our own lives may be a fundamental result of consciousness, built in because of the way our nervous system processes subjective experience: We see, hear, smell, touch, and feel our surroundings as though from our own personal castle, around which the world rotates. Knowing that each of us has our own God-given immortal soul not only gratifies our self-importance but also confirms this illusion of centrality. It is comfortably consistent with our human tendency to deceive ourselves, a phenomenon known to psychologists as motivated perception, or, more accurately, motivated misperception. It commonly happens when we imagine something that isn't there or misinterpret an experience because we bring our own bias to the situation. A troublesome example is the tendency of some men to interpret a woman's friendly smile as sexual interest, when in most cases it is simply being sociable, or merely polite.

On our unavoidable limitations and our penchant for misconstruing our centrality, here is the sixteenth-century French philosopher, Montaigne, in his essay "Of Experience":

> It is an absolute perfection and virtually divine to know how to enjoy our being rightfully. We seek other conditions, because we do not understand the use of our own, and go outside of ourselves, because we do not know what it is like inside. There is no use our mounting on stilts, for on stilts we must still walk on our legs. And on the loftiest throne in the world, we are still sitting only on our own rump.

Writing about the same time, Cervantes lampooned such motivated misperceptions in the figure of Don Quixote, who famously misperceived a windmill for a giant, an inn for a castle and so on, all because he insisted on seeing the world as a romantic, chivalric adventure, with himself as its centerpiece. "Seest thou not yon cavalier who cometh toward us on a dapple-grey steed, and weareth a golden helmet?" said the Don. "What I see," answered Sancho, "is nothing but a man on a grey ass like my own, who carries something shiny on his head." "Just so," answered Don Quixote: "and that resplendent object is the helmet of Mambrino."[4] Never mind that it was just a shaving basin, worn as a hat by an itinerant barber: The soul gives each believer their very own golden helmet, a gifted gratification that human beings adore, especially because science has been reducing our species' centrality and cosmic importance.

It is the height of paradox that the more we learn about our own species and the world around us, the more we are humbled, forced to relinquish some of our most cherished illusions, especially our centrality. Central to this intellectual decentralization was the demotion of our planet to mere peripherality. It is difficult, perhaps impossible, for us in the twenty-first century to realize how painful it was for our ancestors to accept this change. Galileo was hauled before the Inquisition and forced on pain of torture and death to recant and affirm that the Earth was the center of the universe and divinely immobile—although after doing so, he is said to have muttered under his breath "But still, it moves."

The religious philosopher Giordano Bruno was less discrete. Having accepted the evidence that the Earth doesn't occupy a privileged position as center of the solar system, and indeed of the universe, Bruno went on the argue that human beings also lacked a similarly privileged position in God's eyes. For Bruno, the Earth itself was alive and had a soul, as did all things. Moreover, there were an infinite number of worlds, so just as our planetary home isn't unique, each human soul is an instantiation of the Universal Soul, to which it returns after the body's death. Accordingly, we don't have soul-based individuality, because when the body dies, each soul dives into a kind of cosmic, God-infused universal soul-soup: "All spirits are from the sea of one spirit, and all return to that one

Figure 5.1 *Jan Huss being burned at the stake. Source: Painting by Diebold Schilling the Older, Spiezer Chronik (1485).*

spirit." Bruno was burned at the stake, as was another heretic, Jan Hus, a century earlier (Figure 5.1). (We don't know what became of either man's soul.[5])

The Copernican Revolution continues. Take, for example, realization that the universe is at least 13.8 billion years old, and maybe even older because that's the limit of light currently reaching our planet. And that there are billions of other galaxies containing trillions of other stars along with a vast tricolor of red giants, white dwarfs, black holes and, oh yes, our little blue Earth. This planet—and we too, dragged along with it—have therefore become smaller and less cosmically consequential than ever. Moreover, this astronomically inconsequential planet, wobbling around a rather ordinary star (a lowly class G2V Yellow Dwarf), sits on the outskirts of a run-of-the-mill galaxy whose stars contain innumerable planetary systems of their own. (And don't forget the eventual heat death of the universe.)

In the face of all this astrophysical diminution, it takes a lot of chutzpah to maintain the myth of planetary, never mind species-wide or personalized centrality. For true believers, our accumulating insignificance is merely an illusion; if anything, the immensity of the universe highlights God's engagement with *our* planet, *our* species, and *each of us*. Our tiny needle—planetary, species, individual—stands out in the vast cosmic haystack as the special recipient of divine love. (One can imagine this sentence as part of an enthusiastic "God be praised" sermon by a scientifically literate priest, rabbi, or imam determined to make physical reality seem theologically acceptable.)

Our astronomic demotion hasn't been the only blow to our material centrality. Equally devastating was the Darwinian Revolution, with its demonstration that we are one species among many, all connected through evolutionary history and subject to the same biological process. Evolution was resisted by many—although not all—in the West's religious establishment. Much of the opposition was driven by fundamentalists upset that if living things (especially us) arose by evolution, this contradicted scripture's explicit statement that we were created by God, in his image. Accordingly, denial of evolution and embrace of special creation (currently hidden under the anodyne label "intelligent design") is sometimes justified even now as being faithful to the infallible words of scripture; not coincidentally it also coheres with a refusal to give up our golden helmet.

Although many conservative fundamentalist believers continue to reject evolution entirely, for the most part the Christian religious establishment, especially the Catholic Church, refrained from the kind of theological combat that had characterized its response to Copernicus, Kepler, and especially Galileo. This may have been largely a result of the Church having been "burned" by its treatment of the latter (who, although posthumously rehabilitated by the Church, remained an embarrassment). On the other hand, many influential Protestant voices deny basic science even today, especially when it comes to evolution, often maintaining the myth that the Earth is only a few thousand years old and that people coexisted with dinosaurs (who presumably occupied a lot of room in Noah's Ark).[6]

Darwin's religious views have been much debated and discussed. Having initially trained for the Church of England, he subsequently became an agnostic and was averse to public controversy. He didn't write anything about the soul. Darwin had no hesitation, however, when it came to concluding that human beings, like all other living things, arose by evolution. In *The Descent of Man* (1871), we read that

> man with all his noble qualities, with sympathy which feels for the most debased, with benevolence which extends not only to other men but to the humblest living creature, with his god-like intellect which has penetrated in the movements and constitution of the solar system—with all these exalted powers—man still bears in his bodily frame the indelible stamp of his lowly origin.

Darwin left it to others to decide whether the soul, presumably residing within the human "bodily frame," had also evolved—which would result in a kind of "soul gradualism" to go along with the "phyletic gradualism" recognized by evolutionary biologists—in which case either all living things possess a soul to different degrees, or we must face the blasphemous prospect that the soul is a fiction.

In 1999, Pope John Paul II shocked Catholic traditionalists when he acknowledged that human beings might well have evolved rather than been specially created, arguing that maybe God used evolution to do the heavy lifting. But he drew the line at mind and soul. The pope also proclaimed that heaven and hell are not actual, physical places but indications of the soul's communion or lack thereof with God. None of this went over well with old-school, pre–Vatican II Catholics or, no surprise, with Protestant fundamentalists, who stick to heaven and hell as real, and insist that people should look forward to the former and fear the latter. For the sake of—what else?—their souls.

This theological dispute hasn't involved the nature of the soul itself, but rather, whether our soul-selves will spend postmortem eternity in a literal heaven or hell, in an ecstatic communion with or immiserated divorce from God. Monotheistic religions aren't founded explicitly on belief in the soul but, rather, belief in some sort of god. They do share, however, the same assumptions that underpin soul-insistence: that there is an immaterial, immortal world separate from the crude, physical one, and that each human being participates uniquely in that world. Accordingly, our souls are the most immediate and personalized manifestation of this divine centralizing truth and, thus, of God's concern for each of us. As the war-wounded, impotent Jake Barnes concludes in Hemmingway's *The Sun Also Rises*, when his heartthrob imagines that they might have had a lovely life together, "Isn't it pretty to think so?"

We cannot undo the reality of astronomy, ditto for evolution. Nor, it seems, can we overcome the cravings that these insights have undermined. For many, however, there remains our beloved golden helmet.

Christian doctrine maintains that each soul, associated with each body, is permanent, immortal, and unchanging, despite the fact that bodies change, not only from infancy to old age, but even day-to-day, minute-to-minute. As Michael Shermer explains:

> There isn't a single persistent self, so can there be a single, consistent soul? As atoms are replaced, so, too, are molecules, cells, tissues, and organs, by some estimates on average every seven to ten years. There is a wide variation of the replacement process time, from a few days for the epithelial cells that line the gut, to a few weeks for the epidermis skin layer, to two months for

red blood cells, to a year or two for liver cells, to ten to fifteen years for bone and muscle. So the belief that you are the same material person you were years ago—or will be years from now—is an illusion. At most, what stays the same is the pattern of information, and even this changes over time.[7]

Most religious beliefs are not immediately accessible to daily experience. To be sure, some believers see God all around them—in a bat, a baby, a subway turnstile—but in most cases it takes structures, images, or certain rituals to bring the divine to awareness. Hence the importance of regular church, synagogue, or mosque attendance. For believers, God may be everywhere and in everything, but for most people most of the time, he/she/it isn't intimately and immediately apparent. Enter, once again, the soul, which, by contrast, is imaginatively accessible. The soul-satisfied can look into themselves and perceive a conscious entity, with love, hopes, fears, ideas, plans, regrets, experiences that are intensely and directly perceived by each person, readily identified as theirs and theirs alone. It offers a unique personal monopoly of what really counts: one's deeper, truer self, an ineffable me-ness that can't be seen, touched, heard, smelled, or located, but that can't be denied and doesn't even require shared belief in a god. It can even engender, on occasion, a modicum of tolerance: Believe what you want, worship who or what you want, I have my own soul, thank you very much. And you're welcome to yours.

If your life is disappointing and with no positive prospects (perhaps especially in this case), while others are richer, more accomplished, or seem to be happier, your soul is your ticket to a unique status that isn't even canceled when you die. Death levels the playing field: You can't take "it" with you—that is, the stuff of this world (unless you are an Egyptian mummy)—and no one else can, either. But you *can* take your soul; in fact, you're stuck with it. Whether you had been an emperor, courtesan, or street-sweeper, after death, all you have is your soul, just like everyone else. Not just a great centralizer, it's a great equalizer.

Soul-generated equality is a mindset that is not only appealing in its democratic openness, but it also bears a conflicted and ultimately reassuring relationship to what has been called the Copernican Principle. Just as the Earth isn't astronomically unique among planets, in that it orbits the sun just like our fellow denizens of the solar system, human beings aren't unique either (the Darwinian Principle), except insofar as every species is somewhat different from every other one. So far, so devaluing of human centrality, which is where the soul picks up the slack. Leonard Cohen sang that "There's a crack in everything. That's how the light gets in." God's special grace gets into our otherwise diminished cosmic specialness via the crack that admitted our soul. And so, we are bequeathed a doubly exalted status: spiritual specialness shared with all human beings as fellow soul-infused creatures, while at the same time each of us gifted with our own centrality as an individual, our personal, divinely ordained spiritual QRL code. Isn't it pretty to think so?

Earlier, we looked at the seductive appeal of believing that a soul enables one to survive death. Just as there is a kind of paradoxical egotism in assuming that everyone has a soul because you do, the conceit of the soul's undying nature is also gratifyingly self-referential. Transcending death not only responds to a deep, inchoate fear, it also responds to the unspoken assumption that because we have always experienced *something*, it is unimaginable that someday, we won't.

Along with our egocentric insistence that death couldn't possibly be the end of our crucial ego-bounded everything, comes another, related insistence that involves sharing our centrality: the claim that death isn't the end of others, notably those *we* love and care about. Through most of human history, our ancestors couldn't escape the deaths of others, including those important to us. Children and especially infants died young, women died in childbirth, adults didn't only die in wars but also because of predators, accidents, poor nutrition, and especially—given the absence of antibiotics, vaccines and public hygiene—diseases. So, just as our self-centered experience demanded that we couldn't stop having them, in a sense continuing to live even when we die, it seems likely that we have been seduced into thinking that we wouldn't stop encountering the souls of those we have known, loved, and lost. Isn't it pretty to think so?

We've noted that excepting the most devout believers, the existence of God isn't self-evident. There have been precious few theophanies: visible manifestations of God such as Moses's encounter with the burning bush. This may be why organized religions work overtime to establish visible substitutes that represent something not otherwise apparent. Given the soul's importance, it may be significant that the Abrahamic religions all promote images of their God or objects that represent the deity—crucifixes, prayer beads, icons, stars of David, the Islamic crescent and star, and the like—various tokens, trinkets, holy relics, "memento dei" if not *memento mori*, reminders of a deity in whom one believes, but whose immediacy is often less than apparent, or, at least, not directly accessible compared with what people get from their own subjective experience, and that they interpret as their soul. This may be why there are also architectural structures—churches, synagogues, mosques as well as Hindu and Buddhist temples—but no comparable structural monuments to one's soul, no tokens that reinforce confidence in each individual's internal divinity. Maybe this is because we all feel our subjective consciousness (see Chapter 6), which is often more immediate than a sense of God, who can be difficult to perceive in the world around us, and who therefore requires more explicit reminders.

The absence of shared soul-symbols may also be due to the belief that each soul is personal, so there is no one-size-fits-all bit of relevant memorabilia. Or perhaps it's simply because there is no generally accepted symbol for the soul; if this is the case, one might wonder why. Like the soul, God is supposed to defy materiality, yet is often refracted in many material forms. Not so the soul. Perhaps it's because a widespread soul-symbol would diminish the illusion that each person's soul speaks to each person's personalized privacy, at the same time reflecting each individual's secretly longed-for centrality. Like Gollum in *The Lord of the Rings*, we can imagine believers saying to themselves, "My precious!"

And like Gollum, some can be driven to distraction if they lose it and can't get it back.

In a celebrated passage from his *Pensees*, the brilliant sixteenth-century mathematician Blaise Pascal expressed a version of existential isolation, not quite the lament of a Gollum deprived of his Precious (Pascal was an ardent Catholic), but reflecting the anxiety of a believer who has lost confidence in his centrality. "When I consider the brief span of my life," wrote Pascal, absorbed into the eternity before and after, the small space I occupy and which I see swallowed up in the infinite immensity of spaces of which I know nothing and which know nothing of me, I take fright and am amazed to see myself here rather than there: there is no reason for me to be here rather than there, now rather than then. Who put me here? By whose command and act were this time and place allotted to me? . . . The eternal silence of these infinite spaces terrifies me.

The soul-certain don't claim that we have a soul because of some natural process, that we evolved it in the same way we evolved our pancreas, because people with a functioning soul left more surviving offspring than did those who were soulless. No, we have a soul as a gift from God, a supernatural contribution to *each and every one* of us. Let's emphasize this: It's a precious gift to every individual, small and insignificant as they may feel in the context of the wide world, but huge in our private lives. This makes our soul all the more cherished because the bestowal confirms the deep-seated hope that each of us is actually crucially important, not just to one's self, but central to the thoughts and actions of a benevolent deity. One more time: Isn't it pretty to think so?

The widespread insistence on having a soul, with its accompanying support for centralism, is a symptom of what Albert Camus described as humanity's unsatisfying one-way encounter with the universe. Because we want the cosmos to confirm that each of us has a special importance and to care about us, we have a terrible time acknowledging that it doesn't, and that it cannot convey any inherent meaning to our existence. We implore it for a kind of cosmic validation, but it responds with Pascal's "silence of these infinite spaces," which is to say, it doesn't respond at all. And so, a multitude of frustrated meaning-seekers and would-be centrality self-convincers cling their soul as a way of telling themselves that they *really do* matter, that the universe really does care about them so much that it has given each a private, immortal, and infinitely valuable gift.

In his novel, *The Walnut Trees of Altenburg*,[8] Andre Malraux wrote that "The greatest mystery is not that we have been flung at random between the profusion of the earth and the galaxy of the stars, but that in this prison we can fashion images of ourselves sufficiently powerful to deny our nothingness"—the same nothingness that so horrified Pascal. In a way, religions unite people, at least those who profess the same rituals and beliefs, thereby providing connectedness and a feeling of shared purpose via what Malraux identified as our species-wide denial of our nothingness. These cherished connections are based on a commonality of subjective experience, but as we have seen, religions rely on exteriority, rituals and structures orchestrated from the outside to achieve this apparent unity. Not so the soul. Beneath, and more fundamental to that connectedness, is our personal stand-alone soul-supplied specialness.

Although the soul-satisfied find themselves allied with others by virtue of shared belief that everyone possesses one, no two are the same. There's a particular gratification in this. Each is personal and private—except in Hinduism, in which the *atman* or shared cosmic soul predominates. In the Abrahamic traditions, especially Christianity and Islam, each believer's soul is their own unique property, something to guard, often to polish via deeds of devotion so as to achieve salvation, which isn't sought for the good of other believers but for private advantage. In Christian belief, ours is a fallen world and because each of us is enmeshed in that world, it is a problem for each of us, as individuals. Indeed, saving one's soul is pretty much the baseline motivator of Christian devotion. Insofar as the focus is on personal salvation, it reinforces the centrality of each person, while also validating a degree of selfishness that would otherwise be reprehensible.

It is easy to criticize this motivation. After all, social ethics generally lauds altruism and condemns selfishness. But like it or not, a key reason the soul is so attractive to so many people is precisely because of its orientation toward one's self. More than an orientation, it is the entirety of what one is supposed to be, and—when spiritual push comes to psychological shove—all that each individual thinks he or she is.

A soul, then, is a sole possession; more than a private, personal adjunct to oneself, it is supposed to *be* one's self. Although religious commitment provides a dimension of specialness via group affiliation, the soul goes further, embodying nothing less than precious personhood to every believer, something that cannot be trespassed upon or taken away. No wonder it's so popular.

Our species is unique in that we make things up. God and the soul are prominent but not alone in this pantheon of imagined realities. Other comforting fabrications include the bromide that everything happens for a reason, that our group is the best, our leader is uniquely wonderful, each of us is above average. Not all these imagined realities are baseless, however. Things *do* happen for reasons, albeit not because they've been orchestrated by divine providence with us in mind. Most groups are pretty good, and even when they're not, there's often a benefit in thinking that yours is. Before we had effective medicines, we had shamans, and we still have placebos. And so, imagined realities don't necessarily warrant disdain; sometimes, as with placebo some of the time, they work. But they definitely deserve scrutiny.

There is plenty to scrutinize. Make-believe appears to be a human universal, starting with children talking to animals or imagining them conversing with each other. Adults do make-believe too. For example, there is a frequent cross-cultural belief that eating animals conveys their traits (eating lion meat makes you fierce, ground rhino horn conveys sexual potency, etc.), that there is inherent justice in the world (aka *karma* among Hindus), that everything happens for a reason—usually a reason oriented toward oneself as a way of ameliorating personal pain or injustice. And of course, there is astrology, mythology, and a host of supernatural deities. In early childhood, we begin to create a sense of our own identity, which not uncommonly involves making up illusions that are independent of the physical strictures and confines of our body. Moreover, these imaginings often include pipe dreams of heroism, accomplishment, romantic success, and perfect happiness. Imaginary role-playing games—which can involve seeing one's self as separate from our own anatomy—can come from the same illusion that produces belief in an independent soul occupying our body, not unlike how a talented actor "occupies" the character he or she is playing.

It's important to distinguish adult forms of make-believe—novels, games, folk tales, movies, theater, songs, dance, all of which involve a conscious suspension of disbelief in which we know that these things are pretend and we participate in them as though they are true but fully knowing that they aren't—from delusions, in which we take our inventions as bona fide reality. Such reifications of centralistic make-believe include assertive nationalism ("we're number 1"), thinking oneself among the very best drivers, cooks, lovers, athletes, and the like, and also, of course, religion, in which there's often a tension between those who revere its core concepts (love, connectedness, awe, devotion, submission) and fundamentalists who clutch the details as literally true: There is an omniscient, all-powerful, benevolent God who makes specific demands, punishes those who ignore or refuse those demands, who also cares about each of us and answers prayers (albeit sometimes the answer is No). Variously, between the ethereal core of theory and the specificity of fundamentalist literalism reside heaven, hell, and the soul.

Make-believe is usually fun. It can also be liberating, or lethal. Either way, however, reality matters, which doesn't stop human beings from making things up all the time, in order to make the painful more tolerable, feed our ego, provide explanations when none is otherwise available, and often just to amuse ourselves. *Homo fantasia*? Our all-too-human fantasies aren't only of rainbows and unicorns; they can also be dark and terrifying, but altogether "real" in their impact. Whatever the attractions of make-believe, it is important to come up for air. It shouldn't be necessary—but sometimes it is—to point out that no matter how satisfying make-believe can be, it's unwise to live in fantasy, disconnected from things as they really are.

In his poem "The Emperor of Ice Cream," Wallace Stevens urges us to "Let be be finale of seem," that is, let reality, how things *actually are*, take precedence over what seems real. For most people, most of the time, it *seems* that they, courtesy of their very own precious soul, are central to reality. Alas, reality is otherwise.

As living, breathing, metabolizing, reproducing creatures, we and our ancestors have always been engaged with the real world: extracting resources, obtaining safety, finding mates, reproducing, and seeking whatever additional satisfactions we crave. Hence, it seems peculiar that we also rely so heavily on make-believe, although generally this reliance is peripheral to meeting our basic, immediate needs. When immediacy calls, confronting us with a lightning storm, a predator, the risk of drowning or starving to death, threats to our loved ones, even those for whom God or their own soul is a deeply held make-believe construct respond in real time and put their make-believe on the back burner. But afterward, most people, most of the time, quickly pick up where they left off, playing their part in their preferred quotidian fictional script while hardly ever acknowledging that it is made up. It's often less stressful to quietly accept our fictions than to interrogate them. A golden helmet feels good and is always a perfect fit.

Sometimes make-believe works to our benefit, even for adults. William Ernest Henley's panegyric suggests that he really believed he was captain of his soul, and his soul-congratulatory make-believe served him well. If nothing else, it made for a lovely poem.

6

Dueling with Dualism

Are we two creatures in one: the soul of an angel in the body of a beast? Many think so. Belief in this dichotomy—mind versus matter, thoughts versus things—is the basis of dualism, a notion most clearly stated by René Descartes four centuries ago. It remains a key part of the soul's defense even today.

This chapter will look into dualism's appeal. Then, why it's bullshit.

Psychologist Paul Bloom has argued that people are intuitive dualists who readily assume that body and mind are separate and distinct.[1] Nearly all scientists reject dualism, but folk-wisdom embraces it, as do most children—which is Bloom's point. It's not a coincidence that the soul is often taken as identical to mind but different from the body. After all, we experience the seeming paradox that we have, or are, or possess a mind, yet we're equally aware of our physical selves, and the two seem to exist separately. We speak readily about "my brain," or "my thoughts" as though the two are different, a consequence of one entity owning another, rather than the two being one. Try this on: We don't *have* bodies, we *are* bodies. Bodies that don't just act upon the world and are acted upon by it, but that also think, love, imagine, hope, fear, and the like. We nonetheless say that someone has "gone out of her mind" without realizing the implication: that she had previously somehow been "in" her mind, and has then left. Unintended and often unrecognized, dualism creeps in.[2] Insofar as dualists imagine the brain as "the seat of the soul," that's how it is imagined: a seat, someplace where a separate entity sits.

Organ transplants are now well established. People get hearts, kidneys, even lungs and livers from donors, without anyone worrying that a heart recipient also received the donor's soul. That would be unimaginable because, well, the soul doesn't reside there. But imagine a brain transplant. Would the recipient also get the donor's soul? If a brain transplant wouldn't entail a soul transplant, then why not? Perhaps because the soul resides elsewhere, but if so, where? Or maybe the soul-brain connection is delicate and vulnerable to surgical disruption. In that case, what happens to this very vulnerable system, not just the brain but the rest of one's body, when the whole physical substrate is reduced to ash or eaten by worms? (See Chapter 7.)

For now, let's extend our *Gedankenexperiment* from human-to-human transplants to animal-to-human. The surgical implanting of animal organs, in particular genetically modified hearts and kidneys—i.e., xenotransplantation—is proceeding apace. If someone suffering from a terminal brain disease were to get a pig brain, would they also get a pig's soul? When David Bennett Sr., the first recipient of a pig heart, was asked postoperatively how he was feeling, he playfully replied, "Oink, oink!"

We might inquire about a different thought experiment, one less dramatic than a full-on brain transplant. Consider the philosophical chestnut known as the Ship of Theseus. After he killed the minotaur, the hero Theseus rescued the children of Athens by taking them aboard his ship. For centuries after, the citizens of Athens honored this event by bringing the ship on a pilgrimage and, as part of necessary maintenance, regularly replacing worn out components. The question then arises: After its components have all been replaced, and even if the replacement parts are identical to their original versions, is it still the same Ship of Theseus? If at some point the ship's identity shifts, what is that point?

Instead of a total brain transplant, what about replacing brain cells sequentially, like the Ship of Theseus? Whether these off-the-shelf transplanted neurons originated in a pig or another person, does the recipient retain her original soul, or that of the donor? And if there is a soul-switch, when does it happen? Descartes would presumably argue that it takes place when the pineal gland has been transferred—see later in this chapter—although as a devout Christian he wouldn't accept that a pig pineal would do the trick.

Fanciful cases aside, even the most committed dualists acknowledge that we use our brains to taste a strawberry or to read these words. And of course, scientific materialists would agree, but paradoxically, the statement that "we use our brains to think" once again buys unconsciously into the dualist perspective that there is someone or something else—an internal "me"—who uses their brain. Paul Bloom points out that this implied dichotomy was nicely satirized by the comedian Emo Phillips: "I used to think the brain was the most fascinating part of the human body, but then I thought: 'Look what's telling me that!'" Like it or not, and intended or not, closet dualism keeps creeping in whenever we think about mind and body.

This creep makes a kind of sense. Your body can be physically impacted, but not your soul: "Jordan's river is chilly and cold, chills the body but not the soul." Lose a tooth or an appendix and you remain yourself. You can move your fingers upon command, so there must be an inside person issuing those commands, separate perhaps from the body that follows them. We dream, during which some part of us might go away from its body and have adventures while we remain in bed. Dualism is almost unavoidable. We even extend it to physical objects—cars, boats, cell phones, and, of course, computers—readily imagining that they have personalities that emerge out of, yet are somehow separate from, their physical components.

There are other additions to the psychological allure of dualism, whereby body and mind appear to be disconnected. It's well known, for example, that the spirit can be willing but the flesh weak. And vice versa. Men develop erections, sometimes at inopportune times, or fail to do so, also inopportunely. Women undergo menarche, often when they don't expect or look forward to it, certainly unbidden. They also experience menopause, yet another example of the body "behaving" independent of one's mind. Despite changes in our body due to personal growth and development, our memories generate a kind of mental continuity, independent of merely meaty events or transitions.

Also contributing to dualism is our inability to look into our own brains and find therein the source of our mental experience. Philosopher Paul Churchland said it well:

The red surface of an apple does not look like a matrix of molecules reflecting photons at certain critical wave lengths, but that is what it is. The sound of a flute does not sound like a sinusoidal compression wave train in the atmosphere, but that is what it is. The warmth of the summer air does not feel like the mean kinetic energy of millions of tiny molecules, but that is what it is . . . . If one's pains and hopes and beliefs do not introspectively seem like electrochemical states in a neural network, that may be only because our faculty of introspection, like our other senses, is not sufficiently penetrating to reveal such hidden details.[3]

Closely related is what psychologist Julien Musolino calls the first-person fallacy:

Because we are sentient creatures and have access to an inner world of thoughts and sensations, it is easy to assume that our privileged access to this private world provides a reliable guide to our true nature and functioning. In the case of the heart, the fallacy is easy to recognize. A moment's reflection suffices to realize that the third-person perspective offered by science stands in an incomparably better position to tell us how the heart works, compared to our untutored, first-person intuitions. . . . I have direct and private access to the content of my own thoughts and you're not me, dear scientist, so how could you and your third-person perspective possibly know better than me what makes me tick?[4]

The bottom line, once again, is that people readily slip into dualism, however it is labeled. Even as we recognize the absurdity of Gregor Samsa transformed into a giant insect or Odysseus's crew into pigs, we easily accept that Mr. Samsa et al. remain themselves inside. Apsychists, who don't accept that souls exist or that they commute, transmute, travel, try out different bodies, enter heaven, hell, purgatory, the bardo, or nirvana, nonetheless find such stories relatable. We—all of us—may well be intuitive soul-sympathizers, even if we deny dualism *per se*.

But people are also intuitive flat-earthers. Our intuitions are often wrong, which is why this chapter explores how it is that the most skeptical observers, when they relax their rational objections, sometimes resonate with the soul's immateriality. This helps explain why belief in the soul—as factually wrong as belief that the Earth is flat—is so widespread.

For all its remarkable successes, scientific materialism faces real challenges when it comes to the soul, and not just because of the allure of our subjective experiential lives. Medical science puts the kibosh on any kind of life after death, whether in heaven or hell. An afterlife requires that we can and will continue in some kind of conscious state after our component material parts (brain, nerve cells, molecules, atoms) are dispersed. To put it mildly, this is hard to believe. But lots of people insist on it, and so, when science denies this yearned-for outcome, true believers are pushed to deny science itself, preferring fantasy to reality. "Pay no attention to that man behind the curtain"—especially when the curtain is built by scientific materialism, which is sometimes difficult to understand and is all the more unwelcome when it offers unpleasant truths.

In his book, *Ignorance and Bliss: On Wanting Not to Know*, Mark Lilla[5] examines the widespread tendency to avoid uncomfortable truths, which he begins with a modern retelling of Plato's allegory of the cave. A boy has been brought from his comfortable, accustomed dark into the newfound light, whereupon he quickly begs to go back to his deluded state. "I miss my playmates," he cries, "even if they were just pixels on a screen."

Dualism, a close ally of the soul, relies on imagined pixels. Although it is possible to be a believing dualist without also embracing a supposedly explanatory soul, the claim that mind is qualitatively discontinuous from matter requires faith in just this kind of unspecified, immaterial entity, one that requires something supernatural. And the big problem with invoking supernatural forces is that it marks not the beginning of an effort at comprehension, but its end.

Dualism's archenemy, which it shares with belief in the soul, isn't evolution, atheism, or the Devil, but scientific materialism, aka physicalism or sometimes scientific naturalism, which we'll consider shortly (they are interchangeable for our purposes). Most people who believe in the soul are religious; ditto for dualists, although at least some of the latter deny that their dualism is, at its core, supernatural. But it is.

It's possible—although uncommon—to be a dualist but not religious, given the ease of imagining that our minds are distinct from our bodies. It's also possible, but even less common, to be religious but not a dualist. This is rare, however, because the underlying assumption of all religions is that there exist supernatural entities of some sort, which adds to the temptation to apply supernatural forces to the vexatious mind/body problem. Given the elusive nature of our internal mental experience, as well as the standard doctrinal insistence that God is manifest within each of us via our soul, a believer who denies the soul would have to do some complicated mental gymnastics, aside from confronting the problem of dualism itself. So, very few do.

René Descartes, grandparent of today's dualism, was a believing Catholic. It appears that by promoting dualism he intended not only to solve a philosophical problem (the paradoxical existence of ethereal mind in a physical body) but also to elevate humanity by pointing to something we possess—*res cogitans* or "mind stuff"—which has no physical existence and doesn't take up any physical space, and that elevates us above mere *res extensa*, "body stuff," which is extended into three dimensions of reality. As it happens, religious belief

Figure 6.1 *Rene Descartes, a brilliant philosopher and mathematician, who sold his nonexistent soul to dualism. Source: Painting by Frans Hals, late seventeenth century; Photographer: André Hatala [e.a.] (1997).*

was already ahead of him, identifying *res cogitans* with a touch of the divine, while Cartesian dualism served to denigrate animals, who, unlike us, were made of *res extensa*, but nothing else. Hence, they have no mental lives and cannot even feel pain. He vivisected dogs, ignoring their screams. If not for the fact that he is considered the founder of modern Western philosophy and an accomplished mathematical genius as well (inventor, among other things, of Cartesian coordinates), one might suspect that it was Descartes who had no mental life (Figure 6.1).

When it comes to dualism, the Vatican is on board. As we noted previously, Pope John Paul II surprised and disconcerted fundamentalists when in a speech to the Pontifical Academy of Sciences he acknowledged that evolution likely accounted for our bodies. But our minds and notably our souls are a different story: "Theories of evolution which, in accordance with the philosophies inspiring them, consider the mind as emerging from the forces of living matter, or as a mere epiphenomenon of this matter, are incompatible with the truth about man. Nor are they able to ground the dignity of the person."[6] Hence, dualism isn't just psychologically alluring, it is church doctrine.

Herein implied, but not as yet confronted, is that given pontifical acceptance of human evolution, it follows that at some point in the distant past a nonhuman hominin female lacking a soul gave birth to a bona fide human being who had one. Quite a trick, because if (as the Pope acknowledged) human beings evolved via a Darwinian process, then our physical self is the result of a gradual transition from ancestral proto-humans, themselves descended just as gradually from other "lower" and ostensibly soulless primates, who evolved from even lower and thus more soul-deprived mammals... and so on. Yet we are supposed to accept that when biologically modern *Homo sapiens* gradually evolved, at some magical moment they looked around and found that they suddenly had souls. It's a conundrum reminiscent of the dilemma of ensoulment with regard to fertilization, which we explore in Chapter 7. For now, suffice it that there is no thunderclap when *bona fide* human beings instantly appeared, just as there isn't one at which fertilization takes place. And if our evolution was gradual—which it was—then our souls must have been gradually obtained as well. This, in turn, confirms that if evolution is true—

which it is—then either animals have some sort of souls, or they don't and neither do we.

With or without papal pronouncement and even setting the soul aside, it's a heavy lift to connect the two *res-es*—*cogitans* to *extensa*, mind to matter, consciousness to brain, subjective mental experience to neurobiology—because as a purely intellectual challenge our mental phenomena feel qualitatively distinct from that of physical, material events. The two don't seem like apples and oranges; deriving thoughts from bodies feels more like conjuring the nature of love from the nature of fire hydrants. It is this qualitative discontinuity that led Descartes to propose his dualist discontinuity. But as the brilliant Princess Elisabeth of Bohemia pointed out to Descartes at the time, there is no way that *res cogitans* (mind), which lacks extension in space, could push, pull, or otherwise impact the *res extensa* of a physical body. Descartes ducked it, and to this day dualists still have no answer to Elisabeth's cogent objection, no way of explaining how mind acts upon matter. Philosopher Gilbert Ryle pointed out that they're left with "the dogma of the ghost in the machine,"[7] with no way for the ghost to act on that machine.

Scientific materialists have no answer to the reversed conundrum, the traditional dualism dilemma, namely how does matter create mind. In his treatise, *Monadology* (1714), the German polymath Gottfried Leibniz used a striking machine metaphor to argue the dualist cause that mental experience "cannot be explained on mechanical principles, i.e. by shapes and movements" (see Figure 6.2). He suggested:

> If we pretend that there is a machine whose structure makes it think, sense and have perception, then we can conceive it enlarged, but keeping to the same proportions, so that we might go inside it as into a mill. Suppose that we do: then if we inspect the interior, we shall find there nothing but parts which push one another, and never anything which could explain a perception.

Leibniz's challenging image can be extended via today's neurobiology. Can we imagine traveling inside a human brain, wandering among the neurons and thereby seeing how these wet machines produce subjective mental experience?

Figure 6.2 *In mechanical devices such as this, Leibniz seems to be correct: there doesn't appear to be any sign of consciousness. Soure: Part of a printing press in the Musée des Arts et Métiers in Paris; Flickr.*

Two and a half centuries after Leibniz, the 1966 movie *Fantastic Voyage* followed the exploits of a team that was shrunk to microscopic size and tasked to repair a blood clot in a scientist's brain. Alas, they didn't investigate how that brain generated the scientist's mind. But Leibniz was onto something. His armchair speculation, like that of Descartes, italicizes the seeming distance between mind and matter. Leibniz was much influenced by Galileo's emphasis on "matter in motion," so-called mechanical philosophy, at the same time worrying that it could—in his words—result in the "ruin of holy doctrine." (Which it does.)

For a delightful and thought-provoking reversal of the dualist claim that organic matter can't produce mind, consider Terry Bisson's short story, "They're Made Out of Meat." It consists entirely of a dialog between a robotic extraterrestrial space probe and its equally robotic home base. Here is a sample, beginning with the base's incredulity when informed that the human inhabitants of planet Earth are made of meat instead of, presumably, some kind of electronic hardware:

"You're asking me to believe in sentient meat."

"I'm not asking you, I'm telling you. These creatures are . . . made out of meat."

"Thinking meat! You're asking me to believe in thinking meat!"

"Yes, thinking meat! Conscious meat! Loving meat. Dreaming meat. The meat is the whole deal!

As we meat-made creatures struggle with the consequences of Artificial Intelligence, including the dilemma of whether electronic devices could become conscious, it's worthwhile to ask how strange it might be for sentient, intelligent electronic entities to contemplate how meaty critters such as us could possibly be sentient.

If, following Leibniz's lead, we were to shrink ourselves and make our own fantastic voyage inside someone's brain (or our own), all that we'd encounter would be *res extensa:* goopy, chemically infused, electrically charged wet stuff. Meat. We wouldn't see, touch, smell, or hear any thoughts or emotions. "The meat is the whole deal." For Leibniz, this showed that merely material things can't possibly think, feel, or be conscious. But since we do think, feel, and are conscious, Leibniz and other dualists such as Descartes long ago concluded that this feat must be achieved via an immaterial, spirit-infused component. (This is not an option that Bisson's meatless robots bothered to contemplate.)

The soul's immateriality is psychologically appealing in addition to its alleged explanation of how matter produces mind; namely, how matter produces life. The argument goes that something must intervene with sluggish matter to literally enliven it. And conversely, something important is lost when the body dies: Eyes, bright and busy, become dull and unresponsive. Breathing ceases. The body, previously warm, becomes eerily cold. Life has fled, its spark extinguished. Something that had previously animated flesh—a soul?—has departed. No wonder life has long been associated with a kind of magic, insubstantial substance: Now you've got it, now you don't. And no wonder the soul has long been equated with breath and thereby, with life itself. Even people who don't ascribe souls to nonhuman animals are tempted to think that a substance or ineffable force gives life when present and leaves a body lifeless when it flies away. (Interesting that it never crawls, wriggles, wobbles, or squirms away; the immateriality of the soul, or of an imagined animating principle, somehow makes it airborne.)

Although it is oh-so-seductive to pseudo-explain life as due to the infusion of some sort of magical animating principle tightly linked to the soul, trouble arises when it comes to other organisms that are unquestionably alive but allegedly soulless. For a spider to be alive, must it also have a life-giving soul? Spiders are unquestionably alive. If they lack an immaterial soul, is their livingness due to something purely material? On the other hand, "life," according to philosopher Wolfgang Geigerich, "is the dance that makes corpses alive."[8] Giegerich goes on to point out that if he takes someone's wallet, he has it, but if he "takes" someone's life, he has nothing at all. There is no transfer of materiality. In this sense, life is real, yet it is not in any sense a thing.

Like the mind? Neither life nor mind exists by itself, unlike, say, Giegerich's newly acquired wallet. Life, like the mind, is a process that derives from the action of its underlying material bases: how cells interact, notably via their anatomy and electrochemistry. By some interpretations, the soul, although similar to life, isn't quite the same, because it's something that goes on forever, unlike a temporary life-giving interaction among chemicals, electrical signals, and cells. It's not a dance, but an ineffable something within the dancer that makes cadavers into people.

Aside from its alleged explanation of mind and sometimes even of life, part of the soul's dualist appeal derives simply from its immateriality, that is, the fact that it isn't "real," at least not in the way that an elephant is real, or a doughnut, or a rock. It's supposed to be, somehow, a non-thing thing. Clearly, other "things" without physical existence are real, albeit immaterial: love, fear, hope, geometry, and so forth. But the Abrahamic soul is not just a concept.

No one claims that the Pythagorean Theorem is imbued with a divine spark, but believers claim that the soul exists in a way that an immaterial mathematical truth does not. It is more part of the substantive world than is a geometric theorem, yet is not mere dross. Its immateriality opens a door to the divine, while its connection to each individual makes its existence adorably personal and therefore all the more attractive (as I tried to show in Chapter 5).

Immateriality is also useful to the soul's mythology because failure to see, hear, smell, touch, or taste it isn't a dispositive argument against it. After all, something immaterial needn't be detectable by material means. In fact, if you want to make an irrefutable argument, it mustn't be. Call it the China Teapot

Assertion, after Bertrand Russell's critique of unprovable—indeed, untestable—assertions about the existence of God. Suppose, wrote Russell, someone claims that there is a China Teapot in orbit outside Mars. It is too small to be seen by telescopes or any other means, but believe-you-me, it's there! Carl Sagan made a similar point about an immaterial pink dragon cavorting in his closet. You can't see it? Of course not, it's invisible! You can't feel it, hear it, smell it, or in any way verify its existence? Of course not, such is the nature of immaterial dragons! By the same token, no one has scientifically *disproved* the existence of the soul, so its existence can safely be assumed, at least by those eager to do so.

Contrary to the received wisdom that belief in the soul arose as a result of religious belief, maybe belief in the soul—as a mysterious, immaterial mind and life force—came first, which then contributed to the development of religion. If mind and life exist beyond materiality, it's just another step that something else, call it God, similarly exists in its own immaterial realm.[9] This hypothesis is beyond the remit of *The Soul Delusion*, so we'll return to dualism, but first let's have a little talk about tulpas.

First appearing in Tibetan mysticism, a tulpa is a mystical entity produced by intense spiritual practice that is somehow connected to the practitioner and that becomes sentient and to some extent independent of its creator. In the Western occult belief system known as theosophy, tulpas were called "thoughtforms," which may or may not take the shape of the person who created them, having typically (tulpally?) emerged from their own astral plane, whatever that is.

Interest in tulpas is not limited to self-identified occultists. In the late twentieth century, online communities consisting of self-styled "tulpamancers" emerged, with seemingly normal people establishing their own tulpa connections through, believe it or not, such television series as "My Little Pony." Developmental psychologists see parallels between tulpas and children's creation of imaginary friends. And not just children. When fictional characters out of literature—Odysseus, Hamlet, Elizabeth Bennet—"come alive" on the page, which is to say, in the reader's imagination, perhaps they too are tulpas. And of course, maybe each soul is a tulpa (soulpa?), yet another manifestation of how dualism not only appeals to the human mind, but how mind creates whatever it wants.

In addition to mind, consciousness, and tulpas, free will is another chestnut, closely allied to dualism and often synonymized with the soul. Jean-Paul Sartre promoted a kind of atheist dualism. He saw freedom as the key human attribute, arguing that one's body can be imprisoned but not one's will, conscience, or soul, although as a committed atheist, Sartre would never have used this last construction. Neuroscience makes it clear that there is no inner homunculus independent of the physical cause-and-effect interactions that impinge on our neurons and initiate our mental experience.[10] And yet, soul-seduction is so strong that for many it is difficult to overcome, science be damned. But those who succeed will end up better informed and less inclined to brag or worry about the fate of something that doesn't exist.

If you acknowledge that the world is made of matter and energy, cause and effect, all of it subject to natural processes, then you must carve out a huge exception to account for the soul. You'd need to acknowledge the supernatural in a kind of superimposed conceptual dualism. Neuroscientists don't do this; pretty much to a person, they're confident that the mind is something that the brain does. The devout and the dualists find it disconcerting, a case of naïve "scientism" run amuck, but the truth is we're meat, precisely the stuff that so disconcerted Terry Bisson's robotic intergalactic probers: talking meat, thinking meat, worshipping meat, grieving meat, celebrating meat, but any way you slice it, meat.

Neurobiologist Robert Sapolsky begins his book *Determined* by recounting the story of "turtles all the way down."[11] It is said that early in the twentieth century, a famous scientist (accounts vary as to who) had finished a lecture on the makeup of the solar system, whereupon someone raised their hand and said, "This is nonsense. We all know that the Earth rests on the back of a giant turtle." The lecturer responded indulgently, "Very well, what is the turtle standing on?" "Another turtle." "And what is *that* one on?" "You can't get away like that. It's turtles all the way down!"

This vignette is often used to satirize purported explanations that don't explain anything, that rely on illogic stubbornly repeated and indifferent to what we know of reality. Sapolsky brilliantly turns this sarcastic critique on its head, pointing out that when it comes to understanding how the actual, material world of physics, chemistry, geology, and biology works, it *really is* turtles all the way down. Stuff is composed of other stuff, and things happen because of matter and energy. Effects happen because of causes, real physical causes acting in the real world. Even genuine turtles, here on Earth and not floating in the ether, are made of matter and energy. Nothing occurs all by itself, plucked into existence or action by some immaterial Tinkerbell tinsel. This recognition, fatal to the soul, is what philosophers call "scientific materialism" or sometimes "physicalism," and what critics scorn as "scientism."

Biology in particular undermines the dualism-based soul in two basic ways, mechanistically and via evolution. Mechanistically, modern medicine and neurobiology make it stunningly clear that mind comes from matter and not from some airy-flighty nothingness; it's something that nervous systems do.

Evolution is similarly devastating to dualism because it reveals our deep material connectedness with other life forms, thereby obliterating the claim that we are supernaturally special. Other purported human-animal barriers have fallen, or have at least been breached: tool use, tool making, the existence of sociocultural traditions, even perhaps symbolic language, and certainly intelligent problem-solving and various levels of consciousness. The bottom-line evolutionary insight is that all living things share common ancestors and have been materially connected by common descent. Given that the evidence is now overwhelming that animals and not just human beings have minds, anyone equating the mind with the soul must grant that nonhuman animals also have souls. This is not only theologically heretical, but it leads to yet more trouble if we pursue in detail the matter of matter itself and ask about the soul-status of chimps, dogs, cats, horses, pigs, birds, lizards, and octopuses. Worms, anyone? Bacteria? Viruses? There is no clear barrier to arrest the soul's descent down this slippery slope. So, you can either ignore the slope or ditch the soul.

Science studies how real effects are produced by real turtles. The scientific perspective is that there is nothing on Earth and in our bodies but those turtles, all the way down. Nothing here is incompatible with using the word soul as a synonym for mind, consciousness, conscience, imagination, love, empathy, subjective perception, or even spirituality. Let a thousand metaphors bloom! But the theologically infused conception of the soul as a literal *non-thing thing*, possessing some mysterious, metaphysical existence in itself, a magical mystery gizmo hovering in its own spiritual ether, inflated perhaps with phlogiston and not supported by turtles—or by anything—is itself unsupportable and deserves to be discarded along with belief in witches, warlocks, goblins, hobgoblins, incubi, succubi, angels, devils, demons, and fairies. (Also God, although for many, this is a bridge too far.)

Even the Bible occasionally flirts with materialism, as when Genesis points out, "Dust you are and to dust you will return." Carl Sagan substituted "star stuff." In his 1991 book *Consciousness Explained*, Daniel Dennett offered the following assessment:

> The prevailing wisdom, variously expressed and argued for, is materialism: there is only one sort of stuff, namely matter—the physical stuff of physics, chemistry, and physiology—and the mind is somehow nothing but a physical phenomenon. In short, the mind is the brain. According to materialists, we can (in principle!) account for every mental phenomenon using the same physical principles, laws and raw materials that suffice to explain radioactivity, continental drift, photosynthesis, reproduction, nutrition, and growth.[12]

The reality is that we know, to a certainty, that the brain creates consciousness and the mind. Injury to the brain causes injury to the mind. Numerous brain regions, too many to list here, have been identified as responsible for distinct mental experiences. Stimulate them and you evoke subjective sensations. Injure them and you produce mental injury. One of the best-known examples, familiar to generations of physicians, researchers, and undergraduates, concerns Phineas Gage, a railroad foreman who, because of an accidental explosion in 1848, had a metal rod driven through his head, piercing his brain. Astoundingly, he survived and lived somewhat normally for another twelve years. Somewhat, because the injury to his left frontal lobe dramatically changed his personality. Previously sober and responsible, he became capricious, vacillating, unreliable; "Gage," a friend commented, "was no longer Gage."

It is one thing, however, to know *that* brain and mind are tightly connected, quite another to accept it, deep in our what?—our brain, our mind, our supposed soul? Here is Tennyson, from his poem *In Memorium*:

> I think we are not wholly brain,
> Magnetic mockeries; not in vain, . . .
> Not only cunning casts in clay:
> Let Science prove we are, and then
> What matters Science unto men,
> At least to me?

The poet is saying that if science demonstrates that our minds are "wholly brain," then so much the worse for science. If so, then so much the worse for our ability to understand the real world. No one claims that scientific materialism is guaranteed to be easy, or even emotionally comfortable, especially when it demonstrates that long-held beliefs, however comforting, are simply false.

The difficulty is even greater when science-based answers aren't yet forthcoming. Thus, even as we know that Tennyson's "we" (our minds) are "wholly brain," science still doesn't know precisely *how* this wholeness is accomplished. Until then, stubborn dualists will likely keep holding out, claiming that until the actual mechanism of mind-brain connection is unraveled, they are justified in invoking the soul, that because modern science is unable to explain precisely how material stuff generates subjective mental experience, they have an anti-science "gotcha," legitimizing faith in an immaterial soul. This ignores the fact that dualism is completely at sea when it comes to solving or even addressing the riddle that they gleefully accuse neuroscience of failing to unravel. Dualism has nothing to say about how an immaterial entity can undergo or generate mental experience, or how it can induce a material entity (the brain) to do so. Or the body to move. In short, because current neuroscience can't answer the "how" question, dualists claim that their answer—invoking a floating grin that doesn't even pretend to connect to a cat—is as good as any. Moreover, it's somehow better than a real cat.

The physicist Wolfgang Pauli[13] once responded to an especially vaporous proposal in his native German, "*Das ist nicht nur nicht richtig; es ist nicht einmal falsch!*"—often shortened in English to "it is not even wrong." A wrong idea may be useful as a whetstone against which to sharpen thought and if it leads to possible testing. But if something is "not even wrong," it is simply irredeemable. Claims of the supernatural fit this bill. They are not even wrong, because they merely float in the verbal ether and are worse than useless because they inhibit thought and preclude productive investigation. They're not explanations, but evasions.

If a material thinker is unimaginable—more accurately, its mechanism is not yet worked out—an immaterial one is, in Pauli's sense, not even wrong. Yet the immaterial soul enjoys an additional psychological advantage (not a veridical one), beyond the allures of dualism already described. Because we can see the material substance—the brain—whereby and wherein experience is made manifest, we are free to subject that substance to detailed questions, not least: How do you do your job? By contrast, because we cannot even satisfactorily picture a soul, we cannot subject it to any comparable interrogation. And yet, the current inability to explain how neurons produce conscious experience has been brandished as demonstrating inadequacy of the physicalist stance. Sauce for the material goose should be sauce for the goose's immaterial soul. But precisely because of the soul's alleged immateriality, the same sauce isn't applied.

Dualists satisfy themselves that some things, notably the way matter produces mind, will never be solved, so we must engage in magical soul-based nonthinking. By contrast, in his introduction to *The Descent of Man*, Darwin wrote, "Ignorance more frequently begets confidence than does knowledge: it is those who know little, and not those who know much, who so positively assert that this or that problem will never be solved by science." He could have been thinking of Immanuel Kant, genius philosopher and also a scientist who pioneered one of the first theories of earthquakes and who postulated, correctly, that the Milky Way was a huge disc of distant stars, and that "nebulae" were distant galaxies. These insights were new and consequential for the development of modern astronomy. Kant also thought, somewhat less successfully, about the biological world, writing in his *Critique of Judgment* (1790) that "there will never be a Newton for a blade of grass." Well, there have been many such Newtons, notably including Darwin along with researchers successfully unraveling the biochemistry of photosynthesis, details of plant physiology and ecology, and an enormous additional catalog of biological insights.

The gravamen of this book is to criticize supernatural "explanations"—notably those purporting to buttress the soul delusion—as reflecting George Eliot's "power of ignorance." And yet, given that open-mindedness is the hallmark of science, perhaps we shouldn't be too hasty.

According to legend, a visitor to the home of Nobel Prize-winning physicist Niels Bohr was surprised to see a horseshoe (believed by some to bring good luck) above his door.[14] When asked if he really believed in this superstition, the renowned scientist responded, "No, but I am told that it brings luck even to those who do not believe in it." Leaving space in one's imagination for the unknown is crucial to any searching mind, and can, if nothing else, bring a kind of satisfaction or at least hope, maybe even if you don't believe in it. As we bear in mind how wide the differences are between explanations derived from scientific materialism and phony evasions associated with supernatural beliefs, it can be tempting to forget how even great scientists have in the past crossed the line into what we now consider the occult. Only at the time, their subjects weren't considered supernatural or unscientific. Moreover, astrology gave rise to astronomy, and alchemy to chemistry.

Johannes Kepler, notable mathematician and astronomer, believed in astrology; Newton, possibly the greatest physicist of all time, practiced alchemy and wrote as much about the Book of Daniel and the apocalypse of John as in his *Principia Mathematica*. It is said that Robert Boyle, now revered as the first early modern chemist, was fascinated by the possible reality of "second sight," the reported ability of a few Scottish highlanders to predict the future. And William Harvey, justly renowned for figuring out how blood circulates, is known to have once dissected a toad that he believed was a witch's familiar. (Apparently, it wasn't, or if it was, Harvey found no evidence to that effect.)

The above is not to suggest that these people, great scientists all, were on occasion foolish or lacking in the good judgment that modern scientists pride themselves today. Au contraire. Given that so much was unknown (and still is), they reserved mental space for exploring the unknown, even when that space involved what we now realize wasn't science at all. It's a good lesson in open-mindedness, but let's not take it so far that our brains fall out.

Do current unknowns decorate and enliven the scientific quest to understand reality? Of course. Even now, creationists clamor for paleontologists to find the "missing link," ignoring that every time one is found (and many have been: Australopithecines, *Homo erectus*, *Homo ergaster*, *Homo habilis*, and others) success creates two more "missing links," one on each side. The progress of science always creates more questions than it answers.

Back in the matter-to-mind quest, neurobiologists, scientific materialists that they are, have been seriously looking into that deliciously seductive mind-brain problem. Not so dualists. It may be that all the scientists' efforts—slicing and dicing neurons, stimulating brain regions, employing a range of imaging techniques, experimenting with the impact of neurotransmitters and other chemicals—will not yield satisfactory answers. Or maybe they will. There have been stunning successes when it comes to unraveling the neural correlates of consciousness; the actual causative mechanisms, not so much. But the science-saga is ongoing. By contrast, it is impossible even to imagine what sort of research program dualists would mount, beyond pointing to scripture and the widespread sense that somehow the soul does it, because mere matter couldn't possibly. Yet they claim that because science has not yet uncovered the precise details of how the brain produces the mind, this is not only a key weakness of the scientific enterprise but also supports their position, even though they can't even begin to suggest what kind of evidence they might seek. Instead, they rely on abracadabra, while critiquing science for not yet providing the kind of proof that they disdain.

Explaining consciousness via the soul is no different than explaining it via phlogiston.[15] Even if phlogiston had turned out to be real, attributing something to another thing that itself is utterly mysterious hardly counts as an explanation—except for those who have decided that no scientific explanation will suffice. (In that case, why insist that science come up with one?)

Let's assume, just for a moment, that your mind is due to your soul. Would that explain the source of consciousness? Or merely push it back one step? In the movie *Men in Black*, tiny extraterrestrials have invaded Earth and are living inside human-seeming robots, controlling their movements. Positing a dualist soul-mind as something, someone, somehow living inside our human bodies and responsible for our thoughts and actions is equivalent to these little extraterrestrial dudes. But repositioning the source of consciousness in this way "isn't even wrong"; it solves nothing because we need another little critter inside that one, to make sense of *its* mental processes. If the soul solves the mystery of mind, then what solves the mystery of the soul's mind? Thus it goes, as wrote the nineteenth-century mathematician Augustus De Morgan:

> Great fleas have little fleas upon their backs to bite 'em,
> And little fleas have lesser fleas, and so *ad infinitum*.

Denis Diderot was one of the pillars of the eighteenth-century French Enlightenment. In an essay titled "Letter on the Blind for the Use of Those Who See," he urged that we not delude ourselves by thinking that we can solve a mystery by positing a greater mystery, one even less susceptible to rational solution. "If nature offers us a difficult knot to untie,"[16] wrote Diderot, "let us . . . not untie it using the hand of a being who immediately becomes a fresh knot, harder to untie than the first."[17] Diderot was critiquing reliance upon God as explanation for whatever couldn't be otherwise explained. But his warning applies equally to dualistic "explanations" of the mind, whether or not they explicitly invoke the soul.

Echoing Leibniz's machine analogy, dualists argue that we can discount scientific materialism because matter simply cannot produce mind. To repeat: We know that it does. We just don't know precisely *how*. We know, similarly, that like charges repel and opposite ones attract, but not precisely how—yet no one questions the reality of the underlying physics. In any event, for the moment let's turn the dualist claim around as Princess Elisabeth did in her critique of Descartes: How is immaterial mind supposed to influence matter, causing our too too-solid flesh to follow its orders? Descartes feebly suggested the pineal gland, for no particular reason except that it sits midway between the two hemispheres and its function was not otherwise known. Contemporary anatomists were quick to point out that cats, dogs, pigs, and horses had very robust pineal glands, yet no one—and certainly not Descartes—was willing to grant them souls.

The immaterial idea "wiggle my finger," transmitted from your brain along motor neurons, causes your nerves to fire and your muscles to contract. As a result your finger wiggles, without the good offices of the pineal gland. (Or, I daresay, your soul.) We can trace the electrochemical details of how such nerve impulses are generated, how they travel along nerve cell membranes via dendrites, cell bodies, and axons, the anatomy whereby nerves connect to muscles, how muscles respond, and how their contraction causes that finger to move. What we cannot as yet figure out is how the finger-wiggling idea was generated in the first place. In short, we know increasingly, and to remarkably fine detail, the neural correlates of finger-wagging. What we don't know yet are the neural correlates of how this finger-wagging notion is itself produced.

For dualists, the whole magilla was initiated when your soul (or its immaterial equivalent, perhaps your tulpa) acted on your body, with no idea how, and apparently no research program trying to find out. We know that the physical world acts on the body in all sorts of ways, which then acts on the mind: Sound waves tickle the eardrum, stimulating the auditory nerve which then sends signals to the auditory cortex, and you hear something. We have an even better idea what happens when the material world acts on other parts of that same world: billiard balls collide, a car hits a tree, you stub your toe. But how can something that has no physical existence both act on the body and be acted on by it? And why should science lose credibility for not yet knowing how matter produces mind, while leaving dualists free to ignore not only that question but also how mind impacts matter? And what and where is mind, separate from matter? (Answer: nowhere.)

When Newton unearthed the laws of gravity, he had no idea how an immaterial gravitational force could operate on the material world, including the material "heavenly" bodies. Contemporary physicists were initially aghast, troubled by the notion of invisible action at a distance, but they proceeded to study the phenomenon, rather than throw up their hands and announce that they were "gravitational dualists."

Maybe someday a similar claim will be made and confirmed about the human soul: perhaps that it derives from a kind of soul-field, analogous to gravitational fields, quantum wave fluctuations, or something as yet unimagined. In the interest of intellectual honesty, let's admit that this is at least possible, at which point mind and consciousness will have been folded into scientific materialism and another woo-woo prop for soul-belief will have been removed. The physics of gravity, electromagnetic waves, or quantum events, including such weirdness as quantum entanglement—which Einstein once derided as "spooky action at a distance"—have all been validated, not only in theory but via detailed observation and experiment, generating stunning predictive accuracy down to the fifth and sixth decimal places. By contrast, there is presently not an iota (or a quantum) of evidence pointing to the soul or any other basis for dualist imaginings.

Even though we're in the dark about precisely how neurons create consciousness, the fact that matter produces mind is not in doubt. For all their complaints that we can't explain how this happens, dualists have their own dilemma, no less daunting, known as the connectivity problem: How can something immaterial affect something material? Back to Princess Elisabeth. Ideas are indeed immaterial, and they can and do affect actions of all sorts, but they do so by engaging matter in the form of neurons, muscles, and so on. Of course, dualists can argue that this is just what the soul does, but the soul is also supposed to be truly immaterial, like an idea, an intention, a thought, a subjective experience, and the like. Yet, if it survives death and then either cavorts in heaven or suffers in hell, it is necessarily more real than any of these.

Scientific materialism isn't merely the Holy Grail of science, it's the only grail. Christian doctrine in particular has emphasized not only a distinction between the spiritual and the physical but has traditionally devalued the latter—especially the body—as gross, unclean, corrupt, and bestial, compared with the empyrean, angelic realm of the pure and divine, occupied not just by God and the angels, but ultimately, our souls. Compared to this vision of spiritual perfection, our physical bodies are a letdown[18].

Materiality is especially relevant to our inquiry when it comes to the central nervous system. It makes no more sense to separate consciousness from the brain than to separate respiration from our lungs or circulation from our heart. Poke a needle into a brain and you skewer consciousness, subjective sensations, memory, or the ability to move parts of our body: all those mental activities that allegedly depend on nonphysical entities which are supposed to be independent of the body. The connection between our matter and our mind is simply beyond dispute, including not just injuries but also the reality that under normal healthy circumstances the matter of our brains generates our minds. Stimulate different brain regions, and, depending on which ones, you get subjective experiences, including, as will be explored in the next chapter, many of those reported as part of Near Death Experiences. There have also been a gazillion fMRI studies, showing that different brain regions light up in conjunction with different sensory input, motor output, memories, emotional states, cognitive functions; the list is overwhelming. Although the task of generating consciousness is immensely complex, so is the brain. Encompassing upward of one hundred trillion synapses, it, too, is immensely complex, and up to the job.

Here is another dualist argument that has been debunked by modern neuroscience. Descartes pointed out that whereas you can take a knife and cut matter, you can't cut up the mind. The former is divisible; the latter isn't. Just as you can't chop up a ghost, you can't make half a soul. *Ipso facto*, the mind—unlike mere matter—is immaterial. Except that you *can* cut up the mind. One treatment for people suffering from severe epilepsy is to sever the corpus callosum, the brain fibers that connect the two cerebral hemispheres. Such "split-brain" patients literally have split minds, because sensory information that normally crosses over is now restricted to one side of the brain. As a result, these patients can perceive and be induced to act separately upon two conflicting sets of information, because the matter of their brain has been divided, and as the brain goes, so goes the mind.

People with brain injuries experience predictable mental injuries as famously happened to Phineas Gage. For another example, there is something called "prosopagnosia," whereby sufferers cannot identify faces. It is caused by damage to a particular brain region, the fusiform gyrus, located in the temporal lobe. Hence, Oliver Sachs's account of "The Man Who Mistook His Wife for a Hat." On the other hand, when a healthy person's fusiform gyrus is stimulated electrically, the mind attached to that region sees faces "spontaneously." Not really spontaneously, of course, as after a visitation from some mystical force, but because the relevant brain region has been engaged.

The list is almost endless. Damage your auditory cortex, and your hearing is impaired. Similarly for the visual cortex and the ability to see. Michael Shermer writes that a man "who suddenly developed pedophilic feelings was discovered to have a tumor at the base of his orbitofrontal cortex that pressed up against the right prefrontal region of his brain, an area associated with impulse control. When the tumor was resected, he lost all pedophilic feelings. When they returned months later, it was discovered that the tumor had grown back."[19]

While treating patients with severe epilepsy, pioneering neurosurgeon Wilder Penfield discovered that by electrically stimulating various brain regions he could evoke predictable motor responses as well as sensations associated with different body parts. He could even induce patients who were wide awake during the procedure (the brain itself has no pain receptors) to recall detailed memories. The hippocampus is the primary organ tasked not so much with storing memories but with consolidating them. A now-famous patient, HM, whose bilateral hippocampus had been destroyed, lost that ability. Someone could meet HM, share a normal conversation, then leave the room and return a few minutes later, whereupon for the patient it was as though they had never met. HM lived in an eternal present.

It would be a mistake, however, to exaggerate the localization of brain function; diffuse networks involving humongous numbers of complex connections are nearly always involved. Moreover, neurosurgeons have found that the childhood brain is capable of remarkable plasticity such that in some cases, when one of the two cerebral hemispheres has been entirely removed or rendered nonfunctional by disease, patients can live essentially normal lives. On balance, however, the dependence of mind on brain is so screamingly evident that one is tempted to conclude that anyone who denies it may have suffered a stroke in a brain region that specializes in acknowledging the obvious.

Descartes's *Cogito, ergo sum*, "I think, therefore I am," is okay as a statement of philosophical certainty,[20] although more accurate when reversed: *Sum, ergo cogito*.

Francis Crick, co-discoverer of the structure of the DNA molecule, began his book, *The Astonishing Hypothesis*,[21] as follows:

The Astonishing Hypothesis is that "you," your joys and your sorrows, your memories and your ambitions, your sense of personal identity and free will, are in fact no more than the behavior of a vast assembly of nerve cells and their associated molecules. This hypothesis is so alien to the ideas of most people alive today that it can truly be called astonishing.

But it's not astonishing to anyone with a background in neurobiology, nor should it be to anyone with a background in science. Crick, an atheist and dyed-in-the-brain scientific materialist, subtitled his book, "The scientific search for the soul," by which he meant the scientific search for consciousness, an area in which Crick himself worked until his death. It's still going on.

This chapter has readily acknowledged that how consciousness happens, happens to be a very tough scientific challenge. In a nutshell, the "hard problem of consciousness," a phrase initiated by the philosopher David Chalmers, is that we're all made of nonconscious matter, so how can consciousness arise? How can mere stuff think? Or hope? Fear? Love? And taste bananas, smell roses, feel hot or cold, write poems, experience orgasm, worry about consciousness? It's a hard problem indeed, but do we really need woo-woo dualism à la Descartes and Leibniz to "solve" it? After all, hard problems attract science's best and brightest who have learned a tremendous amount about how neurons work, although no one thus far has gotten very far when it comes to cracking this particularly hard-shelled nut. It is even possible that an answer will never be found because the problem just isn't susceptible to scientific unraveling, not because it requires supernatural intervention, but because the question might not be meaningful.

In Douglas Adams's *The Hitchhiker's Guide to the Galaxy*, the supercomputer Deep Thought struggles with the answer to "The Ultimate Question of Life, the Universe, and Everything." It's 42.[22] Maybe the "solution" to the hard problem of consciousness is similar. That is, perhaps the question isn't scientific but philosophical, a function of how we think about consciousness. But we don't know if this is so, and we should all be proud that scientists keep trying to solve it. It's also possible that their efforts, like Zeno's arrow, will continually approach the goal but never quite get there. No matter, the readiness—or rather, the approach—is all. Because scientific truth is always an asymptote, never entirely achieved.

Success in unwinding the scientific materialist basis of consciousness would be terrifically exciting but isn't guaranteed for yet another reason, namely our nature as biological organisms. Because our brains, like our bodies, evolved over many eons during which the selective environment consisted of medium-sized objects moving at medium speeds, it is remarkable how far those brains have gotten when it comes to understanding the universe. This includes such bizarre situations as nearly infinite speeds, nearly infinitesimal particles, invisible energy fields, millions of light-years, biological and geological events occurring hundreds of millions of years ago, all far removed from the environments in which our species evolved.[23]

It is therefore admirable and even a bit surprising how much our wetware mammal-minds have achieved, yet also possible that the hard problem of consciousness is simply beyond our capacity to solve. Our brains evolved to deal with other people, animals, the vagaries of weather, the challenges of reproducing, getting food and shelter—but probably not to figure out how those brains themselves operate, because during 99.999 percent of our evolutionary history, there has been no adaptive payoff in doing so. Our Pleistocene ancestors would not have been more successful projecting their genes into the future if their brains had been able to reveal to the minds that they create how they do it. In addition, we've already considered that it is notoriously difficult to get a deep understanding of how the brain works from inside its own machinery.

Neurologist Antonio Damasio put it this way:

> We can use our minds not to discover facts, but to hide them. One of the things the screen hides most effectively is the body, our own body . . . it's interiors. Like a veil thrown over the skin to secure its modesty, the screen partially removes from the mind the inner states of the body, those that constitute the flow of life as it wonders in the journey of each day. . . . But this has a cost. It tends to prevent us from sensing the possible origin and nature of what we call self.[24]

The best view in Warsaw, Poland, is from the top of the Palace of Culture and Science, an ugly example of Stalinist architecture that long dominated the Warsaw skyline. The reason the view from this Palace is so good is that it's pretty much the only place from which you can't see that building. Just as we don't see the Palace of Culture and Science when we're in it, our brain is incapable of seeing how it works from the inside (recall Leibniz's imaginary thinking machine), and, so, we can't observe how it produces our mind, just as we aren't privy to our pancreas producing digestive enzymes.

There are many more things than are dreamt of in our philosophy, our science, our imaginations. Accordingly, it is at least possible, given the limitations of our own biologically evolved brain, that we will never be able to solve certain puzzles, including the causal mechanisms of consciousness. Some philosophers espouse this view, a perspective known as mysterianism. It suggests that certain phenomena that are currently inexplicable might always remain so, simply because they are beyond our ability as mere human animals to grasp. Mysterians argue that in addition to known unknowns (the ur-stuff of science), there are also known *unknowables*—as well as, presumably, unknown unknowables. But even mysterians don't claim that such phenomena are magical or supernatural, just that as embodied, biologically evolved, meat-headed creatures we can't get our minds around some things, and perhaps never will. But they don't advise that we stop trying. Or that we conscript supernatural forces in lieu of explanations.

Among many potential alternatives to dualism being explored, here is one that sounds like mumbo-jumbo and maybe is, but it has received serious attention, along with equally serious dismissal. Known as "Orchestrated Objective Reduction theory" (Orch OR) and originally proposed by mathematical physicist Roger Penrose and anesthesiologist Stuart Hameroff in the 1990s,[25] it maintains that consciousness arises because of the collapse of quantum wave functions inside microtubules, tiny proteinaceous structures found in human nerve cells (and most other animal cells as well). If there is anything to it, this theory—actually, more of an asserted hypothesis—will have pushed the neural correlates of consciousness into the machinery of nerve cells, where it belongs, so any insight that might result will operate in the realm of scientific materialism—even though by invoking quantum weirdness, Orch

OR seems pretty weird itself. In any event, and no matter how weird, neither it nor any other scientific explanation would support anything approaching a nonphysical, soul-based supposition.

There is, as the Brits would say, "ever so much" that we don't know, aside from the hard problem of consciousness. How do an array of animals achieve their globe-spanning migrations? How is embryonic development so precisely tuned and maintained? Why does the temperature of the sun, about 5,500 degrees Celsius at its surface, increase to one to three *million degrees* Celsius as one moves away from the source of the sun's heat? How do black holes work, not to mention quantum effects? What the heck is dark matter and dark energy? Do they even exist? For that matter, considering just regular matter, if we keep drilling down from molecules to atoms to subatomic particles and keep going, what is matter *made* of? Could there be multiple universes?

And, of course, back to the basic hard problem of consciousness: How does matter create mind? The fact that there is "ever so much" that is unknown doesn't mean that these and other mysteries will never so much be known. What we currently know scientifically isn't nearly all there is to know. We have barely begun to plumb the depths of what we currently think we understand. There is plenty more to know and over time, we'll get our arms around at least some of it—but through logic and science, not by invoking supernatural silliness. Moreover, mysteries do not lose their poetry when solved, because solutions often turn out more beautiful than the precipitating puzzle, and, in any case, as we solve one mystery we uncover others, which sure beats proclaiming "It's a mystery" and then folding our tents in spiritually walled-in, curiosity-defeating, supernatural-evoking self-satisfaction.

To be sure, the history of science includes many cases in which earlier perceptions needed revising. We went from a Ptolemaic Earth-centered solar system to one that is Copernican and sun-centered, from a Newtonian understanding of physics to an Einsteinian one, from confidence in a steady-state universe to one deriving from a Big Bang, from a creationist perspective on the origin of living things to a Darwinian one. It's a myth, moreover, that science's progress always follows a straight line, from ignorance to truth. Thus, Copernicus was persistently skeptical of his own results because his theology demanded that planets moved in perfect circles: Why would a perfect God design heavenly bodies that traveled in imperfect ways? It took unequivocal empirical observations to clarify that planetary orbits were elliptical, never mind how inconvenient this discovery. (Thank you, Johannes Kepler.)

Similarly, there have been numerous tweaks to Darwin's original elucidation of evolution by natural selection, based on subsequent discoveries of genes, advances in the mathematics of population genetics, abundant field and lab studies, recognition of the role of occasional random factors such as genetic drift, epigenetics, even the much-disputed assertion that selection might work at different, competing levels. In these and innumerable other cases, and regardless of occasional twists and backsliding (self-correction is a hallmark), scientific materialism has given us an ever more precise understanding of the real world.

Let's repeat: Scientific advances have never relied on the supernatural. Passing the buck to the occult and keeping it there is precisely what scientific materialism does not do. Not only is it especially good at asking questions, but at answering them without abracadabra. When the answers aren't forthcoming, then—and especially then—relying on divine intervention is particularly unhelpful. Richard Feynman once said he'd rather have questions he can't answer than answers that he can't question.

For our purposes, it's appropriate when considering consciousness that we focus on the hard problem: How does mind arise from mere matter? But first, another question about consciousness is worth mentioning, if only in passing: Why does consciousness exist at all? Biologists distinguish between "proximate" and "ultimate" causation, the former being the immediate mechanism whereby traits are produced, and the latter, the adaptive value of any identified characteristic, namely what is there about it that gave individuals (more precisely, their genes) a reproductive benefit? Sometimes these distinctions are described as "how" (proximate or mechanistic explanations) versus "why" (ultimate or evolutionary explanations).

The hard problem of consciousness is a proximate or "how" question. "Why" consciousness evolved is a suitable issue for evolutionary consideration, although one that has received relatively little attention—nor will it get much here. Despite the theological resonance of the word "ultimate," evolutionary biologists do not invoke supernatural causation but, rather, the physical process of evolution by natural selection. A theist "answer" to why consciousness exists would be that God in his/her/their/its infinite wisdom elected to endow us with it. End of story. Although some theists consider it inappropriate to speculate about God's motivation, others maintain that consciousness was granted to *Homo sapiens* in order to provide our species with free will.[26] Or maybe God imbued us with consciousness as part of a divine plan to create humanity in his/her/their/its image. If we allow God consciousness—which seems a reasonable assumption given that the Bible depicts the Ruler of the Universe possessing such mental states as anger, vengeance, jealously, genocidal murderousness, foresight, and, yes, on occasion forgiveness and love—then perhaps granting consciousness to human beings was part of that celestial mirroring.

Evolutionary thinking looks elsewhere. For example, Nicholas Humphrey[27] has hypothesized that consciousness evolved to enhance subjective appreciation of being alive, thereby increasing efforts to stay that way. My own guess is that the adaptive value of staying alive is sufficient to motivate most living things to keep trying, and that the ultimate, adaptive value of higher-order consciousness, at least in the human case, might be that it provides us with the ability to see (or imagine) ourselves as others see us, and thus to navigate complex social situations more effectively. Or maybe consciousness isn't adaptive at all, given that it has substantial downsides, as when *self*-consciousness gets in the way of "flow," and, not least, belabors us with troublesome anxieties, including fear of death. If not directly selected because of some genetic, reproductive payoff, it is also possible that the conscious mind arose over evolutionary time—to different degrees in different species—as an accidental by-product of having a lot of nerve cells joined together for other reasons, such as responding appropriately to complex stimuli. Consciousness could therefore be what biologists Stephen Jay Gould and Richard Lewontin[28] called a "spandrel."[29] The likelihood, however, would seem to be that something so precisely orchestrated and so widespread, despite being so vulnerable to disruption, is the reslult of positive selection pressures. In any event, why consciousness exists is the best kind of scientific question: an open one.

But the "why" question of consciousness isn't our current focus. The "how" question is, and will occupy us because until it is resolved, the issue of how matter gives rise to mind provides fuel for the dualist embrace of the soul or what passes for it, in the course of what passes for an explanation.

Socrates described himself as the wisest man in Athens because he knew how much he didn't know. But he didn't recommend that we stop trying to know more. "I contend," he remarked in the *Meno*, "that we will be better [people], braver and less idle, if we believe that one must search for the things one does not know, rather than if we believe that it is not possible to find out what we do not know and we must therefore not look for it."[30] He knew, as we do today, that mysteries abound, and that although we may never get to the bottom of everything, we owe it to ourselves to keep looking and not to hide behind a supernatural facade. Just because we cannot intuit something, like the fact that a "solid" wall is mostly empty space, doesn't mean that it isn't so. And similarly, just because we *can* intuit something, like the existence of a soul, doesn't mean that it is real.

No question, consciousness has been giving science a run for its money. (Actually, not all that much money, but one heck of a run.) The following cannot be said strongly or often enough: The fact that we do not currently have a complete and satisfying scientific explanation for something does not warrant attributing it to supernatural entities. Let's go further: Positing a soul, or some comparably immaterial and mysterious entity to explain the hard problem of consciousness is not only unwarranted, but no explanation at all. It replaces a potentially solvable scientific problem with a bigger one, namely what is the soul, where did it come from, how does it do its thing? It also threatens to short-circuit serious efforts to understand consciousness.

Searching for the basis of consciousness in matter and energy isn't even terminally reductionist,[31] because matter and energy are themselves plenty complicated. If we drill down into the nature of mass and energy, we generally answer in terms of their functionality: for example, how mass and energy interact—but not really what they *are*. We might therefore talk about the "hard problems" of mass and energy, but without envisioning that they, too, have souls.

Scrambling to endow their pipe dreams with a patina of scientific legitimacy, dualists sometimes point to the existence of various kinds of fields, such as gravity and electromagnetism, along with energy that is invisible to our unaided central nervous system: cosmic rays, supersonic sound waves, ultraviolet and infrared radiation, and the like, suggesting that the soul may turn out to be another kind of field or invisible energy. But these physical phenomena, although not readily perceivable, are material results of the interaction of matter and energy, and unquestionably real. Nothing supernatural about them. The fact that they exist is not evidence for the existence of other things for which there is literally no evidence and that are expected to defy the laws of physics. This would be like saying that because light has certain physical properties, darkness must be similarly composed.

If someone were transported from, say, the year 500 CE to the twenty-first century, they would doubtless be blown away by computers, cell phones, jet planes, and nuclear weapons (the latter, one hopes, not literally). They might well fall on their knees and worship them and the people who employ them. Arthur C. Clarke once wrote that any sufficiently advanced technology is indistinguishable from magic. But magical as these things may seem to most of us even today, they result from science and technology. Transport someone from today 500 years into the future and they would almost certainly find themselves astounded by whatever advances science and technology will have wrought. We can safely conclude, however, that they wouldn't attribute them to supernatural forces.

For now, those who choose are of course free to "explain" our mind as due to supernatural emanations. They have satisfied themselves this way in the past. Before we understood the causes of infectious disease, communicable illnesses were attributed to various gods, black magic, poisonous vapors, to having violated certain taboos, and so on. Now we know better. Until we get a solid scientific explanation for consciousness, some will doubtless maintain that it is due to dualism, which is to say, some unknown and unknowable intervention beyond the realm of matter and energy.

Enter the theologically fraught concept known as the God of the Gaps. The approach is simple: Consign whatever we don't currently understand—the gaps in our knowledge—to God. More than two centuries ago, a young Percy Bysshe Shelley wrote a tract, "The Necessity of Atheism," in which he argued, "when we say that God is the author of some phenomenon, that signifies that we are ignorant of how such a phenomenon was able to operate by the aid of forces or causes that we know in nature."

Filling explanatory gaps with God is normally avoided by serious theologians because it is risky and not just for Shelley, who was kicked out of Oxford for suggesting that it doesn't solve anything and is simply an admission of ignorance. The theological problem is that as our knowledge increases and the gaps diminish, so does God. And sure enough, the neurobiological gap has been narrowing, leaving us with an ever-shrinking Soul of the Gaps as neuroscience matures and the connection between brain and mind has been cemented beyond any doubt.

In *The God Delusion*,[32] Richard Dawkins pointed out that attributing gaps to God isn't only problematic for believers. It has a pernicious secular impact as well because "[i]t teaches us that it is a virtue to be satisfied with not understanding." Both theists and scientists look for gaps in our knowledge and both are cheered when they turn up, but there is a big difference. The former crow about having a new opportunity to admire God's handiwork—and stop there—whereas the latter are pleased because it gives them more work to do.

For some, the success of scientific materialism has been a major contributor—actually, *the* major contributor—to what pioneering sociologist Emile Durkheim lamented as the "disenchantment of the world." It was an unforced error on his part. If we allow ourselves to see, smell, hear, touch, admire, and immerse ourselves in our real and remarkable world, and to revel in how complex, terrific, and gorgeous it is, not to mention the stunning truth of how much of that real world our limited brains have already begun to understand, the result is nothing less than enchanting. I'll gesture toward some of this enchantment in the final chapter.

"Faith," according to Nietzsche, "means not wanting to know what is true." Among those things that believers and dualists don't want to know, scientific truth—the enemy of soul-certainty—is number one.

There are many forms of truth, not least that love is better than hatred, honesty trumps lying, beauty beats ugliness, and so forth. There are also scientific truths, based on our understanding of material reality. Its fruits have often disconcerted believers seeking to pursue their religious faith untrammeled by truth.

Upon hearing of Darwin's scandalous theory of evolution, the wife of the Bishop of Worcester is said to have exclaimed, "Descended from monkeys? Let us hope that it isn't true, but if it is true, that it does not become widely known." The English critic and essayist John Ruskin also flourished in the Victorian Age, a time when geology was literally unearthing truths of the sort that, thanks to Darwin, so troubled the good bishop's wife. In a letter to a friend in 1851, Ruskin grumbled, "If only the Geologists would let me alone, I could do very well, but those dreadful Hammers! I hear the clink of them at the end of every cadence of the Bible verses."[33]

On occasion, reality wields a dreadful hammer to our cherished assumptions. According to St. Paul, "All flesh is not the same flesh: there is one kind of flesh of men, another flesh of beasts." He is spectacularly wrong, reflecting another of those truths that believers don't want to know. Examine the human body and you will find nothing that reflects special creation, nothing that distinguishes our flesh from that of other creatures, no sign of soulfulness or any other lofty substance beyond the truths of ordinary material reality. Psychologist Nick Humphrey[34] notes that

> Joseph Heller's hero, Yossarian, in the novel *Catch-22*—no scientist he—read this message in the entrails of his dying friend Snowden as countless people must have read similar messages before: "He gazed down despondently at the grim secret Snowden had spilled all over the messy floor. It was easy to read the message in his entrails. Man was matter, that was Snowden's secret. Drop him out of a window and he'll fall. Set fire to him and he'll burn. Open him and seek unsuccessfully for a message in his entrails. Man was matter, that was Snowden's secret. Bury him and he'll rot like other kinds of garbage . . . 'any future,' Snowden said. 'I'm cold.' 'There, there,' said Yossarian. 'There, there.'"

Yossarian was vainly trying to comfort his dying aviator friend, whose abdomen had been ripped open by German antiaircraft fire. Alas for those yearning to find human spiritual essence embedded in our physical bodies, the blood and guts reality of our material situation brings little comfort. There, there.

Of course, the fact that something could be consistent with modern science is no guarantee that it is true. Ivory-billed woodpeckers are believed to be extinct. If a small population were discovered in the Great Dismal Swamp, bordering Virginia and North Carolina, no laws based on physics, chemistry, or biology would have been violated. Ditto for any future insights into how nervous systems produce minds. On the other hand, unearthing proof that souls exist and discovering how they produce mental experience would require a dramatic reworking of all these sciences, and more.

It's the difference between a fly in the ointment and a cockroach in the soup, a distinction made by the philosopher Avishai Margalit.[35] Both happenstances are unfortunate, but the former isn't nearly as bad as the latter. If you choose, you could scoop out the fly and still use the ointment. But a cockroach in your soup is a different matter; you pretty much have to discard the whole thing. Not being able to sort out the physical basis for consciousness is currently a fly in the ointment of scientific materialism. It may eventually be scoop-out-able. Or not. Either way, the underlying ointment will continue to be useful; not only is it the only reliable explanatory mechanism we have, but it has proved immensely generative. But if, somehow, some way, and some time it is *proved* that mind is not and cannot be produced by matter, so that we are stuck with explanatory reliance on a divinely generated, supernatural, immaterial soul—that really would be a cockroach in the soup of science.

When it comes to the existence of the soul, apsychists—including the one writing this book—are expected to show that the soul *doesn't* exist, while those who smugly assume that it does aren't under similar pressure. Where should the burden of proof fall? If someone asserts that the moon is made of green cheese or that Elvis is still alive, whose job is it to evaluate such looney-tunes claims: the person who makes them, or those to whom the claim is directed? Clearly, it's the proclaimer's job, a responsibility that increases in proportion as the assertion is inconsistent with whatever is already known.

Samuel Johnson famously said that patriotism is the last refuge of a scoundrel. When confronted with refutations of their favorite arguments, not to mention more serious confrontations with inconvenient reality, many doctrinaire believers claim divine special privilege for their beliefs: God works in strange ways, beyond our poor ability to understand, so please just shut up and let me take refuge in my invincible faith. Reality must take a back seat. Part of that reality is that science has already identified, time after time, the physicalist cockroach in the spiritualist, theological soul-soup, but believers refuse to acknowledge it and continue to attribute their preferred mysteries to supernatural, God of the Gaps forces.

It is probably unrealistic to expect believers to discard their supernatural soup, and yet, in any confrontation thus far between fantasy and fact, between soul and scientific materialism, the latter has a habit of winning, which is just as well because reality is generally a good place to be. This, too, is fortunate because we have no alternative. In a passage from *Walden*, Henry David Thoreau offers a suggestion:

> Let us settle ourselves, and work and wedge our feet downward through the mud and slush of opinion, and prejudice, and tradition, and delusion, and appearance, that alluvion which covers the globe, through Paris and London, through New York and Boston and Concord, through church and state, through poetry, philosophy and religion, till we come to a hard bottom with rocks in place, which we can call *reality*.

As if the dualist response to the mind-brain problem isn't loopy enough, and sufficiently disconnected from reality, there's another that is even more bonkers. At least at first sight. One newfangled attempted solution to the hard problem of consciousness is called panpsychism; it gets around this problem by proclaiming that even supposedly obtuse matter is conscious.[36] That's right, panpsychism "explains" consciousness by positing that *everything* is conscious: not just people and animals but plants, cells, even molecules, and subatomic particles. Wacky? Yes. But fun to contemplate (especially, perhaps, if you're an electron).

Panpsychists turn the "hard problem" around. Instead of trying to solve it at the level of neurons and brains, they assume that consciousness is ubiquitous, just present in different entities to different degrees. Responding to the scientific materialists, panpsychists say, "You argue that mere physical matter (neurons and brains) can be conscious, but you don't know how. OK, we'll see you and raise you one. What if *all matter* is conscious? Not just other animals—dogs, cats, horses, all the way to worms and amoeba—but also molecules, atoms, subatomic particles. It's just a question of how much consciousness does any chunk of matter have."

Weird, but give them credit for creativity.

At first blush it seems a clever way to solve the hard problem: Duck it by saying that consciousness is everywhere, so there's really nothing to explain. And so, by positing that everything is conscious, panpsychism simply whisks it away by claiming that it is so fundamental it needn't be understood—or even defined. If you think that's crazy, then ask yourself if panpsychism is any more lunatic than claiming that the problem of mind and consciousness is solved by positing a soul.

To their credit, panpsychists don't worry very much about the soul, but if they did, they'd have to deal with another problem, at least as hard as that of consciousness: What sort of soul resides in a molecule, an atom, or a subatomic particle? Perhaps an electron would have a negative outlook, a proton more positive, and a neutron would be, well, indifferent.

Panpsychists claim, counterintuitively, that scientific materialism actually demands their approach, because for them, there is no radical emergence in nature. Although nothing in biology provides any more support for panpsychism than for souls, panpsychism isn't entirely at odds with some serious thinking. Alfred North Whitehead wrote that there are "no arbitrary breaks" in nature, revisiting an older claim—*natura non facit saltum* ("nature does not make jumps")—that's been around for centuries, sometimes attributed to our old friend Gottfried Leibniz. Although quantum physicists would disagree, biologists are on board, at least when it comes to evolutionary change, which is nearly always gradual. If panpsychism is correct, then consciousness *non facit saltum*.

There is something else to be said for panpsychism beyond its too-clever-by-half claim to solve the mind-body problem by ignoring it and denying that any problem exists. According to philosopher Philip Goff, their approach argues against yet another hurtful kind of dualism, that human beings are separate from the natural world:

> Panpsychists believe that consciousness pervades the universe, and is as basic as mass and charge. If panpsychism is true, the rainforest is teeming with consciousness. As conscious entities, trees have value in their own right: chopping one down becomes an action of immediate moral significance. On the panpsychist worldview, humans have a deep affinity with the natural world.[37]

This is all very nice, but one needn't espouse fantasies about conscious molecules to recognize and revel in our deep affinity with the natural world. Evolutionary biology combined with common sense does this beautifully, if only more people had the consciousness to recognize it.

Given that consciousness is present at one extreme (namely us), the panpsychist claim is that it must exist along a continuum with other entities, not only living animals but also various nonliving concatenations of matter. But the real world offers many examples of emergent characteristics when things in combination produce something quite different from each taken separately. Hydrogen atoms and oxygen atoms all have their own physical traits, but when two of the former and one of the latter combine, the resulting water has its own qualitatively different, emergent characteristics. Similarly, life emerges from nonliving atoms and molecules.[38] On the other hand, the problem of emergence can be bypassed, at least in theory, by pointing out that in the case of water, for example, its nature is already predictable and inherent in the atomic characteristics of hydrogen and oxygen, just as life—like consciousness—is inherently available to be generated via the suitable combining of nonliving atoms and molecules.

Even devotees of panpsychism acknowledge that the consciousness of molecules, atoms, electrons, and so forth must be of a very primitive sort, presumably less developed as one proceeds down the material ladder. They admit, nevertheless, that they have a "combination problem," namely how do tiny, minimally conscious bits and pieces come together to produce the macro-consciousness we identify in ourselves and, increasingly, in other animals? And why is this only true of living organisms and not of chairs and tables? (Maybe some believe that, too. And maybe chairs and tables believe it as well.) Let's grant that neurobiologists have a similar problem explaining how bits of no-nonsense matter called neurons, glial cells, and so on come together to produce consciousness. But whereas their efforts have generated highly productive research, panpsychism—like dualism—has simply produced a lot of mental masturbation.

For now, believers in panpsychism have much in common with believers in the soul. Both are versions of dualism, although each works from a different direction, postulating the primacy of wherever they put their faith. Soul-belief privileges the soul as the seat of consciousness, while panpsychism radically decentralizes it by placing consciousness in everything. Sadly, neither comes close to explaining anything.

7
Purported Proofs and Practical Problems

In 1907, Dr. Duncan MacDougall of Haverhill, Massachusetts, weighed patients immediately before and after they died, seeking to determine the heft of their departed souls. He reported, to great public interest, that immediately after death a corpse loses 21 grams. He published his results in the journal *American Medicine* under the title "Hypothesis Concerning Soul Substance Together with Experimental Evidence of the Existence of Such Substance."

Julien Musolino has skewered these findings, pointing out that MacDougall's work has so many problems it would never pass muster today:

> For starters, his sample size was too small (only six human patients), his instruments too imprecise (he had trouble determining the exact moment of death and could not measure differences in weight precisely enough), and his results were too variable to allow him to draw any meaningful conclusions. The results from two of his patients had to be discarded and of the remaining four one showed an immediate drop in weight; two showed that the initial drop in weight increased over time (how many souls are there in a human body?); and one showed an immediate drop in weight, followed by an increase in weight, and then another drop (maybe the soul had trouble making up its mind). All in all, there was simply too much noise and uncertainty in MacDougall's results to even conclude that the

body loses weight at the moment of death, let alone that the weight loss was due to anything like the soul leaving the body.[1]

Nevertheless, these flaws haven't prevented enthusiasts from latching onto the MacDougall report as definitive. It is referenced to this day. As a kind of control, the good doctor killed fifteen otherwise healthy dogs and reported that there was no postmortem loss of weight. Evidently Descartes was right: We have souls and animals—or at least, dogs—do not. (Or if they do, theirs are weightless.)

Despite the public enthusiasm with which Dr. MacDougall's initial report was received, church authorities were understandably more cautious, because it would have been theologically troublesome if an actual physical weight had been attached to the human soul. Because the soul exists on a plane separate from the material world, it should not have any discernible mass, just as God is without physical qualities that can be measured in the secular realm.

Moreover, if the soul is a material object with weight, it would follow that it has some sort of structure, along with traits such as size, texture, color, smell, and so forth. Soul-believers can't have it both ways: Either it weighs something or it does not. If yes, then it is some*thing* by definition and hence not immaterial. Even Carl Sagan's alleged pink dragon was immune to being measured. But in this regard at least, the soul-certain are off the hook: There is no evidence that the soul has any weight at all. Its materiality (i.e., its actual existence in the real world) has never been confirmed and, let's face it, never will be, although some have claimed success. No one, alas, will prove the existence of unicorns. One *bona fide* unicorn would do the trick, or even a small DNA sample, but don't hold your breath. At the same time, no one can ever conclusively disprove them either. "We haven't found a unicorn (or Bigfoot, Lock Ness monster, or Yeti), but that doesn't mean they don't exist." Granted, absence of evidence isn't evidence of absence—but the more persistent the absence, the more this speaks to likely nonexistence.

Although Dr. MacDougall appears to have been sincere, there is a long history of grifters, mountebanks, phonies, and other con-men and women who batten off the credulous and the recently bereaved, holding seances, writing books, giving well-paid lectures and purporting in various ways to "communicate with the dead"—which is to say, with the souls thereof. Arthur Conan Doyle's signature creation, Sherlock Holmes, became an avatar of laser-focused logic. But when his son died in the First World War, Conan Doyle became a fervent spiritualist, desperately trying to communicate with him via seances and Ouija boards, orchestrated by mediums whose mediation was well compensated.

Most people believe in souls, perhaps even more than believe in God, and we probably owe it to our fellow human beings to respect their motives. We are not obliged, however, to be similarly respectful of the assholes who have long pretended to link the living and the dead—for a fee, of course—and who have engaged in massive flimflammery toward that end.

Carl Sagan cautioned that "extraordinary claims require extraordinary evidence," and when it comes to purported miracles, the evidentiary base is—to put it mildly—thin. Claimed proof of the soul's existence goes beyond its supposed weight and the phony testimony of mountebank mediums and Ouija Board brandishers. It starts with a nontrivial example, at least for Christianity: resurrection of the dead. Interestingly, such stories aren't terribly abundant, aside from Jesus himself and his reputed raising of Lazarus. But the former claim is so central to Christian belief that the story is literally a key article of the faith. "You ask me how I know that my soul will be resurrected when I die? Easy, because Jesus said it would happen, and, of course, it happened to him!" Miracles happen.

Or do they? In his 1758 work, *An Enquiry Concerning Human Understanding*, the Scottish philosopher, David Hume, penned the gold standard for evaluating any claim of a miracle. He argued that one should ask which is more likely, that the proclaimed miracle happened, or that the claim itself is incorrect. A miracle, by definition, is something exceedingly unlikely, that might never have occurred before and that departs from common sense and/or available evidence, which may go a long way toward explaining why people yearn for them.

Canonization within the Roman Catholic Church requires evidence of a bona fide miracle, which often involves healing people previously suffering from a serious illness. For example, when former Pope John Paul II was canonized in 2014, his case consisted of healing one Sister Marie Simon Pierre, a French nun with Parkinson's disease, who had prayed for the deceased pope to intercede on her behalf. She recovered, after which several doctors were consulted, whereupon their testimony was notarized and the committee certified the miracle.

Parkinson's disease nearly always gets worse over time, although sometimes it remains unchanged for months, even years. Cures are rare and worth noting when they occur. But just a few minutes of Googling makes it clear that remissions and possible cures for this illness have been reported and attributed to all sorts of things: changing one's diet, consuming herbal remedies, getting more exercise, and, of course, praying. (One should also add the real possibility that sometimes Parkinson's had been wrongly diagnosed in the first place.)

In any event, "miracle" cures always pertain to maladies such as cancer, stroke, Parkinson's, and the like, illnesses that are known to occasionally remit in the absence of divine intervention. Never—at least in recent times, such that they can be genuinely evaluated—do they involve something that is truly impossible, such as spontaneously regenerating an amputated limb. Which poses this question: Why doesn't God cure amputees? Given the horrendous carnage experienced by many presumably God-fearing people, who have lost hands, feet, arms, and legs—not uncommonly because of accidents or military service—at least some of whom have doubtless prayed in good faith, why hasn't God cured them? Skeptics would settle for just one. Nor has someone beheaded sprouted a new one. Now, *that* would really be a miracle.

Maybe the absence of miraculous limb or head-regeneration is because the likes of Pat Robertson are correct, and God is punishing his children for society's sins. Or maybe God only chooses to do the easy stuff, that which coincidentally turns out to be consistent with biomedicine and probability. Or maybe he doesn't like doing anything really unlikely because this would smack of pandering to the disbelievers. God doesn't regenerate foreskins either, maybe because he is Jewish and approves this amputation. (Well, maybe Muslim, too.) On the other hand, it isn't clear that anyone circumcised has ever prayed for reversal. Then again, there don't seem to have been any cases in which female genitalia have regenerated after the barbaric practice of "female circumcision," yet one hates to think that God approves of it.

Figure 7.1 *An adorable axolotl, with limbs intact. If one is amputated, the experimental subject will promptly proceed to grow it back. Because this species is found only in Mexico, we can assume that its prayers are uttered in Spanish. Soure: Photo by Ruben Undheim, Flickr.*

The simplest conclusion? For whatever reason, either God hates amputees or miracles that do occur aren't so miraculous. God evidently has a soft spot, however, for starfish and certain lizards who autotomize their tails, after which they often grow back, presumably without prayer. (Or—leaping lizards!— maybe there are praying lizards, too.) Finally, don't forget the numerous limb-regrowing salamanders, especially the regeneration champion among vertebrates, the adorably appealing axolotl, *Ambystoma mexicanum*. Modern researchers are looking into the mechanism whereby they readily regrow lost limbs (Figure 7.1).[2] Someday, perhaps, that miracle will be made flesh and provide secular succor to humans in need.

Thomas Hardy, novelist and poet, was somewhere between an agnostic and an atheist. Yet he understood, from his own experience, the appeal of miracles. Here is part of Hardy's poetic meditation on the traditional English belief that on Christmas Eve cattle go down on their knees at midnight in homage to the Christ child:

"if someone said on Christmas Eve
come see the oxen . . .
our childhood used to know
I should go with him in the gloom,
hoping that it might be so."

People can be credulous, especially when "hoping that it might be so." This adds the troublesome phenomenon that psychologists identify as "confirmation bias" to any attempt at honestly assessing things as they are.[3] It is simple, powerful, and widespread: When we want something to be "so," we are disposed to ignore contradictory evidence and latch onto whatever confirms our preexisting conviction. As a child, Thomas Hardy would have been thrilled to see the oxen bow down to Jesus on Christmas Eve. It would be similarly thrilling to know that after death, our souls would live on in a state of eternal bliss. But wishing, hoping, and thrilling, alas, doesn't make it so.

Confirmation bias, no matter how eagerly indulged, is just one of many factors that lead to false claims of the miraculous. Claimants need not be intentionally dishonest—although that happens so often that when it does, it assuredly isn't a miracle. Eyewitnesses can be notoriously inaccurate, even when reporting ordinary events, and more so when it comes to extraordinary ones. We readily deceive ourselves, as with a visual mirage, imagining sounds or voices that are only "in our heads," when under the influence of psychedelic drugs, or social pressure, and for hundreds of other reasons. No wonder we are so easily bamboozled. Michael Shermer is the world's premier professional skeptic; over the years, he has performed a great public service by uncovering cranks and conspiracy theories, shining the light of reason and data on questionable claims. "We have very little evidence for miracles," he points out, "but lots of evidence that people misunderstand, misperceive, exaggerate, or even make up stories about what they think they witnessed or experienced."[4]

Writing 250 years before Shermer, David Hume courageously took as his prime example claims of the dead being revived. Hume pointed out that despite literally hundreds of millions of cases in which people have died, there has not been a single documented example of a real-world resurrection. In some cases, notably after drowning or a severe concussion, , people have been thought dead only to be alive. But never has anyone been documented to be truly cold and dead, then to rise again, a modern-day Lazarus. Which is more likely, Hume asked: that someone has been genuinely dead and miraculously revived, or that they were *perceived* to be dead, but were actually comatose for a time? Drowning victims, for example, can stop breathing for minutes, then revive. Heart attack victims can flatline, and then recover: wonderful events, but within the realm of normal medical experience.

In the case of Jesus, who may have really lived and been really dead when taken down from the cross and then interred in a crypt, after which the crypt may have really been found empty, which is more likely, that his soul and body ascended to heaven or that someone removed the corpse? When—unlike Jesus—a seemingly dead body remains accessible, which is more likely: a dead person has miraculously come back, or they weren't dead to begin with? Sad to say, when it comes to proclaiming a miracle, falsehood (whether intentional or not) is far more likely than is an actual miracle. Here is Hume:

> When anyone tells me that he saw a dead man restored to life, I immediately consider with myself, whether it be more probable that this person should either deceive or be deceived, or that the fact, which he relates, should really have happened. I weigh the one miracle against the other. No matter how remarkable and apparently incontrovertible the evidence, I would still reply that the knavery and folly of men are such common phenomena, that I should rather believe the most extraordinary events to arise from their concurrence, than admit to so signal a violation of the laws of nature.

No surprise that very few religious believers have been convinced by Hume's argument. Their most frequent response is to ignore it altogether. A close second is to bypass it by relying on a distinction between logic and empiricism on the one hand and on the other, faith. The bottom line here is sometimes called "fideism," which seeks to cut through the former by asserting the latter's primacy: "It doesn't matter what facts or rationality might say, this (the resurrection of Christ, the immortality of the soul, etc.) is what I believe. Case closed."

Earlier we met Blaise Pascal, the mathematician and ardent Catholic who flourished roughly a century before Hume and who expressed terror at the universe's "eternal silence" and "infinite spaces." Pascal anticipated the skeptical claim that returning from the dead defies logic, and he sought to respond with logic of his own. In this, he worked within a Catholic tradition especially associated with Aquinas, who had been at pains to argue that belief in scripture needn't rest on faith alone because it is consistent with rationality. Pascal cleverly pointed out that being conceived and born—transitioning from nonexistence to existence—is profoundly, unimaginably illogical, and yet it happens all the time. He then asked: "Which is harder, to be born or to rise again? That what has never been, should be, or that what has been, should be once more?" The world is full of everyday miracles, so why resist adding one more?

Next, we come to the soul-certifying claims embodied—rather, out-bodied—in near-death experiences (NDEs). These often report out-of-body events in which someone's soul departs and flies around and/or hovers above the subject. (There don't seem to be any accounts of a soul crawling on the floor or doing jumping jacks.) Sometimes, the near-dying person's soul sees a lovely light, and, less commonly, goes through a tunnel, often dark with light at the end (Figure 7.2).

Using Hume's perspective, let's hover briefly, soul-like, above these claimed NDEs. No one doubts that many people have been near death. The question is whether some NDEs, when publicly proclaimed in bestsellers such as Raymond Moody's *Life After Life*,[5] or Eben Alexander's *Proof of Heaven*,[6] accurately reflect a genuine miracle—if not proof of heaven, then proof of a soul independent of one's body. So independent, indeed, that it emerges and takes a little tour on its own before returning and relating its experience.

Assuming that accounts of these soul-certifying NDEs are not ginned up for publicity or other forms of personal gain—an unjustified assumption in the best-known cases—it seems reasonable that at least some of these people truly perceived what they report. After all, they were at death's door and their physiological functioning doubtless reflected it. Bear in mind, as well, that unlike when Dorothy's house lands on the Wicked Witch of the East and the munchkins announce that she is "really, truly dead," people reporting their

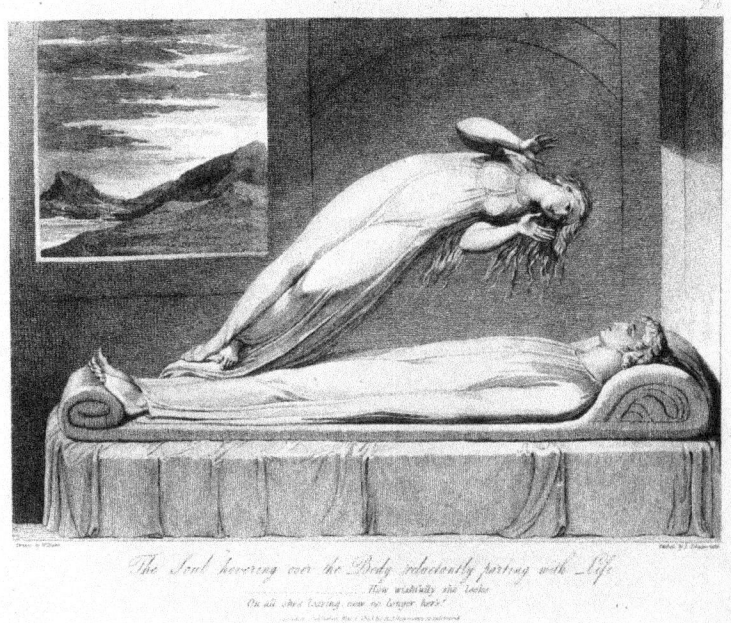

Figure 7.2 *A soul leaving its body at the time of death. In this case, the soul is said to be doing so "reluctantly," unlike NDEs, in which the emotional attitude of the soul isn't usually described. Source: The Soul Hovering over the Body, Reluctantly Parting with Life, from "The Grave," a Poem by Robert Blair; painting by Luigi Schiavonetti 1810).*

NDEs weren't really, truly dead. Rather, according to reliable hospital reports, in most cases they really, truly had an NDE. To repeat: People can and do survive several minutes of a nonpumping heart or a temporarily flatlined EEG. They really, truly do.

When this happens, what someone genuinely perceives isn't necessarily what is actually happening to their real, physical bodies in this real, physical world. Which is the greater miracle, that their souls really did float around and have diverse experiences—after which they returned to their bodies to debrief their body-based central nervous systems—or that under conditions of great physiologic stress, notably hypoxia in which their brain was critically deprived of oxygen combined with a flood of emergency and rarely evoked neurochemicals, they had *subjective experiences* that certainly felt real to them? As to why many of these accounts of NDEs involve similar parameters (bright lights, sense of peace, lots of floatation), consider the shared cultural and religious anticipation of what dying ought to be like, and how one's imagined soul would behave. Someone should compare NDEs from entirely different cultural traditions and see where reports are similar and how they diverge.

In *Paradise Lost*, John Milton wrote that "the mind can make a heaven of hell and a hell of heaven." Milton acknowledged that attributing such power to the mind is a form of heresy, but only if one takes switching between heaven and hell as literal. On the other hand, Milton's poetry is altogether accurate insofar as it captures how the mind—our only source of subjective experience—generates all that we remember, all that we perceive and interpret, all that we wish were true, all that we choose to deny, all that we create or forget, all that constitutes our internal world: in short, all that we feel, all that we know, all that we can know, including our imagining of heaven and hell, and any mental mirages of an airborne, peregrinating soul when the body is *in extremis*. If our mind proclaims that something, somehow floated about independent of our corporeal self, then how can such a perception not feel utterly, absolutely, undeniably, unquestionably real? We literally have no other way to perceive reality than via our minds, and when near death, the brains that produce those minds aren't functioning at their best.

It might help at this point to take a brief detour to visit Wittgenstein's beetle. In his *Philosophical Investigations*, philosopher Ludwig Wittgenstein posed this thought experiment. Imagine that everyone had a box and could look inside their own, but no one could look into anyone else's. Let's say you had a blue beetle in yours and you announced this fact. Other people might state that they, too, have a beetle in their box, but they could report a different color, a different size, or maybe that they didn't have a beetle at all. Wittgenstein's mental game lends itself to different interpretations, of which one—for our purposes—is that everyone's consciousness is their own personal, private box, to which no one else has access. As a result, we should be cautious when it comes to evaluating, and certainly when it comes to criticizing, someone else's subjective experience, whether perceptual or (Wittgenstein's particular concern) linguistic. We don't know and perhaps never will know what sort of beetle they have, or if they have anything at all. Nonetheless, we are entitled to believe or disbelieve another's report if it contradicts other things that we know to be true. If someone claims, for example, to have a twenty-ton garbage truck inside their little box, we might be more than a bit skeptical.

In addition, let's face it, people love to make up stories. We do it all the time; it's a big part of being human (see Chapter 5). Sometimes, and especially if we are rewarded for doing so, we even come to believe it ourselves. Michael Shermer points out that the "improbably named Alex Malarkey" acknowledged that his account, *The Boy Who Came Back from Heaven*,[7] originally said to be nonfiction, was made up out of whole cloth. (This particular malarkey was made real when the author made a pile of money before fessing up to the deception.)

Compared to the expectation of literally surviving death, something that we'll examine later, claims of soul-voyaging NDEs seem downright reasonable. And yet, they aren't. NDEs leading to out-of-body-experiences in which something purported to be one's soul exits their body and explores their immediate surroundings, never mind more empyrean realms, have never—repeat, *never*—been validated, just as, aside from Alice, no one has ever seen a grin floating independent of a cat. (In Alice's case, at least, the Cheshire Cat seemed otherwise healthy and wasn't undergoing a near death experience.) To their credit, some empirically minded researchers have tried to investigate NDEs. In *Heavens on Earth*, a deeply researched assessment of these and other claims, Michael Shermer described

> an ongoing experiment by Sam Parnia and others in rooms located in fifteen different hospitals in the United States, the United Kingdom, and Austria where cardiac arrest patients will likely undergo resuscitation efforts. They placed images high on a shelf facing the ceiling so that if an OBE [Out of Body Experience] occurs during an NDE and the patient is "up" by the ceiling looking down, they should be able to see the image and later report what it is. So far the researchers have recorded a total of 2,060 cardiac arrests, 330 survivors, 140 interviewees, 9 remembered NDEs, and only one OBE, the patient in this case saying he floated up to a corner of the room where he watched the staff try to resuscitate him.

This last account coincides with the resuscitation efforts made at the time, namely a flurry of emergency procedures, but it hardly demonstrates that the purported out-of-body experience accurately described what the patient's airborne soul witnessed while he was unconscious. Shermer points out that "most of us have seen television shows and movies depicting doctors using a defibrillator to start someone's heart after cardiac arrest, so any description even remotely close is going to sound 'eerie' to those who want NDEs to be real." To be clear: There's no question that NDEs, if we employ this phrase literally, are real; these patients really and truly were near death. What's much less likely to be real and true is the claim that during these near misses their souls left their bodies and then, when those bodies weren't dead after all, they scurried back inside.

Here are some real questions that we might ask the relevant souls: Why did you leave in the first place? Did you mistakenly think that your body had died or was about to do so? Perfect, divine entities like you shouldn't have been deceived, although maybe as the flesh nears death, your ability to assess it diminishes. Or were these peripatetic travels the supernatural equivalent of rats leaving a sinking ship—only to reboard once it righted itself? Curious minds want to know (Along with any souls debating their next excursion).

During surgery on a patient suffering from severe epilepsy, neurosurgeons found that electrical stimulation of a particular brain region, the right angular gyrus, induced the still-conscious patient to feel that she was hovering several feet above her surgical bed.[8] Emily Dickinson wrote that "the Brain—is wider than the Sky." It is also exquisitely sensitive. Do we really need to be reminded that this same brain is a highly functioning, hugely complex organ that pound for pound is the most metabolically demanding of our body parts? And that it relies on a delicate array of chemicals and electrical impulses and is highly vulnerable to oxygen deprivation as well as to disruptions in its circuitry along with imbalances in its chemistry? Think about the effect of concussions, alcohol, sleep deprivation, certain kinds of migraine headaches, extreme dehydration, or starvation, all of which can produce hallucinations. Not to mention psychedelic drugs.

Research in the journal *Neuroscience of Consciousness* examined a cohort of people who had an NDE and who had earlier experimented with psychedelics. Many of these subjects reported significant subjective overlap: a sense that they had left the material world, that time and space were altered, frequently amid a sense of ineffable peacefulness. There were also some differences, notably more visual hallucinations with psychedelics and more out-of-body sensations during their NDEs.[9]

Let's be clear: These accounts, whether NDE or drug induced, are all attributable to physical and biochemical events occurring in the subjects' brains. In all such cases, the experience is so intense as to seem real, with the persons genuinely feeling, at the time, that they are seeing more deeply than otherwise into the nature of reality, really and truly floating above their bodies, merging with the cosmos (or at least, whatever part is immediately nearby). Drug-induced perceptions and insights notoriously appear brilliant while under the influence but are considerably more mundane when revisited after the chemicals wear off. Don't overlook, as well, the impact of tumors and brain lesions, which, as described by Oliver Sachs among others, lead to dramatic and convincing subjective experiences. Dr. Sachs could as well have described "The Very Sick Patient Who Thought That His Soul Had Taken a Trip."

It would be remarkable—although a bit short of a miracle—if under severe physiological stress, just as when bathed in psychoactive chemicals, human brains *didn't* generate some rather peculiar and powerful subjective sensations, which feel altogether real. When people experience a visual hallucination, whatever its cause, the regions firing in their visual cortex are identical to those engaged when undergoing real visual input, mediated by their optic nerve which stimulates various parts of the optic cortex and elsewhere. Ditto for auditory hallucinations. Therefore, someone's subjective experience, as it unfolds in real time, seems unquestionably "real."[10] Most people, however, when they return to normal after experiencing an intense hallucination, recognize that no matter how genuine it may have felt, it was a result of temporarily altered brain activity. Of course, some insist that such events, especially those induced by psychedelic drugs, provide genuine insight into aspects of reality behind and beyond the everyday, that by proceeding through what Aldous Huxley called "The Doors of Perception,"[11] they encountered some sort of cosmic truth not otherwise available.

Alas, they're almost certainly wrong. The resulting experiences are often dramatic and mind-boggling because they result from what are correctly called mind-altering drugs. (The mind being altered when the brain is altered.) There is growing evidence that some psychedelic drugs, when administered carefully and under close supervision, can help alleviate certain mental disturbances such as post-traumatic stress disorder. But there is no basis for concluding that insights thereby obtained exceed what "straight" but medically stressed minds sometimes cook up when it comes to supposedly soul-certifying claims about NDEs.

The soul's alleged weight, along with claims of resurrection and the testimony of some people's NDEs, pretty much exhaust the purported empirical evidence adduced for soul-support. We turn now to arguments against.

Let's start with the fraught question of when and how the soul arises in an individual. This has long been an issue for theologians and philosophers, but has recently become politically fraught as well. If the soul is real and if everyone has one, then there must be some time when each person gets theirs; yet it is impossible to specify exactly when or how. This isn't merely a scholarly debate over how many souls can dance on a fertilized egg. It has immense practical implications, notably when it comes to abortion.

In the annals of ancient Chinese medicine, the mother provided blood and the father, semen, thereby producing a child, without specifying when, exactly, this union produced a soul. Ancient and medieval Christianity also didn't wrestle significantly with the question of timing until Aquinas in the thirteenth century, who concluded that the uniquely human rational soul (the divine component of Aristotle's trichotomy) develops gradually, but according to a different schedule for males and females: something like forty days for a male fetus and eighty days for a female. This was supposed to coincide with "quickening," when a pregnant woman first feels movement within her uterus, although in this respect there is no difference between male and female fetuses.

Julien Musolino plausibly suggests that because miscarriages and spontaneous abortions were likely common in pre-obstetric days, delaying the time of ensoulment helped to salve worry about the fate of unborn embryos or fetuses, which was a particular problem for some Protestant sects, notably Calvinists, who maintained that unbaptized souls couldn't be saved (Figure 7.3).

Figure 7.3 *An angel and devil fighting for the soul of an unbaptized child; not clear who won in this case. Source: Early seventeenth-century painting by Giacinto Gimignani, Web Gallery of Art.*

According to Catholic teaching, unbaptized infants were sent to permanent limbo, but in 2007 Pope Benedict downgraded limbo from doctrine to a "theological hypothesis."

By the last few decades of the nineteenth century, microscopists began observing the details of fertilization. Scholastic observers since Aquinas, along with biologists today, agree that there is steady, consistent development from fertilized egg to full-fledged human being, although there is no agreement about when the developing organism is "alive" as a distinct being, not to mention when it gets a soul. Islamic doctrine generally holds that embryos become soul-possessing human beings precisely 120 days after fertilization. (Some argue for forty days.) Jewish tradition generally maintains that humanity begins only at birth and not before, with little or no reference to the arrival of a soul—or for the existence of one later.

Catholic doctrine, enshrined in canon law, is quite different. It was enunciated on October 12, 1869, by Pope Pius IX, who specified that anyone who participates in aborting an embryo, at any stage of development, warrants excommunication, because "ensoulment" was proclaimed to occur at fertilization. This makes a kind of sense, if only because fertilization appears to provide a sharp line, with presumably soulless eggs and sperm on one side and a fully soul-full person on the other.

There are alternatives, each carrying its own baggage. One could grant a separate soul to every sperm[12] and egg, which raises the question of when and how in the ovaries and testes of women and men that endowment occurs. Add to this the awkward problem that somehow the two merged souls must eventually combine or degenerate into one. Then there's the alarming notion that a single male ejaculation would include a hundred million or so unsaved souls. Ditto for a healthy woman, although each is granted fewer: a mere one to two million oocytes at birth. In either case, there would seem to be a lot of souls consigned to heaven, purgatory or hell.

Alternatively, every gamete could be carrying one-half of a soul (each presumably weighing 10.5 grams). All of this awkwardness would appear to be bypassed by current doctrine that enshrines the moment of conception—when sperm combines with egg—as the instant when a new soul is created. On the other hand, it leaves untouched the question of *where, how,* and *when* this sudden soul-insertion takes place. As to "where," perhaps the nucleus, specifically the chromosomes, or maybe in the mitochondria or ribosomes? (Church doctrine doesn't say.) As to "how," maybe some super-sharp angelic hypodermic needle, too tiny to be observed even with an electron microscope. (Again, crickets.) Or via holy spiritual means (apparently the default mechanism). The most likely encompassing reply, and, as we've seen, the one commonly employed when difficult questions arise, is that these issues are answerable only through faith, because they involve divine intervention, with God using his unique holy powers, incomprehensible to mere mortals. As for the nitty-gritty of ensoulment, he does it in ways that only he can perform, beyond our ability to grasp in merely empirical, scientific, debased material terms. Hence the above speculations come across as sarcastic and absurd, seeking as they do a physical basis for a spiritual event, mixing gross bodily apples with sublime godly oranges. But the *when* of ensoulment-at-conception is different, because for all its spiritual provenance, it specifies a precise materiality: the moment when sperm encounters egg and achieves fertilization. Accordingly, it warrants being interrogated as such.

Moreover, the *when* question has practical medical and social consequences, so we are not only entitled to look into it, but obligated. It is also a claim that is much more fraught and much less clear than the simple doctrine of ensoulment-at-conception appears to be.

Antiabortion activists like to point to a continuous biological transition from a single celled-fertilized egg to birthed baby, challenging pro-choice activists to distinguish abortion from murder. But just as there is no bright line after which a fertilized egg becomes a person, there is no thunderclap moment of fertilization after which we might conclude that a soul has been created, planted, or perhaps inserted fully grown into a not-yet-established embryo. If the Vatican had dictated that the human soul resided in, say, the mitochondria, and then declared that as a result certain medical treatments for mitochondrial disease were prohibited, it would be appropriate to look carefully at mitochondrial anatomy and physiology. Given the claim about the timing of ensoulment and its significance for abortions, it would be irresponsible to do less.

So, if ensoulment happens at conception, let's ask when, precisely, it takes place. We can start when a flotilla of sperm contacts the egg (now?), after which one lucky or predestined-for-greatness pollywog penetrates the egg cell membrane and makes it into the cytoplasm (now?). Note that fertilization hasn't yet taken place. The sperm's entry into the egg generates a response whereby a tiny barrier arises that prevents additional sperm from forcing their way inside (now?). The winning sperm then adheres to the egg's nucleus (now?), and eventually enters it (now?), whereupon the sperm's head is incorporated into the egg's nucleoplasm (now?), after which the paternal and maternal nuclear material perform a series of choreographed intranuclear dances, but without the two genomes physically merging (now?), which doesn't happen until roughly twenty-four hours later (now?). Not so fast, because even at this point, paternal and maternal chromosomes remain distinct and *never* actually meld together.

Sex determination at birth is controlled by X and Y chromosomes. If the maternal X is joined by a corresponding paternal X, the resulting XX zygote will be female; if maternal X meets paternal Y, the result is male. Either way, throughout the life of the new indiviual we can identify which chromosome came from which biological parent, a distinction that remains true for each sperm- and egg-bestowed chromosome across the rest of the genome, except for crossing over, when corresponding segments of two chromosomes occasionally switch places. (Religious literature has never hypothesized that ensoulment happens after a certain number of chromosomal crossovers.) And so, there is *no* instant when male and female genomes literally merge to mark or achieve ensoulment. Fertilization becomes biologically complete but is never theologically consummated.

In the real world, theologians are stuck with announcing that a presumably soulless sperm encounters a presumably soulless egg, after which, some time or other and some way or other, and in some cellular place or other, a key spiritual event takes place. Just don't ask about it.

To repeat: There is no thunderclap moment that enables us to say, "Now— from this time on— this zygote, this embryo, or this fetus has a soul." (Accordingly, what about each zygote, embryo or fetus once it has become a human being?) Just as antiabortion activists proclaim (correctly) that there is no instant when a one-cell zygote becomes a human being—or when a microscopic, one-cell zygotic hippopotamus becomes an abundantly fleshed one—there is no way to identify a time of ensoulment, much less force women to maintain a pregnancy because of such arbitrary nonsense, analogous to what the philosopher Alfred North Whitehead called "the fallacy of misplaced concreteness." One might argue that we deal with gray area transitions all the time. For example, there is no moment at which day becomes night and vice versa, yet the transition takes place. A key difference, however, is that whereas delineating the precise passage from day to dusk to night is merely a question of semantics, the matter of ensoulment has life-and-death implications.

The hard-core Vatican perspective, based on the doctrine of ensoulment-at-conception, fervently maintains that every zygote (eight-cell, four-cell, two-cell, even presumably a single fertilized egg) has a soul, so it must be cherished and preserved. To do otherwise is murder. This explains not only the church's hard-core attitude toward abortion at any developmental stage but also the discomfort occasioned by *in vitro* fertilization, which involves producing many early zygotes, most of which are discarded as medical waste and don't end up being implanted into a receptive uterus.

The doctrine of ensoulment ends up implanting yet more problems. What to do, for example, when the life or well-being of a pregnant woman conflicts with the life or well-being of a zygote or early-stage embryo that she is carrying? In such cases, the "baby" isn't a baby at all, and certainly not a human being in any meaningful sense, given that it is unformed and lacking anything approaching a functioning brain. But if it has a soul, it must be given its due and perhaps even priority over the mother. If it was the result of rape or incest, that's not its fault, so how can this otherwise spotless soul[13] be cut short? And what if the ensouled embryo is nonviable and destined to die either *in utero* or immediately after birth? Is aborting it a straightforward medical procedure and thus part of health care? Or murder? A side bar, rarely considered, asks whether such souls go to heaven. If not, why not? And if so, what sort of body are they ultimately united with?

It is estimated that roughly 10–20 percent of live births are preceded by spontaneous abortions, although the number may well be considerably higher because many early natural miscarriages go unnoticed. Does this mean that heaven, limbo, or purgatory is populated by billions of zygotes and embryos? (If so, then they are overwhelmingly male, because that is the statistical make up of spontaneously aborted early embryos.) Thus, ensoulment presents a serious dilemma in its own right, even disregarding its entanglement with abortion, whether induced or natural. If souls are to be taken seriously, and not just assumed to exist and then ignored when important implications and complications arise, the question of when and how they are installed demands a serious response. None has been forthcoming.

We should also consider cloning. At present and likely into the future, it is illegal to create human beings this way. However, cloning is a well-established biomedical technology, already used on many mammals, and there is no technological barrier to some unethical practitioner applying it to *Homo sapiens*. The first successfully cloned mammal, Dolly the sheep, was derived from a normal adult sheep's mammary gland cell. (She was named for Dolly Parton; 'nuff said.) Given that every cell in an adult body is derived from preexisting cells, tracing back to the original cell that had allegedly been ensouled, would the newly created individual have the same soul as the one from which it was derived? That seems theologically unmanageable, not made easier by Aquinas's claim that the soul is distributed throughout the human body. Or would a clone get a new soul of its own? If so, when would this happen?

The Catholic Church isn't alone in opposing human cloning, but the Vatican's reason is noteworthy: A cloned individual wouldn't have its own soul. Sure, biomedical engineering could produce a human body, but as Joyce Kilmer might have written, "Clones are made from cells to whole, but only God can make a soul." Let's agree that for many reasons human cloning is a very bad idea and shouldn't be done. But the reality is that it probably will, somewhere and sometime. The fact that it appears immoral—at least, for now—doesn't avoid the issue: When (not if) it happens, what will be the soul-status of the resulting person? It seems unlikely that they will be a zombie or Frankenstein's monster. At least, let's hope not.

Here's another problem. If two different eggs are ovulated and each fertilized by a different sperm, the resulting twins are "fraternal" or "dizygotic," sharing the same maternal and paternal contributions as would two siblings produced at different times. They don't pose a unique ensoulment dilemma. But what about when human clones appear naturally, namely in the case of identical (monozygotic) twins? Identical twins derive from a single fertilized egg, which presumably had been endowed with just one soul, which subsequently divided and separated into two individuals.

The twins' ancestral one-cell fertilized egg had ostensibly been ensouled somewhere, somehow, and sometime around conception. Do they share that soul? (The Yoruba people believe this.) Does each have its own newly created version, in which case what happened to the immediately prior one? Was it obliterated? If so, was it a natural, spontaneous murder? And what becomes of that very short-lived, just-deceased soul? Or was there divine foresight whereby a particular egg, destined to split in two after being fertilized, was held back and not ensouled in the first place? Alternatively, does each of the newly separated one-cell identical twins start off with half a soul, derived from its share of the original fertilized egg, thence to each grow its own missing half? In this case, the twins go through life sharing half of their soul-stuff. Or does one of the identical twins get all of the original soul-allotment while the other gets freshly ensouled with a brand new one? Or maybe one of the twins is fully ensouled, while the other ends up soulless, a kind of collateral-damage zombie.

The reality is that when we drill down into the mythology of ensoulment, we find nothing there but that mythology, along with a whole lot of confusion and—for many women and their families—unnecessary misery.

At the end of the Book of Job, our eponymous character had been complaining about the unfairness of his situation, asking God to justify his suffering given that he had always been righteous, whereupon the "voice from the whirlwind" chastised Job, pointing out how powerless and ignorant he is compared to God. Maybe the only theologically acceptable answer to the question of ensoulment is God's response to Job: "Don't ask. And besides, who the hell are you to question me?"

Maybe this is also the only allowable theological answer to science's troublesome habit of asking questions.

8
Soul-Free!

Napoleon once asked Pierre-Simon Laplace where God fitted into his system. The renowned mathematician and astronomer responded, "I have no need of this hypothesis."[1] Do we need the hypothesis of a soul? Some people probably do, but that's not the point. Some need assurance that they are the center of the universe, but alas, they aren't. People who need their soul, or think they do, are simply out of luck. There are also wants, as opposed to needs. Some people want a million dollars but can't get it. Many want to escape death, but no one will. As The Rolling Stones sang, "You can't always get what you want."[2]

What I want is for readers to understand that recognizing their soullessness isn't a loss but a gain. A big one. It's not just that we don't need a soul, but we're better off without it. Much better off. In this final chapter, we'll explore some of these positives: how, by divesting ourselves of the misbegotten notion that the divinely granted soul is necessary for us to have an ethical compass, we gain an appreciation of our own, wholly human morality. How, recognizing ourselves as material, wholly natural creatures freed from afterlife-based fantasies, we are free to revel in the here and now. How dropping the soul delusion is conveys far more gains than losses.

Scientific materialism underlies these gains. The natural nature of the material world was taken as gospel—as better than Gospel—by Laplace and other Enlightenment thinkers and is currently embraced by the great majority of scientists along with most modern philosophers. Nevertheless, and particularly insofar as it is perceived as atheistic, we need to acknowledge that seeing the world in naturalistic terms is even now regarded by many as deeply unsatisfying: scary, bewildering, insulting, demeaning, dispiriting, confining. The view from science is sometimes seen as denying us what we want and need. John Keats, reacting in 1819 to the scientific revolution, voiced a common Romanticist horror: "Do not all charms fly / At the mere touch of cold philosophy?" No, they don't. (By "philosophy," Keats meant "natural philosophy," which was equivalent to what we mean today by science.)

Keats was despondent that Newton had destroyed the poetry of the rainbow by reducing it to prismatic colors. His poem, "Lamia," lamented:

There was an awful[3] rainbow once in heaven:
We know her woof, her texture; she is given
In the dull catalogue of common things.
Philosophy will clip an Angel's wings,
Conquer all mysteries by rule and line,
Empty the haunted air, and gnomed mine—

Materialists have been accused by the likes of Keats of a terrible crime: scientism, seeing the world as composed of matter and energy acting according to the laws of physics. And then, at higher organizational levels: chemistry, geology, astronomy, and biology. In short, they have fallen prey to a destructive reductionism, in the process depriving life of its joy and wonder. But scientific materialism has done precisely the opposite, making real our understanding and admiration of reality itself. In its stunning multicolored magnificence, a rainbow is certainly wonderful. Full stop. Knowing that white light is the source of all those colors, which are then separated out when passed through floating water droplets only adds to the wonder.

Galileo made some of the earliest telescopes and was apparently the first to use one to examine the night sky. Doing so, he made a crucial discovery: The moon had bumps, ridges, valleys, and craters, all rough-hewn and resembling landforms known on Earth, with no sign of the crystalline perfection that had been anticipated in a "heavenly body" produced by a sublime Creator. How strange that an omnipotent god would make a moon horribly pock-marked with geologic acne scars! In *Paradise Lost*, Milton was later to sing of the "ethereal quintessence of Heaven," none of which was apparent when early premodern scientists actually looked.

Galileo was also the first to see that Jupiter had moons, which orbited that planet much like how our moon responds to the Earth, thereby suggesting that the same basic physical principles operate on distant worlds. He made the first detailed observations of sunspots, thereby further confirming the nature of messy reality, with its undeniable, far-from-divine imperfections. Prior to this discovery, the sun was assumed to be a perfect entity, befitting its creation in the heavenly firmament by a perfectly spotless, heavenly God. But despite the close-mindedness of some of Galileo's notable colleagues at the University of Padua—who simply refused to look through his "spyglass" so as to avoid seeing what they didn't want to be true—only today's close-minded are likely to refrain from awe and wonder at the immensity of the universe that Galileo and his astronomic descendants have opened up.

Let's turn the Keatsian, Romanticist criticism around. Reductionism is genuinely troublesome not in the hands of science but when, owing to theistic cant, it shrinks our appreciation of the natural world, claiming that to recognize its wonders we must invoke supernatural nonsense rather than seeing reality for what it is. In "Catalog of Unabashed Gratitude," the contemporary poet Ross Gay exulted "Friends this is the realest place I know, / it makes me squirm like a worm I am so grateful,"

It's a shame that John Keats, brilliant poet that he was, couldn't see the beauty, wonder, and, yes, the poetic grandeur of the natural world unless it were reduced to mystery and mysticism, which is like saying he couldn't enjoy a delicious meal if he knew the chef, the ingredients, and the recipe—that to savor it he needed to believe that it was magical manna from heaven. To be sure, Keats wasn't hesitant to extol the glories of nature, whether of autumn or nightingales. This is the same renowned poet who wrote that "'Beauty is truth, truth beauty,'—that is all / Ye know on earth, and all ye need to know." He is correct, despite himself. There is beauty in truth, including the truth that underlies—and in no way undermines—how the world is put together.

Knowing musical theory isn't required to appreciate a Beethoven symphony, but it certainly doesn't diminish one's enjoyment, either.[4] Knowing evolutionary biology generates yet more delight at a flower, a bumblebee, an ecosystem. Knowing physics doesn't make a rainbow any less bright. Quite the opposite.

Here is one of the great physicists of the twentieth century, Richard Feynman:

Poets say science takes away from the beauty of the stars—mere globs of gas atoms. Nothing is "mere." I too can see the stars on a desert night, and feel them. But do I see less or more? The vastness of the heavens stretches my imagination—stuck on this carousel my little eye can catch one-million-year-old light. A vast pattern—of which I am a part—perhaps my stuff was belched from some forgotten star, as one is belching there. Or see them with the greater eye of Palomar, rushing all apart from some common starting point when they were perhaps all together. What is the pattern, or the meaning, or the why? It does not do harm to the mystery to know a little about it. For far more marvelous is the truth than any artists of the past imagined! Why do the poets of the present not speak of it? What men are poets who can speak of Jupiter if he were like a man, but if he is an immense spinning sphere of methane and ammonia must be silent?[5]

Why be silent over the majesty of a rhinoceros, the precision of a spiderweb, the astounding complexity of a brain, or the immense power of a black hole? Imagine the mass of the Earth shrunk to the size of a marble, so dense that its gravitational field does not allow even light to escape. Now add that there are millions of these things in our Milky Way galaxy alone! Rewriting Walter Scott: "Breathes there a mind with brain so dead who never to itself hath said 'Holy shit! This world is fucking amazing.'"

And here is Richard Dawkins, one of the great biologists of the twentieth and twenty-first centuries:

> After sleeping through a hundred million centuries we have finally opened our eyes on a sumptuous planet, sparkling with colour, bountiful with life. Within decades we must close our eyes again. Isn't it a noble, an enlightened way of spending our time in the sun, to work at understanding the universe and how we have come to wake up in it?[6]

A bit of Keats-bashing one more time. In a letter he wrote to his brothers George and Tom in 1817, Keats coined the term "negative capability," which he described as the capacity to live in "uncertainties, mysteries, doubts, without any irritable reaching after fact and reason." Humanist scholars recognize that negative capability is desirable, something to cultivate as we explore imaginative literature. But we can also engage in too much negative capability, satisfying ourselves with mysteries and doubts when we'd be better off reaching (whether irritably or not) for fact and reason, which not only enable us to navigate reality, but to appreciate it even more.

Scientific materialists can do no better than to channel the master of combining science with appreciation for the natural world, Mr. Darwin:

> It is interesting to contemplate an entangled bank, clothed with many plants of many kinds, with birds singing on the bushes, with various insects flitting about, and with worms crawling through the damp earth and reflect that these elaborately constructed forms, so different from each other, and dependent on each other in so complex a manner, have all been produced by laws acting around us.... Thus, from the war of nature, from famine and death the most exalted object which we are capable of conceiving, namely, the production of the higher animals, directly follows. There is grandeur in this view of life, with its several powers, having been originally breathed into a few forms or into one; and whilst this planet has gone cycling on according to the fixed law of gravity, from so simple a beginning endless forms most beautiful and most wonderful have been, and are being, evolved.[7]

It is only a small step from enhancing our appreciation of the world by embracing scientific materialism to enhancing our lives by rejecting soul-silliness. But for many, this is a large step indeed, one that could be psychologically unmooring. Without our soul, what would we be? Someone newly apprised of their soullessness, and having therefore pulled a key piece out of their supernatural Jenga Tower, would have to deal with its collapse.

In addition to the deep disappointment of being deprived of a hoped-for heavenly reward and one's own self-constructed centrality, there is this widely imagined horror: being reduced to an empty shell, essentially a zombie. It is thought that the word "zombie" derives from the word "nzambi," meaning soul in Haitian tradition, according to which when someone dies violently, body and soul part company, whereupon the latter can be captured by an evil sorcerer who then makes the empty soulless body into a mindless automaton.

Whatever their origin, the zombies of our nightmares lack an internal life. Devoid of joy and morality, they are the iconic case of soulless evil, or evil because soulless. They're also terrifying not simply because they kill people and eat their brains (which seems bad enough), but because they freakishly move without being alive and act without any sign of subjective awareness or moral constraint. They are purely material—hence wicked—rather than soul-infused and spiritual. No souls, no awareness, no morals, no good (Figure 8.1).

Paul Bloom recounts a possibly apocryphal story that makes an important point.[8] Rene Descartes had an illegitimate daughter, Francine, who died at age five and to whom the philosopher had been deeply devoted. So distressed was Descartes that he constructed an automaton that resembled Francine and that moved and gestured in a lifelike manner. He took the mechanical Francine with him wherever he went. Once, when Descartes was asleep, a boat captain was curious about the contents of the box that his passenger always kept with him. He opened the box, and the Francine automaton

Figure 8.1 *Zombies, from the movie* Night of the Living Dead, *1968, one of the earliest zombie movies. They're all soulless. Source: Film Night of the Living Dead by George A. Romero.*

started moving, whereupon the captain was so appalled that he threw it into the sea. This story italicizes the horror of a body that lacks a soul, what is sometimes today called an "uncanny valley," when something looks human but isn't quite there.

It seems worse yet to kill people without compunction, whether or not you stagger around with eyes that are blank and opaque rather than windows unto the soul within. And maybe that's what happens if you lack a soul. After all, "without God, anything is possible." That's the claim of Dostoyevsky's Ivan Karamazov, which is about as meaningful as "Without persimmons, anything is possible." Nonetheless, many people agree, believing that God is our guardrail, the only reliable source of personal morality and social ethics, with the soul providing our internal compass, without which we are doomed to sin. And you know where that gets you. It's also important that the soul is immortal because without the promise of heavenly reward for good behavior and hell-based punishment for bad, we are especially liable to stray.

And so, God uses the soul to keep us on the straight-and-narrow, a kind of one-stop shop or multipurpose carrot-and-stick, keeping our nose to the grindstone of morality, either directly by summoning the better angels of our nature (helped along by the promise of heavenly reward) or indirectly by generating fear of what will happen if we transgress and let our soul down, big-time and forever. What we might call the Ivan-ian stance assumes that there are no sources of moral behavior other than God and his soulful emissary residing in each of us. Without the soul, anything—including universal zombification—is not only possible but unavoidable.

If we take a *Time Machine*, à la H. G. Wells, to visit a soulless future, will we find that we've devolved into either immoral, predatory Morlocks, or childlike Eloi, or—yet later, as the novel ends—will there be an utterly inhuman world featuring immense predatory crabs? (The souls of the latter, we must assume, would be excluded from even a hard-shelled crustacean heaven, and, perhaps for that reason, downright crabby.)

Earlier, I noted the claim that the Devil's best trick was convincing people that he doesn't exist, and that maybe the soul's best trick has been convincing so many people that it does. Maybe the soul's next best trick has been the Ivan-ian stance: convincing people that without it zombification looms. Or each Jekyll will transform into his Hyde.

In most Western traditions, the soul embodies whatever inherent goodness we can muster. So without it, we're irretrievably bad. This ignores a great deal, not least that religious believers do not have a monopoly on morality. Evolution, like religion, has equipped human beings with an array of both negative and positive inclinations, ranging from violence to love, from murder to altruism. On the positive, prosocial side of evolution's ledger, we find a range of affirmatively moral inclinations, including what biologists call reciprocal altruism (being generous and even self-abnegating as part of an adaptive, reciprocating system), kin selection (benevolence toward relatives), empathy (a prosocial inclination to walk a mile in another's shoes), reputation effects (a social payoff to publicly evident morality and kindness), and more. As a result, all human beings acquire a sense that some behaviors are good and right while others are bad and wrong; they don't need a stone tablet or a supernatural soul to tell them that. Natural selection plus cultural traditions do just fine. Insofar as we have an inherited package of ethical tendencies courtesy of evolution—and we do—one might suggest that our DNA constitutes a kind of biochemically packaged soul. (Just don't suggest this to a *bona fide* biologist.)

In summary, there is no reason to worry that deprived of a soul, people would be especially cruel and murderous toward each other—or rather, more cruel and murderous than sometimes they, including the most soul-saturated, already are.

In addition to our biological bequeathal, morality is also conveyed by parents, friends, social rules, and expectations. After all, societies that condoned lying, theft, rape, and murder would not have lasted long, whatever their religious guidance or prohibitions. Morality isn't an airy-fairy set of disconnected, socially irrelevant concepts; it has an adaptive function and has persisted not because it was inspired by God but because it has been useful to people worldwide, regardless of their mythologies. Anthropologist Richard Wrangham has made a strong case that human prehistory also involved self-monitoring whereby individuals who were unacceptably violent and lacking in moral restraint were, as a last resort, either ostracized or killed.[9] As a result, although the methods were sometimes violent, the paradoxical outcome was a kind of societal cleansing that has led to differential survival of the socially responsible, along with respect for culturally conveyed expectations of acceptable behavior. There are many routes to human morality—all of them soulless.

In his masterful *The Invention of Good and Evil: A Global History of Morality*,[10] philosopher Hanno Sauer concluded that "it is simply not true that at the most fundamental level, different cultures have different values." Rather, globally shared moral expectations include but aren't limited to "personal safety and freedom, care and tolerance, happiness, autonomy and self-fulfilment." Sauer concludes that because "we all share the same history of morality, our political disagreements are often shallow; underneath them are deep-seated, universal moral values that all people share with each other."

When it comes to prosocial inclinations, let's not overlook love: romantic love, to be sure, but also love of one's children, family, friends, pets, other animals, natural environments, even more distant entities such as one's nation. You don't need a death-and-torture cult that worships ancient crucifiction to manifest love.

Please don't forget, as well, that trait of which most people are appropriately proud: reason. The ancient Greeks lauded it and for, let's call it, good reasons—because reason isn't just reasonable, it's really good. It enables us to figure out the world, to assess our inclinations, to decide which of our emotions are hurtful and which are worth following. Not that it always works, but for most normal, healthy people, it's powerful and available.

The German philosopher Immanuel Kant identified what he called the "categorical imperative," a basic rule of thumb that he felt was universally accessible to all rational human beings as a guideline for moral behavior. It simply states that when you find yourself debating a course of action, ask yourself whether you would choose to be part of a society in which everyone did the same. Is it okay to lie? Would you like to be part of a society in which everyone lied? Is it okay to steal, or to murder? What sort of world would you, and others you love and care about, be inhabiting if this were the norm? Granted, Kant's categorical imperative is easier to describe than to follow, but that doesn't make it any less valid. And it doesn't rely on your soul, just your mind.

Being good is thus instilled deeply into the human psyche by our evolutionary heritage—which includes our capacity for empathy plus rational thought—along with cultural teaching and traditions, which could certainly include those coming from organized religion as well. Also deeply inscribed, unfortunately, is being bad, behaviors to which organized religion has often contributed and that the alleged human soul has not notably restrained. Nonetheless, given the widespread tendency to perceive the soul as not just the repository of cherished beliefs but also their source, it is easy to see why it has long been lionized as the fount of personal morality.

But the soul might well be on its last legs, if only because in the twenty-first century it occupies much the same place as God in the well-trodden God-of-the-Gaps argument. As noted in Chapter 6, the problem for believers has been that the more we learn, the smaller the gaps that God is called upon to fill, and therefore the smaller is God. The same is likely true of the soul, as neurobiology continues to show that the mind is neither more nor less than what the brain does: hence the Soul-of-Smaller-and-Smaller-Spaces. By the same token, the more we learn about biological and social-based sources of human morality, the less need for the soul to fill that ever-diminishing gap. Morality isn't something floating about (such as, for instance, souls). Nor is it bestowed *upon* human beings; it arises *from* human beings.

One of the most successful con jobs by Abrahamic religion, and, to some extent, society at large, is that supernatural belief (aka being "spiritual") indicates unique moral virtue, and, conversely, being an unbelieving scientific materialist—not just a God-denying atheist but also a soul-denying apsychist—reveals a corresponding ethical emptiness. Attributing human ethics to a religion-based soul requires not only that we ignore our underlying prosocial biology and social teachings but also that we look only at how the soul is reputed to infuse our good behavior while ignoring the long, sad history of religion-powered hatred and violence. Examples are legion, including but certainly not limited to the Crusades, the Inquisition, witch burning, Hindu-Muslim horrors in India notably manifested during the slaughter of hundreds of thousands following religion-based partition of that subcontinent, the vicious "troubles" between Irish Catholics and Protestants, and current outrages between mostly Jewish Israelis and mostly Muslim Palestinians.

In 1209, a Papal army besieged the French city of Béziers, initiating the Albigensian Crusade to eliminate Catharism, a sect deemed heretical by the church largely because it embraced the Pelagian Heresy that original sin—which meant that the souls of even newborns were damned until baptized—was unworthy of a good and just God. Evidently this notion was so heretical that all who believed it deserved to be killed. The city was sacked, after which the attacking force was perplexed about how to distinguish Catholics from Pelagian heretics; the crusaders worried that the Cathars would pretend to be good Catholics in order to save their lives, only to later sink back into heretical sin. The Papal legate, Cistercian abbot, and military commander, Arnaud Almaric, accordingly ordered: "*Caedite eos. Novit enim Dominus qui sunt eius*," which translates literally as "Kill them, for the Lord knows those that are His," more often rendered as "Kill them all; let God sort them out"—presumably by examining their souls and sending them to heaven or hell as appropriate. Roughly 20,000 men, women, and children were slaughtered.

Amid the presumption that possessing a soul is key to human morality, only rarely has soul-belief been tasked with its burden of *immorality*. In his book, *Why I Am Not a Christian*, Bertrand Russell pointed out, "the more intense has been the religion of any period and more profound has been the dogmatic belief, the greater has been the cruelty."[11] Much of this cruelty has been soul-powered, with perpetrators burnishing theirs while legitimizing cruelty and the murder of victims who are soul-deficient. It's what happens when bad thinking happens to good people.

When our benighted species goes about dehumanizing others, we consistently deprive them of souls, often identifying them with animals and thereby creating monsters of our own imagination.[12] This enters into the uncanny valley of our confused perceptions whereby some humanoids are considered especially troublesome because they are close to us real folks, but they don't quite make the grade. It may also be connected to the long-standing African American cultural celebration of their souls as a response to the self-serving White slave-holder assertion that Black people aren't quite human because they lacked souls, which was part of the justification for enslaving them in the first place. It is noteworthy that even as racist, soul-infused nonsense provided ammunition for some of humanity's worst impulses, it generated useful pushback via "Negro spirituals" along with a raft of positive, soul-assertive cultural messaging. In *The Souls of Black Folks* (1903), W. E. B. Du Bois wrote of African Americans: "In those sombre forests of his striving, his own soul rose before him, and he saw himself, darkly as through a veil; and yet he saw in himself some faint revelation of his power, of his mission."

Du Bois went on to develop his concept of "double consciousness," through which

> One ever feels his twoness,—an American, a Negro; two souls, two thoughts, two unreconciled strivings; two warring ideals in one dark body, whose dogged strength alone keeps it from being torn asunder. The History of the American Negro is the history of this strive-this longing to attain self-conscious manhood, to merge his double self into a better and truer self. He simply wishes to make it possible for a man to be both a Negro and an American, without being cursed and spit upon by his fellows, without having the doors of Opportunity closed roughly in his face.[13]

Thus viewed, we have not only Du Bois's double consciousness but something of a two-edged soul-sword, whereby in the hands of White racists soul belief was used to justify the horrors of slavery and dehumanization, while on the other, Black traditions used it to assert their *bona fide* humanity and value.

This benefit wouldn't be relevant if belief in the soul and in its absence among certain target populations didn't exist in the first place. Insofar as the soul provides some surcease for battered people, it hardly compensates for the harm already done. It is demeaning to have to assert, as a response to what early abolitionists called "soul murder," "You're wrong. We really do have souls, just like you." Moreover, it offers no recompense for the frequent soul-sourced justification for other massacres, in addition to the horrors of slavery.

When religious fundamentalists kill in the name of their convictions, nearly always they are motivated by confidence that as a result of their actions, their souls will be rewarded in the heaven of their imagination, including, for example, the seventy-two virgins infamously promised to the 9/11 terrorist murderers. (It is likely that the fanatical hijackers who carried out those attacks—a faith-based initiative if ever there was one—were more religiously devout than anyone else on those planes.) Medieval Christian crusaders were no less homicidally deluded, inspired by the expectation that their souls would know eternal bliss in proportion as they killed infidels and died in the process. Suicide bombers, kamikaze "patriots," and no end of devout killers have been buoyed by confidence (no, certainty) that their souls will benefit from their actions. What's a little massacre, especially if the victims lack souls and therefore aren't losing much by being murdered? Or if they have souls that have been led astray, they may even be ultimately saved, as was widely believed during the Inquisition, when heretics benefited by being burned at the stake. (The beneficiaries just didn't feel that way at the time.) And if some worthy souls were erroneously murdered, well, God would sort them out.

Alleged witches are still murdered in certain parts of Africa and Asia, although no longer in the West. But even in our supposedly enlightened times, some people abhor taking a tiny ball of human stem cells and using it to seek cures for some of humanity's most devastating diseases. Why the opposition? Because those cells embody someone's soul, so it's better to let real people suffer and die than to disrupt fairy dust. And, as we saw in Chapter 7, the dogma of ensoulment has powered opposition to abortion, even when the health of the mother is at stake. All of this is part of the sad, larger story whereby actual lives—whether of victims or perpetrators—are devalued in favor of some sort of pie-in-the-sky expectation of future punishment or reward. By contrast, as Emily Dickinson wrote, "That it will never come again is what makes life so sweet."

In his book *The Better Angels of Our Nature*,[14] Steven Pinker urged us to celebrate "the shift from valuing *souls* to valuing *lives*." He points out that "the doctrine of the sacredness of the soul sounds vaguely uplifting, but in fact it is highly malignant . . . [because] it discounts life on earth as just a temporary phase that people pass through, indeed, an infinitesimal fraction of their existence." As a result, this life becomes disposable. On the other hand, recognizing that life is short and that, as Ms. Dickinson pointed out, it will never come again, sets the stage for seeing it as sweet and infinitely precious, precisely because it is not infinite. Mary Oliver ended her poem "The Summer Day" with this challenging recognition:

Doesn't everything die at last, and too soon?

Tell me, what is it you plan to do
with your one wild and precious life?

It's a good bet that people who stop imagining that they have an immortal soul and stop worrying about how to convey it to heaven and keep it from hell will be more tuned in, here and now, to their wild and precious lives, and better off as a result. In *Enlightenment Now*,[15] Pinker emphasized that "Belief in an afterlife implies that health and happiness are not such a big deal, because life on earth is an infinitesimal portion of one's existence, and so coercing people into accepting salvation is doing them a favor, and martyrdom may be the best thing that can happen to you." Giving up the illusion of an afterlife frees us—moreover, obliges us—to conclude that *this* world is what we have and all we have, including the opportunity and/or duty to make the best of it, for ourselves and others.

Earlier, we met Gilgamesh in his epically unsuccessful pursuit of immortality. He did, however, get some advice from Siduri, a kind of divine barmaid:

> Gilgamesh, where are you roaming? You will never find the eternal life that you seek. When the gods created mankind, they also created death, and they held back eternal life for themselves alone. Humans are born, they live, then they die, this is the order that the gods have decreed. But until the end comes, enjoy your life, spend it in happiness, not despair. Savor your food, make each of your days a delight, bathe and anoint yourself, wear bright clothes that are sparkling clean, let music and dancing fill your house, love the child who holds you by the hand, and give your wife pleasure in your embrace. That is the best way for a man to live.[16]

Echoing Siduri is Albert Camus: "If there is a sin against life," he wrote, "it consists perhaps not so much in despairing of life as in hoping for another one and in eluding the implacable grandeur of this one."[17]

It is a fool's errand to construct a detailed balance sheet for belief in the soul, but here's a quick-and-dirty summary. On the plus side, there is the appeal of dualism, the satisfaction of seeming to bypass death, belief that the soul is the fount of morality, and, for many, the anticipated delight of eternal heavenly bliss, along with the prospect of meeting one's deceased loved ones in that empyrean neighborhood. Even, for some, the schadenfreude consolation that bad actors who seem untouchable in this life will eventually receive eternal punishment. On the negative is the "soul-crushing" fear of hell as well as how fundamentalist religions have used this fear to manipulate their followers, the destructive impact of soul-belief on needed medical procedures and research, the horrors of soul-sanctioned killing, the marching orders soul-belief has provided for cruelty and abuse of animals, and the degree to which the promise (and threat) of an afterlife diminishes appreciation of existence in the here-and-now.

Soon we'll consider another downside, the cost of living a lie and, on the positive sdie of the ledger, the benefit of truth for its own sake.

In *Civilization and Its Discontents*,[18] Freud wrote: "The whole thing is so patently infantile, so foreign to reality, that to anyone with a friendly attitude to humanity it is painful to think that the great majority of mortals will never be able to rise above this view of life." His subject was religion, but Freud's regret applies equally to the soul and how it deforms our expectations of life no less than death. Freud was a pessimist when it came to human nature and our ability to outgrow belief in God. Most likely he would have concluded similarly when it comes to the deity's lesser handmaiden, the soul. Freud was an atheist; I predict he was an apsychist too.

If we kill the soul, would it mean the death of Abrahamic religion? Possibly, but don't hold your breath. Which came first, the soul-chicken or the religion-egg? Is belief in the soul a result of religious ur-stuff? Or vice versa: Is religion a result of the same preexisting belief in dualism, immateriality, and the human yearning to cheat death that birthed the story of the soul? There is no way to know whether soul-belief will increase or diminish in the future, but the latter is at least possible.

Human beings seek meaning but also understanding, because not everyone is comfortable residing in Keats's "negative capability." As information-seekers, we are often befuddled when presented with situations for which we don't have a solid explanation, and so we have a healthy inclination to reach for reason and science. Where we lack solid explanations, however, it remains tempting to turn to supernatural stuff to fill troublesome gaps in our understanding. Moreover, as Diderot pointed out nearly three centuries ago, by invoking supernatural "explanations" we revert to others that, rather than explaining anything, merely engage a fiction that obviates explanation. The philosopher Henri Bergson "explained" the nature of life as based on "*elan vital*," which, the biologist Julian Huxley pointed out, is as useful as attributing the power of a train engine to its "*élan locomotif*."

In an essay titled "The Perimeter of Ignorance,"[19] astrophysicist Neil deGrasse Tyson explained that scientists "invoke divinity only when they reach the boundaries of their understanding." He went on to suggest that scientists "appeal to a higher power only when staring into the ocean of their own ignorance. They call on God only from the lonely and precarious edge of incomprehension. Where they feel certain about their explanations, however, God gets hardly a mention."

Diminishment of divinity as an explanatory mechanism has served well when it comes to understanding the origin of disease (pathogens instead of black magic), organic evolution (instead of special creation), meteorological events (thunder is no longer attributed to Olympian gods rolling celestial bowling balls), and pretty much everywhere that scientific materialism has been applied. The soul, too, is finally on science's chopping block.

In 2005, Richard Dawkins[20] predicted that in fifty years science will have killed the soul as it is theologically conceived: immaterial, immortal, God-given, and explaining consciousness and whatever else we don't understand. I don't usually disagree with Richard, whom I have known and admired since 1969 when he was a postdoc at UC, Berkeley, and I was a graduate student at the University of Wisconsin. But from my perspective, science has already killed the soul, notably when it comes to dualism. Neurobiology has demonstrated, time and again, that all human consciousness—emotion, cognition, the whole gamut of subjectively experienced personal sensations—derives from and is entirely dependent on material causes: specifically, neural activity. To be sure, it is possible to maintain that something—call it the soul—exists independent of the material stuff of the world, just as it is possible to maintain that the Earth is flat or that Elvis still lives. Some people hold these views. But the soul is as dead as Elvis. We needn't wait until 2055.

People—even the truest of true believers in the supernatural—can run from science, but they can't hide. Or maybe they can; at least, they try. It's easy to underestimate the stubborn refusal of many to base their views on what is empirically, scientifically, and logically evident. I write this twenty years after Richard's prediction, and must conclude, with regret, that even with another thirty years many will probably still believe in the mystical, theological soul, precisely what this book is intended to dispel. Refusing to be buried—or to stay buried—despite an avalanche of contrary evidence, the soul staggers on, covered with flies, a genuine zombie (soul-stuff without a soul?) that should be dead but isn't. In Frank Kermode's words, it seems that the soul's demise is "more immanent than imminent."[21]

In *A Contribution to the Critique of Hegel's Philosophy of Right* (1843), Karl Marx is renowned—in some circles, reviled—for having called religion the "opiate of the masses" (a more accurate translation would be "the opium of the suffering"). Just a few sentences later, Marx wrote, "To call on [people] to give up their illusions about their condition is to call on them to *give up a condition that requires illusions*" (italics in original). For our purpose, giving up soul-infused religion would require that individuals give up the illusory hope of immortality, and that organized religion give up the expectation—which, regrettably, has never been illusory—of scaring the bejesus out of its followers via fear of hell. Good luck with both.

The United States is an anomaly among highly developed Western nations when it comes to its attitudes toward religion and science. During the nineteenth and early twentieth centuries, the US was not a worldwide leader in science. In fact, Americans interested in pursuing science often went abroad—typically to the UK, Germany, France, Scandinavia—to learn from the likes of Charles Darwin, Louis Pasteur, Robert Koch, Max Planck, Marie Curie, Nils Bohr, Albert Einstein, Werner Heisenberg, Erwin Schrödinger, and many others. The United States was responsible for many innovative technologies (think Thomas Edison), but relatively little in the way of world-class, creative scientific thinking. Today in the twenty-first century, budding scientists from around the world come *to* the US, which in recent decades has been the fount of more Nobel Prizes in the sciences than the rest of the world combined. There is no question that the United States is the international leader in science.[22]

The US is also, paradoxically, the most religious of all developed countries, which is difficult to explain given that education levels generally and scientific sophistication in particular correlate inversely with religious commitment: Worldwide, the better the education and the greater the grasp of and appreciation for science, the less the religious devotion. The reasons for American religiosity have been studied intensely, and, although no single factor has emerged as determinative, some likely causes have been identified. The United States was founded at least in part as a haven from religious persecution and has long been more tolerant than most other countries of religious diversity.[23] The absence of a state-supported religion (unlike, say, the UK's Anglican Church, Italian Catholicism, German Lutheranism, etc.) has not only fostered diverse varieties of religious experience in the US, but has also encouraged competition among denominations, which has spawned aggressive efforts to attract parishioners to a degree not found, for example, anywhere in Europe. Significantly, that continent has been spared anything like the American epidemic of mega-churches.

Whatever the root causes of American religiosity, the confluence of religious commitment and scientific accomplishment isn't the only US-based paradox involving the two. For a country uniquely accomplished when it comes to science, the United States is also unique in the extent to which a large proportion of its population—higher than in any Western nation—actively *rejects* science. The reasons for this disturbing pattern are also unclear, although once again, there are several plausible explanations. For one, Americans cherish the image of rugged individualism, which inclines them to distrust authority, sometimes including accomplished scientists. Such disdain of expertise is unimaginable in most other advanced Western countries and even more so in sophisticated Asian societies such as Japan and South Korea. (Oddly enough, religious Americans tend to accept a different manifestation of authoritarian expertise, namely the spoutings of religious leaders.)

The US is also unusual when it comes to the large and growing impact of religious fundamentalism, which, by definition, takes the Bible literally. This, in turn, leads to seeing science generally and evolution particularly as tainted with the special immorality that atheism allegedly brings. Although there are no relevant survey data at present, it seems likely that compared to their European counterparts, Americans are also more soul committed.

In any event, one upshot is this stunning fact: A high proportion of a country that is the world's most advanced scientifically is not only ignorant of science but sometimes even disdainful of it, as shown by denial of such bottom-line, well-established truths as anthropogenic climate change, the effectiveness of vaccines, and the reality of evolution. This can only be discouraging for those who hope for the triumph of apsychism. But hope springs eternal, especially if buttressed by that bugaboo of religious belief: reality.

When Pope John Paul II shocked Catholic traditionalists by acknowledging that human beings had likely evolved rather than been specially created, he suggested that maybe God used evolution to do the heavy lifting. In addition to drawing the line at mind and soul, the Pope proclaimed that heaven and hell are not actual physical places but indications of the soul's communion, or lack thereof, with God. None of this went over well with old-school, pre–Vatican II Catholics or, no surprise, with Protestant fundamentalists, who stick to heaven and hell as physically real, with heaven supposed to be way, way aboveground while hell is deep, deep underground. They also, of course, insist that people should look forward to the former and fear the latter. For the sake of—what else?—their souls.

The theological dispute over the location of heaven and hell hasn't involved the nature of the soul, but rather, how our soul-selves will spend postmortem eternity, either literally in a physically real heaven or hell, or spiritually in ecstatic communion with or immiserated divorce from God. Monotheistic religions aren't founded explicitly on belief in the soul but, rather, belief in some sort of God. They do share, however, the same underlying assumptions that underpin soul-insistence: that there is an immaterial, immortal world separate from the crude, physical one, and that each human being participates personally and uniquely in that world.

It would be strange indeed if we need belief in some sort of airy nothingness to enjoy human beingness as living, breathing, fully experiencing, warmly alive, totally organic creatures. Love doesn't require the notion that we've been impaled by an arrow sent by Cupid, and it isn't diminished by the reality that it involves certain brain regions along with a surge of hormones, including but not limited to oxytocin.

Arthur Koestler, journalist and wide-ranging author, wasn't anti-science, but he had his own idiosyncratic perspective, lamenting what he saw as an intellectual revolution whereby human behavior was structured from the bottom up rather than divinely, from the top down:

> As a result, man's destiny was no longer determined from "above" by a super-human wisdom and will, but from "below" by the sub-human agencies of glands, genes, atoms, or waves of probability. This shift of the locus of destiny was decisive. So long as destiny had operated from a level of the hierarchy higher than man's own, it had not only shaped his fate, but also guided his conscience and imbued his world with meaning and value. The new masters of destiny were placed lower in the scale than the being they controlled; they could determine his fate, but could provide him with no moral guidance, no values and meaning. A puppet of the Gods is a tragic figure, a puppet suspended on his chromosomes is merely grotesque.[24]

Many people assume that the soul is the seat of our emotions and deepest feelings, bequeathed to them, top-down, by God. Perhaps this accounts for the widespread belief that without a soul human beings would be demoted to mentally vacant zombies, or, as Koestler worried, puppets suspended by their chromosomes, hormones, prior experiences or—most crucially and bottom line—their brains.

Psychologist Julien Musolino is having none of it. He has a nice argument for why we shouldn't worry that without the soul, we'd stop falling in love, appreciating beauty, behaving morally, and the like.[25] Professor Musolino suggests that we consider apples falling. For Aristotle, they did so because the ground is their natural place (and, incidentally, they accelerate on route because they become increasingly "jubilant" as they get closer). For Newton, it was because of gravity. For Einstein, it's because of the nature of space-time.

But apples fell then, and do so now, regardless of our scientific materialist explanations. There is similarly no reason to think that we'll stop falling in love, seeing beauty, or feeling wonder just because we increasingly understand the nature of what we are reacting to and what's going on as we do so. You don't need to think that your soul is being stirred when you are feeling deeply about something—any more than it matters what an apple thinks when it falls.

Musolino also invokes Dumbo's feather, something that Dumbo thought was responsible for his ability to fly but that had nothing to do with it. The feather simply bucked up his self-confidence. When he dropped it, Dumbo was terrified, but he quickly discovered that he could zoom around just fine without it. And so can all of us, simply because we are human, with brains and as a result, minds, that take wing without any supernatural feather to catch the wind. And, contra Mr. Koestler, we get plenty of moral guidance from our biology (bottom up) as well as our social and cultural experiences, top-down.

People cling to their supposed soul not just because they worry that morality depends on it (earlier in this chapter), but, as we have already seen, in hope of surviving death (Chapter 3), in fear of hell (Chapter 4), because it panders to the human need to feel central (Chapter 5), because it seems to explain the puzzle of consciousness (Chapter 6), and despite a variety of nonsensical, disproven "proofs" (Chapter 7), but also because of the well-established psychological phenomenon known as "loss aversion." Behavioral economists have shown that we really, really hate losing what we have, more than we seek to gain what we don't. It's well established that when birds hassle about real estate, the territory owner nearly always wins. The proprietor is more invested in not losing his property than the intruder is in gaining it. Living things value what they have, or what they think they have. Those who believe that they have a soul really, really hate the idea of losing it.

Whether the soul exists, however, isn't tied to preferences, beliefs, whether it benefits us, or whether we'd be worse off without it, just as the existence of a sunset isn't predicated on whether it's good or bad for us, or whether we are convinced that it happens when the sun god drives his chariot below the horizon. Will the truth hurt? Some people might go through their lives pining for their lost souls. Perhaps ignorance of one's soullessness is a source of bliss, or at least a way to avoid the misery of finding oneself consigned to miserable materiality. Worse yet, maybe some of the newly soul-free, no longer believing that they are composed of sparkly soul-stuff, will adopt Ivan-ian, immoral lives. Fundamentalists especially have been outraged that we evolved from and in fact *are* animals.

The Republican majority leader, Tom DeLay, attributed the horrifying 1999 school shooting in Columbine, Colorado, to students being taught that they are "nothing but glorified apes who are evolutionized [*sic*] out of some primordial soup of mud."[26] Many people resist seeing themselves as they really are: biological organisms with an existential responsibility for how they live, no longer buoyed up by that part of themselves that allegedly absorbs God's grace and that also holds out the prospect of redemption.

Blaise Pascal, brilliant seventeenth-century mathematician and ardent Catholic who we have already encountered several times, proposed a wager regarding the existence of God that can readily be extended to the soul. Pascal suggested that God either exists or doesn't, and we might believe in him or not. This generates four possibilities: (1) God exists, and we believe in him, (2) God exists, and we don't believe, (3) God doesn't exist, and we believe nevertheless, and (4) God doesn't exist, and we don't believe. Pascal argued that the consequence of options 3 and 4 are trivial, with number 3 resulting in some wasted effort unnecessarily following church doctrine, and number 4 being altogether beside the point, except for a slight payoff because nonbelievers will have been liberated to go about their lives without worrying about their responsibilities to God. But the outcome of number 2 could be disastrous, namely eternal damnation. Hence, the best bet is number 1, protect yourself by believing.[27]

Maybe it's a similarly good Pascalian bet to assume that you have a soul, even if you probably don't. This would be equivalent to what statisticians call a Type 1 error: a false positive, believing that something is true when it isn't. The alternative, Type 2, is a false negative, believing something isn't true when it is.[28] The difference may seem abstruse but can be crucial, and sometimes one or the other is more adaptive. Think of a fish biting at a worm. Here, the cost of a false positive is high (thinking wrongly that the worm is safe to eat and being impaled on a hook), but the probability of that happening is very low, because, as William James pointed out, "There are more worms unattached to hooks than impaled upon them; therefore, on the whole, says Nature to her fishy children, bite at every worm and take your chances."[29]

For most of human evolutionary history, erring via Type 1 has probably been a better bet than committing Type 2. The classic example is that protohominid hearing a faint rustle in tall grass. Is it just the wind or a predator? Better to act as though that rustle is real (i.e., a genuine danger) and avoid it than disregard it and perhaps be eaten. Better to waste a bit of energy—in this case, moving away from the stimulus—than run the Type 2 risk and maybe die as a result. Better safe than sorry. Which boils down to this: Perhaps people are well advised to make a soul-supporting Type 1 error and assume that they have one rather than indulging in Type 2 and denying their soul's reality. Nope.

When it comes to denying one's soul, the equivalent of Pascal's Wager is much less dire than is abandoning belief in God. He may be pissed off if you deny His existence, but there is no theological basis for thinking that your soul would be similarly outraged or vindictive. In the movie version of *Peter Pan*, Peter's disconsolate fairy sidekick, Tinkerbell, is revived from near death by the asserted faith of viewers: "If you believe in fairies, clap your hands!" But even the most devout believers don't imagine that their soul is a Tinkerbell, liable to fade away if you don't proclaim your belief. If you have a soul and lose faith in it, your unbelief will not make it go away; you're stuck with it, no matter what.[30] It's supposed to be a crucial part—for some, the most fundamental—of yourself. Perhaps you could sell your soul, à la Faust, but you can't simply lose it by not clapping your hands. If it's real, then real it is, whether you believe it or not, just as living things have evolved whether or not you are a creationist. And if the soul isn't real, accepting that fact won't do it, or you, any harm.

Au contraire, it will do a lot of good. Among the beneficiaries will be other animals.

The most fundamental take-home message from evolution is the continuity of living things. Yet, one of the consistent messages of monotheistic religion is *discontinuity*: There are soulful human beings, and soulless everything else. It is intellectually challenging to acknowledge our evolutionary continuity with other organisms and at the same time to demand that we have souls and they do not. There was no single event at which a nonhuman hominin, *Homo not-quite-us*, gave birth—Voila!—to a *Homo sapiens*. So, at what point in our phylogenetic continuity with other primates did a soulless hominin give birth to a soul-filled human being?

We are supposed to be the sole ensouled ones, never mind that we share basic patterns of genomics, anatomy, physiology, biochemistry, neurobiology, embryology, and the like with the rest of the organic world. As Rudyard Kipling's Mowgli understood, "We be of one blood, ye and I." We converge with the rest of life in every way imaginable, except, we are told, when it comes to souls: We got 'em, they don't. (Notwithstanding that my dogs look at me with undeniably soulful eyes.) If we could drop the destructive, limiting perspective whereby *Homo sapiens* are uniquely ensouled while other animals are soul-deficient, we would open ourselves to what philosopher Peter Singer calls "expanding the circle"[31] of ethical concern to embrace the rest of the living world.

Biological continuity demands that either souls are fictions and no one has them or we have souls and they do, too, perhaps to varying degrees. If each person has 100 percent of a soul, then do chimps and bonobos have perhaps 99 percent and capybaras 85 percent? Earthworms? Avocados?

The above will not warm the hearts of the devout. More troublesome yet would be if humanzees (or chimphumans), hybrids between chimpanzees and human beings, were produced. I have written—admittedly somewhat tongue-in-cheek—to encourage this,[32] if only as a thought experiment, suggesting that such hybridization could be a stake in the heart of the hurtful mythology that human beings are qualitatively distinct from other animals, a despicable insistence that has provided the marching orders for our species to mistreat animals because lacking souls, they don't count. Or even if they have a divine whiff, their soul-quotient isn't up to snuff.

Rene Descartes, patron saint of dualism, whose hurtful speculation we met in Chapter 6, was so eager to distinguish human beings from other living things that he claimed the "lower animals" (i.e., all of them) were mere automata. Kick a dog and its whimpering was simply a reflex, like a machine that needs some grease. It's ok to cut open live animals—which he did—because lacking souls, they don't really feel pain (see Chapter 6). Although modern researchers in animal behavior never did vivisections, for the most part they followed Descartes's grotesque lead and denied mental lives to animals. This has changed dramatically. (Thank God?) It has finally been acknowledged that many nonhuman animals can learn complex tasks and that a substantial number of species think, are conscious, feel pain, and anticipate the future; in short, their mental lives are not qualitatively discontinuous from our own.[33] They certainly have minds, albeit different kinds for different critters, and those who insist that minds require souls must conclude that animals, too, have souls[34] or no one does, although so far no one has unearthed evidence for salamander souls or described the inhabitants of a hippopotamus heaven.

It's a safe bet that our animal colleagues would cheer the demise of human soul-certainty. Anyone who loves and values them should do the same. There are many other positive payoffs to going soul-free.

Not least is reproductive freedom. As we reviewed in Chapter 7, according to the doctrine of ensoulment, when sperm fertilizes egg, a supernatural thunderclap takes place—albeit only audible to the one-celled zygote—after which its soul somehow pops into existence. Hence, this single cell is endowed with all the legitimacy of a full human being, and, so, killing it is homicide, zygoticide, cellicide. If this sounds absurd, it is. But the reality goes beyond absurdity, into tragedy visited upon women who are denied control over their bodies, forced to carry a pregnancy that is often not only unwanted, but potentially lethal. No matter: The newly created soul must be protected, no matter what.

A similar outrage occurs at the other end of life, when euthanasia—that is, the freedom for someone suffering a terminal illness and in intractable pain to end their life on their own terms—is foreclosed because it's more important that the sufferer's soul be given free rein and allowed to depart on *its* own terms, even if those terms contradict the will of the person to which it is putatively attached. (Until its body dies, whereupon the soul departs, or maybe is kicked out.)

According to a cliché often evoked as a way of mitigating distress when something bad has occurred, "Everything happens for a reason." This is usually intended to soothe the sense of being singled out for ill fortune and is therefore proclaimed on behalf of a suffering individual, pandering to the illusion that one's private, subjective self is so central that the cosmos—most often, God—has orchestrated events specifically with regard to the sufferer in question (Chapter 5). Everything really does happen for a reason, as scientific materialism has demonstrated time and again. It doesn't help a struggling ego, however, to be told that the reason is cause and effect, via the unfolding of physical and biological laws rather than part of a grand design directed at them, ultimately somehow for their benefit.

This drags us back to the problem of painful truths and whether we are better off knowing them. When Odysseus's ship was about to pass by the Sirens, whose enchanting song lured mariners to their death, our hero instructed his men to plug their ears with wax, so what they didn't know (in this case, hear) wouldn't hurt them. But Odysseus wanted to experience the song. To do so safely he left his ears unobstructed but had himself tied to the mast. These are two Homerically approved ways to avoid inconvenient truths: plug your ears or get the information but restrain yourself from acting on it. There's a third option, however: face reality and then, after what may or may not be a bracing—even painful—cold shower, discover that it's likely not as destructive as you had thought. In fact, it may be liberating, and may also demand action on your part. In any case, the reality you'll encounter is, well, real.

In his book, *Chance and Necessity*,[35] Nobel Prize-winning biologist Jacques Monod confronted the affront that the universe isn't structured with human beings in mind, a truth that he urged his fellow primates to embrace: "Man must at last wake out of his millenary dream and discover his total solitude, his fundamental isolation. He must realize that . . . he lives on the boundary of an alien world; a world that is deaf to his music, and as indifferent to his hopes as it is to his sufferings and his crimes." Monod's point is consistent with one of the basic ideas of existentialism, that we often look to the universe to endow our lives with meaning, but the universe is completely indifferent.

This was a key argument of Albert Camus (another Nobelist, and not coincidentally a close friend of Monod), who pointed out that people seek meaning in—and from—the universe. The problem is that plug our ears, or tie ourselves to the mast, or not, the universe just doesn't give a damn. It is altogether aloof from human beings and, indeed, from anything other than itself. (Pascal's "eternal silence" and "infinite spaces" redux.) Hence, the situation is "absurd," not ridiculous, but rather, paradoxical in that people seek cosmic consolation and significance when there simply isn't any to be had. At least, not outside oneself and one's actions. Better to hear the song of reality, regardless of whether you find it seductive.

The redoubtable Lucien Musolino, with an assist from Bertrand Russell, said something similar, acknowledging what may appear to be some painful truths, namely that

> being locked into our mortal bodies we are inexorably locked out of eternity—and hence, it seems, locked out of any wider frame of meaning. That if we suffer now, we shall have no later pleasures to set against it; if we strive for perfection, we shall receive no reward; if we do harm, we shall not come to judgement. . . . That the entire history of our individual presence in the universe will, when all is said and done, have been the trail left by this little human comet that burned so prettily but insignificantly and—like all the others—finally burned out. What would people be getting in return for losing their hoped-for future? Bertrand Russell elegiacally said what. "That man is the product of causes which had no prevision of the end they were achieving; that his origin, his growth, his hopes and fears, his loves and beliefs, are but the outcome of accidental collisions of atoms; that no fire, no heroism, no intensity of thought and feeling, can preserve an individual life beyond the grave; that all the labours of the ages, all the devotion, all the inspiration, all the noonday brightness of human genius, are destined to extinction in the vast death of the solar system."[36]

Rather than dispiriting, however, for Monod, Camus, and for most existentialists,[37] the bottom line is bracing: Our human project is ours to create, to establish meaning in our lives by how we live, not by looking to a mythic top-down God or an equally make-believe soul, ready to guide us, from the inside out. Here is Bertrand Russell yet again: "It is not the whole duty of man to slip through the world so as to escape the wrath of God. The world is our world, and it rests with us to make a heaven or a hell."[38]

Which brings us to yet another thing that points toward abandoning the soul: Truth. Truth isn't trivial. Sometimes it's hard to accept, simply because it goes against our own first-hand experience (e.g., that the sun goes around the Earth, that we have bizarre out-of-body adventures while asleep). In his *Essay*

Concerning Human Understanding (1689), philosopher/physician John Locke recounted a story told to him by a Dutch ambassador.

> who, entertaining the king of Siam with the particularities of Holland, which he was inquisitive after, amongst other things told him that the water in his country would sometimes, in cold weather, be so hard that men walked upon it, and that it would bear an elephant, if he were there. To which the king replied, Hitherto I have believed the strange things you have told me, because I look upon you as a sober fair man, but now I am sure you lie.

The King of Siam's incredulity didn't appear to do any harm, except insofar as it diminished his confidence in the reliability of the Dutch ambassador. In other cases, denying the truth because we haven't directly experienced it can lead to terrible errors such as denying the Holocaust, refusing to acknowledge global climate change or the danger of nuclear war. Truth is a tribulation when it requires us to accept something that we yearn to deny or deny something that we yearn to accept. Either way, and like it or not, truth persists.

Time now for a quick visit with the sixteenth-century Danish astronomer Tycho Brahe, one of the finest scientists of his day and probably the greatest naked-eye astronomer of all time. According to Brahe's paradigm and consistent with Copernican reality, the five then-known planets—Mercury, Venus, Mars, Jupiter, and Saturn—all circled the sun but that conglomeration, including the sun itself, departed from the Copernican system and revolved around an immobile Earth.[39] In some ways, Brahe's Blunder reflects a very human inclination to give way to undeniable facts (e.g., the known planets revolve around the sun) while also retaining a deeply desired belief: that the Earth remains central to the whole shebang. Modern astronomers note, incidentally, that Brahe's proposed system was a good fit with the data available to him, and his "blunder" wasn't so much a result of prevailing religious belief as an understandable reluctance to discard the reigning Earth-centered system and replace it with the newer solar one unless the evidence was indisputable. (Which it wasn't until later.)

Such an adjustment, bowing to indisputable astronomic reality, ultimately proved to be a necessary part of the broader and deeper realization exemplified in the core discovery by Galileo (Brahe's contemporary) that the material world lends itself to human understanding based on evidence that human beings obtain: objective as distinct from subjective, natural rather than supernatural. Not everyone approved, then or now. In *The Myth of the Machine*, the twentieth-century historian Lewis Mumford complained:

> Galileo committed a crime far greater than what any dignitary of the Church accused him of; for his real crime was trading the totality of human experience for that minute portion which can be observed and interpreted in terms of mass and motion. In dismissing human subjectivity Galileo had excommunicated history's central subject, multi-dimensional man. Under the new scientific dispensation, all living forms must be brought into harmony with the mechanical world picture by being melted down, so to say, molded anew to conform to a more mechanical model.[40]

When not caught in the coils of either painful recognition or stubborn denial, most people agree that truth is worth knowing, if only because in most cases there are practical benefits associated with facing reality and accepting it. Leon Trotsky once observed that whether or not you are interested in war, war is interested in you. Whether or not you are interested in truth, truth is interested in you. And in fact, most people *are* interested in truth. Worrying about the benefits and liabilities of acknowledging reality is like worrying about the pros and cons of gravity or mathematics. Dostoyevsky's Underground Man, an avatar of stubborn, self-destructive irrationality, refused to accept that $2 + 2 = 4$[41], demanding that it was his right, as a free human being, to define reality as he chose. It may be discouraging to recognize that if you drop a brick on your toe, gravity will have an unfortunate effect, but you're better off knowing it. Adhering to truth beats living with lies, some of which are immensely deleterious: that is, Trump won the 2020 election, vaccines are dangerous, Ukraine isn't a real country.

But what of falsehoods that have no conceivable consequence, or that might even be beneficial? For example, what about the morality of white lies? Is it okay to refrain from disputing with a dying person who ardently believes in an afterlife? Almost certainly. In fact, it is likely immoral to deprive anyone of such consolation. What about keeping secret someone's terminal diagnosis?

Probably immoral, at least in most cases. How about letting a young child believe in Santa Claus? Probably okay. But what about buttressing that belief with other falsehoods as she gets older?

It is sometimes said that we live in a "post-truth" era. Not that truth has disappeared, but it has been muddied in many people's minds by forgetfulness, closed-mindedness, misunderstandings, and, in some cases, a blizzard of outright lies such as science denialism, wacky conspiracy theories, "alternative facts," and the like. But truth matters; it gives us purchase on the world. There is adaptive value in knowing it ("There's a saber-tooth in that cave," "Those pretty berries aren't good to eat"); hence, a premium on accurate knowledge. But what about truths that are not especially useful, or maybe not useful at all? Last year, the apple tree in my backyard produced, by my count, twenty-seven apples. What if it was actually twenty-eight? Even if it doesn't "matter," there's a case to be made that it is inherently good to know what's what.

In Goethe's *Faust*, Mephistopheles points out that although fewer people believe in the Devil as a real being, this hasn't made people happier because even without the Evil One secular evil ones still populate the world, and along with them, crimes, lies, temptations, and the like. Similarly, even for those who no longer formally believe in a literal, metaphysical, theological soul, an aura of mostly pleasant mysticism often lingers. Time to dispel it, whether or not it makes people happier.

There are some key philosophical issues at work here. It may be corny, but we ought to consider the value of truth for its own sake. Jesus first urges his followers to "Know the truth" and then reassures them: "and the truth shall set you free" (Jn 8:32). He meant the "truth" of God and, not surprisingly, of himself. But what about literal, actual, honest-to-reality truth? Some of it, perhaps most of it, is damned important, whether it sets us free or not. It is true that gravity exists. Evolution by natural selection is true. It is true that if you walk carelessly into a busy street, you might get hit by a car. Two plus two really and truly equals four. Truth matters. But does it matter if you believe that the constellation Great Bear really is a great bear, rather than the truth: that it is a conglomeration of stars whose orientation is due to various gravitational and centrifugal effects, and no more a great bear than a Great Ping Pong Table?

Our species has had to deal with painful truths in the past and for the most part we've weathered them quite well. It is almost impossible for inhabitants of the twenty-first century to understand how disorienting it was for our European ancestors to go from a Ptolemaic (Earth centered) view of the universe to the Copernican one, with our planet demoted from gratifying centrality to peripheral truth.[42] Ditto for absorbing the truth of evolution, which removed *Homo sapiens* from our cherished status as specially created favorite children and relegated us to one species among many, "created" like all the others by a purely natural process.

Dropping all pretense about possessing an immortal soul looms now as a blow to humanity's yearned-for defeat of death (Chapter 3) and to our cherished self-importance (Chapter 5), a downgrading that may be more painful than giving up our astronomic or biologic centrality. These, after all, merely impacted our generalized planetary and species identity, whereas to lose belief in one's soul would be, for many, to suffer an intensely personal affront.

In most intellectual traditions, truth was exalted. Plato anointed truth as the goal of philosophy and indeed of human life. "Assuredly we must be bold to speak what is true," Socrates averred in the *Phaedrus*, "above all when our discourse is upon truth. . . . It is there that true being dwells, without color or shape, that cannot be touched; reason alone . . . can behold it, and all true knowledge is knowledge thereof." Truth is the highest thing, identical to the good and the just.

Jesus appears to have agreed (albeit with no small amount of egotism), proclaiming himself in Jn 14:6 to be "the way, the truth and the life." But what if he isn't? Granted, the truth sets us free—from falsehood. But not from death. What if the truth is that the truth—for example, there is no heavenly afterlife—makes you miserable? Falsehoods, as we've seen, are often comforting, but the truth can be, too. (And even when it isn't, the truth is, well, true.) There is much to be said for recognizing ourselves as we really are, which includes accepting our materiality. Ditto for how being soul-free means that our minds emerge from our material brains and not from supernatural fairy dust, and how releasing us from any overarching, soul-infused divine pattern requires a sometimes painful disconnect, namely giving up the Golden Helmet of Centrality. At the same time, there is plenty of Good News, an apsychist

Gospel, such as how being soul-free liberates anyone imprisoned within the guilt-ridden hell of original or personal sin, while giving up the myth of immortality helps us focus on *this* life and its wonders. So, go ahead and throw out all that soul-infused bathwater. You won't find a baby in the slop.

Repurposing Martin Luther King, Jr., how wonderful to be "Free at last! Free at last! Thank reality we are free at last!"

Notes

Chapter 1

1. My apologies to genuine, biological toads, which are for the most part admirable creatures.

2. Warren Hays, *The Price of Reason: Evolution, Free Will and Humanity's Fate* (Auckland: Diadema Press, 2019).

3. Joseph Conrad, *The Shadow Line*—author's note (Hagerstown, MD: Wentworth Press, 2016).

4. I discarded "asoulism," because it lends itself to its own vulgar built-in critique.

5. Perhaps there is also room for a soul-infused version of "agnostic," a word invented by "Darwin's bulldog," the early evolutionary biologist, Thomas Huxley, as a description of those who maintain that they do not know whether God exists and doubt if anyone does, or will. For some people, "agnostic" likely does double duty, referring to uncertainty about the soul as well as about God.

6. American Psychiatric Association, *Diagnostic and Statistical Manual of Mental Disorders 5* (Washington, DC: APA Publications, 2022).

7. Whether or not one believes in God, confining discussion to his, her, its, or their existence or nonexistence grants special importance to the presumed entity in question. Ideally, therefore, the word "atheism" should be retired and replaced with something that doesn't concede the intellectual arena to theists. Scientific materialism, naturalism, or physicalism would seem better labels, but neither trips off the tongue and perhaps I've already gone too far by suggesting apsychism.

8. "Looking up at the stars, I know quite well / That for all they care, I can go to hell" (W. H. Auden, "The More Loving One").

Chapter 2

1. My proposed soul-denying version of "atheists" (see Chapter 1).

2 Moses Maimonides, *The Guide for the Perplexed*, trans. M. Friedlander (Mineola, NY: Dover Publications, 2000).

3 We know that even stars don't last forever. So, let's take the literal route: Stars such as our Sun, with low mass, will end their lives as white dwarfs, while high-mass shiners will explode into supernovae and then end up either as dead neutron stars or black holes. Sadly, Daniel didn't specify which fate applies to those souls that "turn many to righteousness."

4 Diogenes Laërtius, *Lives of Eminent Philosophers*, vol. IX, Democritus, 44, trans. C. D. Yonge (London: Henry G. Bohn, 1853).

5 The ensoulment of animals—or at least, of some animals—would be more than a little problematic, especially if in a shared afterlife we encounter Bossie, whose body we ate during our mortal existence, and at the end of her's.

6 Jean-Paul Sartre, *Existentialism is a Humanism*, trans. Carol Macomber (New Haven, CT: Yale University Press, 2007).

7 So has the Christian soul; we'll get to that in Chapter 8.

8 Perhaps the present book should have been titled *Arsenic for the Soul*.

9 Radek Trnka and Radmila Lorencova, "Indigenous Concepts of Consciousness, Soul, and Spirit: A Cross-Cultural Perspective," *Journal of Consciousness Studies* 29, no. 1–2: 113–40.

10 "Indigenous concepts," ibid.

11 L. D. Arnett, *The Soul: A Study of Past and Present Beliefs* (Champaign, IL: University of Illinois Press, 1904).

12 "Funerary Monument Reveals Iron Age Belief That the Soul Lived in the Stone," *UChicago News*, 2008, https://news.uchicago.edu/story/funerary-monument-reveals-iron-age-belief-soul-lived-stone.

Chapter 3

1 Thomas Hobbes, *Leviathan* (London, 1651; Project Gutenberg, May 1, 2002), 6, https://www.gutenberg.org/cache/epub/3207/pg3207-images.html#link2HCH0006.

2 Word has it that some wag once wrote on a wall, somewhere, "God is dead"— Nietzsche, followed by "Nietzsche is dead"—God.

3 Sigmund Freud, *The Future of an Illusion* (New York: W.W. Norton, 1989).

4 Ibid.

5 Miguel de Unamuno, *Tragic Sense of Life*, trans. J. E. Crawford Flitch (New York: Dover Publications, 1954).

6   Ernest Becker, *The Denial of Death* (New York: Free Press, 1997).

7   Thomas Browne, "Urne Burial." published in 1658 (New York:, New Directions, 2010).

8   *The Dhammapada*, trans. Ananda Maitreya (Berkeley, CA: Parallax Press, 2001).

9   If so, then there must be many inconvenienced souls these days, because widespread administration of the anti-inflammatory drug diclofenac to cattle resulted in Indian and Nepali vultures eating dead cows and then dying in vast numbers. Fortunately, the drug has been banned, and the vultures have been slowly repopulating. Researchers have found that the vulture die-off resulted in an increase in human mortality, attributed to an epidemic of disease transmitted to humans from unconsumed carrion. Or maybe it's the revenge of angry souls deprived of their liberation because the vulture apocalypse prevented so many sky burials.

10 George Santayanna, *The Life of Reason* (New York: Charles Scribner's Sons, 1954).

11 In her book *Playing Possum: How Animals Understand Death* (Princeton, NJ: Princeton University Press, 2024), philosopher Susana Monsó makes a strong case that some animals have a concept of death, although it seems unlikely that even chimpanzees and elephants believe they have a soul.

12 Elias Canetti, *The Book Against Death*, trans. Peter Filkins (New York: New Directions, 2024).

13 Woody Allen, *On Being Funny* (New York: Charterhouse, 1975).

14 Erik Trinkaus, Alexandra Buzhilova, Maria Mednikova, and Marvia Dobrovolskaya, *The People of Sunghir: Burials, Bodies, and Behavior in the Early Upper Paleolithic* (Oxford: Oxford University Press, 2014).

15 Julien Musolino, *The Soul Fallacy: What Science Shows We Gain from Letting Go of Our Soul Beliefs* (Amherst, NY: Prometheus Books, 2015).

16 Bertrand Russell, *Why I Am Not a Christian* (New York: Simon & Schuster, 1957).

17 Michael Shermer, *Heavens on Earth: The Scientific Search for the Afterlife, Immortality, and Utopia* (New York: St. Martin's Griffin, 2019).

18 Michael Shermer, *Heavens on Earth* (New York: Robinson, 2018).

19 Except in Goethe's version in which, rather unexpectedly, he is redeemed at the last moment by God and the "eternal feminine."

20 Ludwig Feuerbach, 1890, quoted in *The Fiery Brook: Selected Writings, Radical Thinkers* (New York: Verso, 2013).

21 von Wernsdorff, M., Loef, M., Tuschen-Caffier, B., and Stefan Schmidt, "Effects of Open-Label Placebos in Clinical Trials: A Systematic Review and Meta-analysis," *Scientific Reports* 11 (2021): 3855. https://doi.org/10.1038/s41598-021-83148-6

22 Leon Festinger, Henry Riecken, and Stanley Schachter, *When Prophecy Fails* (Mansfield Centre, CT: Martino Publishing, 2009).

Chapter 4

1 Laurie Goldstein, "Falwell: Blame Abortionists, Feminists and Gays," *The Guardian*, September 19, 2001. https://www.theguardian.com/world/2001/sep/19/september11.usa9.

2 Eugene Scott, "A White House Faith Adviser Is under Fire for Appearing to Suggest Coronavirus Is Due to God's Wrath over Homosexuality, Environmentalism," *The Washington Post*, March 27, 2020. https://www.washingtonpost.com/politics/2020/03/27/top-white-house-faith-adviser-is-under-fire-suggesting-that-coronavirus-is-due-gods-wrath-over-homosexuality-environmentalism/.

3 Travis Mitchell, "2. Views on the Afterlife," *Pew Research Center* (blog), November 23, 2021. https://www.pewresearch.org/religion/2021/11/23/views-on-the-afterlife/.

4 "Do You Believe in God, Angels, Heaven, Hell or The Devil?" *Statista*, June 2016. https://www.statista.com/statistics/245496/belief-of-americans-in-god-heaven-and-hell/#:~:text=As%20of%202011%2C%20about%2075%20percent%20of%20respondents%20believed%20in%20hell.

5 Shariff, A. F., and M. Rhemtulla, "Divergent Effects of Beliefs in Heaven and Hell on National Crime Rates," *PloS one* 7, no. 6 (2012): e39048.

6 Shariff, A. F., and L. B. Aknin, "The Emotional Toll of Hell: Cross-national and Experimental Evidence for the Negative Well-being Effects of Hell Beliefs," *PLoS One* 9, no. 1 (2014): e85251.

7 Holbach wasn't the first to point this out. Among the ancient Greeks and Romans, Epicurus and Lucretius expressed similar views when they dissented from reigning visions of the afterlife, but these "pagan" perspectives weren't nearly as gruesome as those concocted by subsequent followers of Jesus.

8 Baron d'Holbach, *The System of Nature* (Calgary: Theophrania Publishing, 2011).

9 Ara Norenzayan, *Big Gods: How Religion Transformed Cooperation and Conflict* (Princeton NJ: Princeton University Press, 2015).

10 Voltaire, *A Pocket Philosophical Dictionary* (New York: Oxford University Press, 2011).

11 Not all of Voltaire's pronouncements in his Philosophical Dictionary were optimistic, although all are challenging. Consider this: "What can you say to a man who tells you he prefers obeying God rather than men, and that as a result he's certain he'll go to heaven if he cuts your throat?"

12 To me, this sounds more like hell.

13 Stephen Greenblatt, "Damn it All," *The New York Review of Books*, December 20, 2018, https://www.nybooks.com/articles/2018/12/20/damn-it-all-book-of-hell/

14 Quoted in Scott G. Bruce, ed., *The Penguin Book of Hell* (New York: Penguin Classics, 2018).

15 Must one be an atheist to ask what kind of God, allegedly love incarnate, would demand *eternal* torture for anybody, no matter how egregious their earthly misbehavior? How and why does eternal love translate into eternal anger? Barrels of ink, and, these days, oodles of electrons have been spilled attempting to answer the related dilemma of theodicy (why a good and all-powerful God permits terribly bad things to happen in this life; e.g., the Holocaust, thousands of people dying in tsunamis, earthquakes, and the like). Almost as much effort has attended the question of why a good and loving God might order the torments of hell. Many anguished souls still await an answer—to both questions.

16 Although the word "Malebranche" sounds singular, it refers to plural claws, as in "the Malebranche are."

17 As it happened, he made a mistake in calculating that thickness, because having determined its span, he simply scaled up his estimates from the most famous dome existing in Florence at the time. But, as Galileo later realized, to maintain adequate strength, the thickness of a supporting structure must increase more rapidly than simple linear extrapolation from its width: the thickness cubed divided by the span squared must stay constant. Galileo's square-cube law is still used by structural engineers today, so regardless of whether he got hell right, he at least obtained one hell of a useful result.

18 In Joyce's telling, young Stephen—who had recently lost his virginity to a prostitute—is utterly mortified, horrified, guilt-ridden, and grief-stricken by this vision of his future punishment, which induces him to connect all the more strongly with the church, for a time.

19 Robert Burton, *Anatomy of Melancholy* (New York: Penguin Classics, 2023).

Chapter 5

1 It's worth noting that during his twenty-seven-year imprisonment in South Africa, Nelson Mandela recited "Invictus" to himself and others, reporting later that he derived strength from it.

2 The title of Stephen Jay Gould's book, *Wonderful Life*, is homage to the movie, although its message is quite different. *Wonderful Life* describes the wild profusion of living things during the Cambrian, a period of extreme phylogenetic diversity. It emphasizes the importance of historical contingency, concluding that if the videotape of evolution were rewound, human beings almost certainly would not appear again. We may seem special—to ourselves—but in the great scheme of evolution, we're not.

3   Bertrand Russell, *An Outline of Intellectual Rubbish* (London: Haldeman-Julius Publications, 1943).

4   Readers might enjoy the delightful song "Golden Helmet of Mambrino"—https://www.youtube.com/watch?v=eQ8iZu-BAVM—from the musical "Man of La Mancha."

5   Fearing retribution, not so much divinely instigated but at the violent hands of church and state, most early modern unbelievers kept mum. One of the most notable—and someone regrettably unrecognized even today—was Jean Meslier (1664–1729), a French Catholic priest who confided his thoughts to a personal testament, suitably titled *Testament*, which was only discovered posthumously. This appears to have been Meslier's intent, because in it he dangerously denounced religion, including any doctrine involving an immaterial and immortal soul. Meslier also opposed killing animals, although he evidently had some violent inclinations, wishing that "all the great men in the world and all the nobility could be hanged, and strangled with the guts of the priests." In this regard, he presaged Diderot's famous pre-French Revolution pronouncement. Meslier deserves to be reincarnated today, in reputation if not his soul.

6   In the twenty-first century, fundamentalist Christians make archeological pilgrimages to Mount Ararat, in Turkey, looking for signs of that boat (as yet undiscovered), and to special creation theme parks such as Ark Encounter in Williamstown, Kentucky, which, according to its website, Features a full-size Noah's Ark, built according to the dimensions given in the Bible. Spanning 510 feet long, 85 feet wide, and 51 feet high, this modern engineering marvel amazes visitors young and old." In addition, "You'll learn how Noah might have cared for all the animals and how the Ark was big enough to fit them all on board."

7   Michael Shermer, *Heavens on Earth* (New York: Henry Holt Co., 2018).

8   Andre Malraux, *The Walnut Trees of Altenburg* (Chicago: University of Chicago Press, 1992).

Chapter 6

1   Paul Bloom, *Descartes' Baby: How the Science of Child Development Helps Explain What Makes Us Human* (New York: Basic Books, 2005).

2   Something similar takes place in other domains as well, when a kind of intuitive common sense trumps reality. For example, we refer to "sunrise" despite knowing full well that the sun doesn't actually do so.

3   Paul M. Churchland, *Matter and Consciousness* (Cambridge: MIT Press, 2013).

4   Julien Musolino, *The Soul Fallacy: What Science Shows We Gain from Letting Go of Our Soul Beliefs* (Amherst, NY: Prometheus Books, 2015).

5   Mark Lilla, *Ignorance and Bliss: On Wanting Not to Know* (New York: Farrar, Straus and Giroux, 2024).

6   Pope John Paul II, *Address to the Plenary Session on "The Origins and Early Evolution of Life"* (Vatican City: The Pontifical Academy of Sciences, 1996).

7   Gilbert Ryle, *The Concept of Mind* (Cambridge: MIT Press, 2000).

8   Wolfgang Giegerich, *What Is Soul?* (London: Routledge, 2020).

9   How it would have come to dominate this realm, and even create it, is another question.

10 See Robert Sapolsky's book, *Determined*, for a magisterial demolition of free will.

11 Robert M. Sapolsky, *Determined: A Science of Life without Free Will* (New York: Penguin Press, 2023).

12 Daniel C. Dennett, *Consciousness Explained* (New York: Back Bay Books/Little Brown and Co, 1992).

13 He is known for the Pauli Exclusion Principle, which states that no two electrons in the same atom can have the same quantum values. Embracing the supernatural produces another kind of exclusion: excluding rational thought.

14 I've tried, unsuccessfully, to corroborate this story, which in some versions places the horseshoe above the desk in Bohr's office, while others deny it altogether. No matter. In this case, the story is the point.

15 Phlogiston was a substance believed to be contained within flammable material, which, when sufficiently heated, was responsible for fire. In ancient times, it "explained" fire by invoking a word. Sounds familiar?

16 Quoted in Kate E. Tunstall, *Blindness and Enlightenment. An Essay, with a New Translation of Diderot's Letter on the Blind* (London: Continuum, 2011).

17 Diderot's observation can be flipped on its head, resulting in something more optimistic. When science solves a mystery (as distinct from theology refusing to solve it and invoking the supernatural instead), science unearths yet more mysteries, many of which are even more interesting than the original one.

18 Is it possible that souls, with all their spotless immaterial perfection, also feel let down, given that they are encased in yucky material bodies? Maybe this explains why near-death experiences (see Chapter 7) invariably describe the near-dying person's soul leaving their body and flying around, if the soul perceives the body's *extremis* as presaging forthcoming liberation from its fleshly prison, in which case the fact that these people don't die might be a big disappointment for their souls: "Damn, back I gotta go—at least for a little while!"

19 Michael Shermer, *Heavens on Earth* (London: Robinson, 2018).

20 Ambrose Bierce revised Descartes's Dictum as follows: "I think I think, therefore I think I am," noting that this is the closest any philosopher has ever come to articulating truth.

21 Francis Crick, *The Astonishing Hypoothesis: the scientific search for the soul* (New York: Scribner, 1994).

22 This is a lovely example of something that is "not even wrong," but is delightful rather than destructive. Further delight, and suitable confusion, comes from the subsequent revelation that the real question was, "What do you get when you multiply 6 by 9"—for which the answer isn't 42, but 54.

23 Reading a draft of this chapter, a colleague (alas, I lost track of who) commented at this point:

> this seems like a realm in which scientists are like superstitious peasants—believing in things that are too little to be seen, in things like continental drift moving too slowly to be perceived as such, to think about things inconceivably long in the Big Bang-ish past or death-of-the-sun future. The obvious difference, of course, is it's not superstition if it's falsifiable and you're interested in seeing if it is.

24 Antonio Damasio, *The Feeling of What Happens* (New York: Harcourt Brace Jovanovich, 1999).

25 Stuart Hameroff, and Roger Penrose, "Consciousness in the Universe," *Physics of Life Reviews* 11, no. 1 (2014): 39–78. https://doi.org/10.1016/j.plrev.2013.08.002

26 If so, there's good reason to conclude that this gift was a failure, because just as scientific materialism puts the kibosh on the soul, it similarly dismisses free will.

27 Nicholas Humphrey, *Soul Dust: The Magic of Consciousness* (Princeton, NJ: Princeton University Press, 2011).

28 Gould, S. J., and R. C. Lewontin, "The Spandrels of San Marco and the Panglossian Paradigm: A Critique of the Adaptationist Programme," In *Shaping Entrepreneurship Research*, eds. Saras D. Sarasvathy, Nicholas Dew, Sankaran Venkataraman (London: Routledge, 2020).

29 A "spandrel" is originally an architectural term, referring to the structural wedge required in Renaissance architecture in order to install an arch within the right angle formed between a vertical wall and a horizontal ceiling. Although spandrels, once incorporated into a structure, are typically decorated or inscribed, they were not produced for that purpose. Gould and Lewontin proposed that many biological features are spandrels that have not been directly selected for.

30 Plato, *Five Dialogues: Euthyphro, Apology, Crito, Meno, Phaedo*, trans. John M. Cooper (New York: Hackett Publishing Co., 2002).

31 Although some consider reductionism a bête noire, the truth is that most of science's most notable advances have arrived by reducing complex issues to their smaller and thus more tractable components. Einstein said that the grand aim of all science is to cover the greatest number of empirical facts by logical deduction from the smallest possible number of hypotheses or axioms.

32 Richard Dawkins, *The God Delusion* (New York: Mariner Books, 2008).

33 John Ruskin, *Selected Writings* (Oxford: Oxford University Press, 2009).

34 Nicholas Humphrey, *Leaps of Faith: Science, Miracles, and the Search For Supernatural Consolation* (New York: Basic Books, 1996).

35 Avishai Margalit, *On Compromises and Rotten Compromises* (Cambridge: Harvard University Press, 2009).

36 William Seeger, ed., *The Routledge Handbook of Panpsychism* (London: Routledge, 2021).

37 Philip Goff, *Galileo's Error: Foundations for a New Science of Consciousness* (New York: Vintage, 2019).

38 The physicalist take on consciousness would also interpret it as an emergent quality in which combining things produces an outcome that appears qualitatively different from its component parts, although it is nonetheless derived from the interaction of those parts.

Chapter 7

1 Julien Musolino, *The Soul Fallacy: What Science Shows We Gain From Letting Go of Our Soul Beliefs* (Amherst, NY: Prometheus, 2015).

2 The axolotl is named for an ancient Aztec god, Xlotl. Maybe that explains everything.

3 See Chapter 3 for more on confirmation bias when it comes to belief in immortality.

4 Michael Shermer, *Heavens on Earth* (New York: Henry Holt, 2018).

5 Raymond A. Moody, *Life After Life* (San Francisco: Harper One, 2015).

6 Eben Alexander, *Proof of Heaven* (New York: Simon & Schuster, 2012).

7 Alex and Kevin Malarkey, *The Boy Who Came Back from Heaven: A Remarkable Account of Miracles, Angels, and Life beyond this World* (Carol Stream, IL: Tyndale House, 2010).

8 O. Blanke, S. Ortigue, T. Landis, and M. Seeck, "Neuropsychology: Stimulating Illusory Own-body Perceptions," *Nature* 419, no. 19 (2001): 269–70.

9 C. Martial, R. Carhart-Harris, and C. Timmermann, "Within-subject Comparison of Near-death and Psychedelic Experiences: Acute and Enduring Effects," *Neuroscience of Consciousness* 2024, no. 1 (2024): niae033.

10 Eben Alexander, whose grandiosely titled book, *Proof of Heaven*, which recounted his NDE as nothing less than a proof of heaven, sold a gazillion copies. Dr. Alexander, as he doesn't hesitate to point out, is a neurosurgeon. I would bet that if he stimulated

the brain of a conscious surgical patient, who reported the sensation of floating, flying, or entering a new realm of consciousness as a result, Dr. Alexander would attribute these perceptions to what was happening in the patient's brain, rather than their soul having suddenly been electrically inspired to take a quick out-of-body excursion. And yet, when recounting his own experience, Dr. Alexander is adamant that it "really happened." Such is the power of personal experience, especially when coupled with promoting a best-selling book.

11 The counter-culture rock band, "The Doors," was named in honor of Huxley's book. Huxley, in turn, had derived the phrase from William Blake's *The Marriage of Heaven and Hell*: "If the doors of perception were cleansed, every thing would appear to man as it is, Infinite. For man has closed himself up, till he sees all things thro' narrow chinks of his cavern."

12 For a good laugh, listen to the Monty Python song, "Every Sperm is Sacred."

14 In some versions of Christianity, notably Calvinism, a soul—even of a newborn and presumably a "preborn" as well—is far from spotless. Rather, it is debased by virtue of humanity's original sin.

Chapter 8

1 This has been variously interpreted as Laplace meaning that he didn't need God in a narrow sense as part of his mathematical astronomy model or more generally that he didn't need God at all, period. I don't know if Laplace wrote about the soul.

2 The Stones added that "But if you try sometime, you'll find/ You get what you need," something that, sadly, is also less than certain.

3 By "awful," Keats didn't mean terrible, but deserving of awe.

4 My musically sophisticated friends tell me that it increases both their appreciation and their enjoyment.

5 Richard Feynman, *Feynman Lectures on Physics* (New York: Basic Books, 2011).

6 Richard Dawkins, *Unweaving the Rainbow: Science, Delusion and the Appetite for Wonder* (New York: Mariner Books, 2000).

7 Charles Darwin, *On the Origin of Species by Means of Natural Selection,* 150th anniversary ed. (New York: Signet, 2003).

8 Paul Bloom, "Natural-born Dualists," *Edge: The Third Culture*, May 11, 2004, https://www.edge.org/conversation/paul_bloom-natural-born-dualists

9 Richard Wrangham, *The Goodness Paradox: The Strange Relationship Between Virtue and Violence in Human Evolution* (New York: Vintage, 2019).

Notes

10 Hanno Sauer, *The Invention of Good and Evil: A World History of Morality* (New York: Oxford University Press, 2024).

11 Bertrand Russell, *Why I Am Not a Christian* (New York: Simon & Schuster, 1957).

12 David Livingstone Smith, *Making Monsters: The Uncanny Power of Dehumanization* (Cambridge: Harvard University Press, 2021).

13 W. E. B. De Bois, *The Souls of Black Folks* (New York: Penguin, 1903).

14 Steven Pinker, *The Better Angels of Our Nature: Why Violence Has Declined* (New York: Penguin Books, 2012).

15 Steven Pinker, *Enlightenment Now* (New York: Penguin Books, 2018).

16 *Gilgamesh: A New English Version*, trans. Stephen Mitchell (New York: Washington Square Press, 2006).

17 Albert Camus, *Summer in Algiers* (New York: Penguin Press, 2005).

18 Sigmund Freud, *Civilization and its Discontents* (New York: W. W. Norton, 2021).

19 Neil deGrasse Tyson, "The Perimeter of Ignorance," *Natural History Magazine*, November 2005, https://neildegrassetyson.com/essays/2005-11-the-perimeter-of-ignorance/

20 Richard Dawkins, *Science in the Soul* (New York: Bantom Books, 2005).

21 Frank Kermode, *The Sense of an Ending: Studies in the Theory of fiction* (London: Oxford University Press, 1968).

22 It remains to be seen whether this will continue, given the depredations occurring under the know-nothing second Trump administration.

23 Sadly, as with the uncertain future of US science supremacy, it is also uncertain whether religious tolerance will continue to be a hallmark of the United States, given the Christian nationalism promoted by the second Trump administration.

24 Arthur Koestler, *The Sleepwalkers: A History of Man's Changing Vision of the Universe* (London: Penguin, 1968).

25 Julien Musolino, *The Soul Fallacy: What Science Shows We Gain from Letting Go of Our Soul Beliefs* (Amherst, NY: Prometheus Books, 2015).

26 Quoted in Chris Mooney, "Darwin's Sanitized Idea," *Slate*, September 24, 2001, https://slate.com/culture/2001/09/darwin-s-sanitized-idea.html

27 Did he really think that God would be fooled into letting someone into heaven if that person's belief was merely predicated on their bet that it was the best way of getting in? We'll never know.

28 Richard Dawkins has introduced a type 3 error, to which most of us, even the statistically literate, are prone: forgetting which is which!

29 William James, *The Principles of Psychology* (New York: Dover Editions, 1950).

30 Of course, you'd be stuck with God, too.

31 Peter Singer, *Expanding the Circle: Ethics, Evolution and Moral Progress* (Princeton, NJ: Princeton University Press, 2011).

32 David P. Barash, "It's Time to Make Human-Chimp Hybrids" *Nautilus*, March 5, 2018, https://nautil.us/its-time-to-make-human_chimp-hybrids-237003/

33 Frans de Waal, *Are We Smart Enough to Know How Smart Animals Are?* (New York: W. W. Norton, 2016).

34 Different kinds of souls for different kinds of critters? Perhaps busy souls for bees and lazy ones for three-toed sloths, ferocious souls (now blessedly extinct) for *T. rex*, and kindly ones for my golden retriever.

35 Jacques Monod, *Chance and Necessity: Essay on the Natural Philosophy of Modern Biology* (London: Fontana, 1974).

36 Julien Musolino, *The Soul Fallacy: What Science Shows We Gain from Letting Go of Our Soul Beliefs* (Amherst, NY: Prometheus Books, 2015).

37 Camus maintained that he wasn't an existentialist, a claim that didn't fool anyone.

38 Bertrand Russell, *Why Men Fight* (New York: The Century Company, 1920).

39 Irrelevant fact about Mr. Brahe: The bridge of his nose had been sliced off in a duel with his cousin, precipitated by a dispute over a mathematical formula. As a result, he had three prostheses—gold, silver, and brass, which he wore depending on the social occasion. Brahe's prosthetic model of the solar system, however, turned out to be less useful.

40 Lewis Mumford, *The Myth of the Machine* (New York: Harcourt, 1967).

41 Coincidentally, perhaps, this is the same logic-based equation that George Orwell's Winston Smith kept insisting was true while Big Brother's torture henchman kept demanding that he accept that the answer was 5.

42 Historians have argued, by the way, that not all contemporary theologians and philosophers felt that the center of the universe was such a good place to be. Thus, the physical middle of the Earth was widely considered to be the abode of hell and the center of the universe, not much better. Also noteworthy is that church authorities initially greeted the Copernican system (published in 1543) with indifference. It was only about a half-century later that its troublesome implications were seriously considered, just in time for the church to persecute Galileo.

Bibliography (Actually, Suggested Further Reading)

The God Delusion is above all a trade book, so I've limited academic references and am doing something similar here, focusing just on some of the books I've used and that I think nonspecialists might value and enjoy.

Chapter 1 "Grappling with the Grin"

For the Cheshire Cat's grin (which came close to being this book's title), see Lewis Carroll's *Alice in Wonderland*, always worth reading and not just aloud to children. It provides many examples of make-believe situations and characters, all of them more fun and more believable than silly soul-stuff. Richard Dawkins's *The God Delusion* does a superb job of demolishing God, while also inspiring the title of the present book. For another very effective attack on theism, I recommend Christopher Hitchens's *God is not Great*, along with Sam Harris's *The End of Faith* and Daniel Dennett's *Breaking the Spell*. These four books initiated what became known as the new atheism, and although none of them deal especially with the soul, that fiction lurks behind each. I haven't written previously about soul-stuff, but it can be found behind some of my books as well, notably *Through a Glass Brightly: Using Science to See Our Species as We Really Are*.

Chapter 2 "What Is It?"

For a detailed, scholarly, yet accessible treatment of the history of the soul, and especially its use and abuse with regard to mental illness, see George

Makari's *The Soul Machine*. Kocku van Stuckrad's *A Cultural History of the Soul*, provides just that: a review of how the concept of the soul has manifested in popular culture, especially in Europe and the United States. For a claim that the soul is more important in Judaism than I have suggested, see Elie Kaplan Spitz's *Does the Soul Survive?* In *The Soul's Longing*, Mary Ford takes the reader back to early Christian soul doctrine, comparing it with more recent perspectives. Mehmet Kulic's *The Sense of Soul in Islam* reviews, well, the sense of soul in Islam. For a refreshing view of Hindu soul-thought, and how it can be made more socially progressive, I happily recommend Bhimrao Ambedkar's *Riddle in Hinduism*. And for the soul in Buddhism, I hope I'll be forgiven for suggesting my own *Buddhist Biology: Ancient Eastern Wisdom Meets Modern Western Science*.

Chapter 3 "Escaping Death: The Cosmic Carrot"

Tons of ink have been expended (and these days, electrons hijacked) providing book-length treatments dealing with fear of death and hopes for heaven. For a near-poetic treatment of how death anxiety is reflected in day-to-day psychology, I recommend Ernest Becker's *The Denial of Death*. Among the myriad volumes seeking to reassure Christians that they won't "really" die, a reasonable example is found in Clay Jones's *Immortal*, with which I wholeheartedly disagree, although I understand that many believers have found it and comparable efforts reassuring. Less than reassuring, for those of us with a rational, scientific mind, but downright entertaining and far more accurate, is *Spook: Science Tackles the Afterlife*, by Mary Roach, in which the author tackles the question of "life" after death and thus, indirectly, the soul. Although ostensibly an objective investigation, *Spook* is highly critical—not so much of the supposed existence of the soul (although that, too, by implication), but of those mountebanks who have bilked a gullible public by claiming to provide evidence for an afterlife. It's an often-hilarious first-person account of Ms. Roach's investigation into the zany, infuriating world of liars and frauds. I can't recommend it strongly enough! A reviewer of Elias Canetti's *The Book Against Death* wrote that "Every page is alive with animus, ardor, humor, sufferance, with venom for death and its posturing acolytes." The best treatment of heavenly mythology is Michael Shermer's *Heavens on Earth* (suitably plural, because there are so many different takes on the longed-for afterlife). If you're intrigued by placebos—and why not?—a good review is Jeremy Howick's *The Power of Placebos*.

Chapter 4 "The Cosmic Stick: Hell"

As with heaven, there are bookshelves dealing with hell, most of it Christian apologetics and—IMHO—forgettable. If you must pursue this, in *Four Views on Hell*, Christian scholars J. Walvoord, W. Crockett, C. Pinnock, and Z. Hayes do a credible job of presenting four different Christian perspectives. Although Ari Norenzayan's *Big Gods* doesn't deal directly with details of hell, it is a marvelous and readable work of scholarship, ranging through anthropology and history to reveal how "big gods"—notably including threats of postmortem punishment—have provided a mechanism of social control. Miriam Van Scott's survey, *The Encyclopedia of Hell*, covers an immense cross-cultural field, and does so with scholarship along with surprising flashes of humor. Similarly, Bart Ehrman's *Heaven and Hell* shouldn't be missed by anyone looking for a scholarly, critical, and yet tolerant account by a highly regarded and prolific scholar who is also a serious Christian skeptic. Eight hundred years after its publication, Dante's *The Divine Comedy* remains the most notable Christian version of hell; I especially like the Clive James translation. Read James Joyce's *A Portrait of the Artist as a Young Man* for more on the hellish indoctrination of young Mr. Joyce, including more of the horrifying kinetic sermon than I was able to include in the current book.

Chapter 5 "The Golden Helmet of Centrality"

Alas, I'm not aware of any books (aside from my own *Through a Glass Brightly*) that deal explicitly with this issue. In writing this chapter, I pulled together a variety of otherwise disparate sources. For an account of the Copernican Revolution, I'd recommend *Heaven on Earth: How Copernicus, Brahe, Kepler, and Galileo Discovered the Modern World*, by L. S. Fauber, and for the impact of the Darwinian Revolution, go past my fondness for alliteration and do dive into Daniel Dennett's *Darwin's Dangerous Idea*.

Chapter 6 "Dueling with Dualism"

For some suggestions on how children in particular tend to be intuitive dualists, see Paul Bloom's *Descartes' Baby*. Paul Churchland's *Matter and Consciousness* provides a solid overview of mind-out-of-matter, showing how key ideas in cognitive psychology, neurobiology, and philosophy support a scientific materialist perspective. Similarly, and more combatively, Julien Musolino's *The Soul Fallacy* argues persuasively against the myth of the human soul generally (it's among my very favorite anti-soul writings); Musolino is especially devastating about the fallacy of dualism. There have been many—far too many—books alleging to "prove" dualism, nearly all with an unacknowledged religious underpinning. If you feel that you need a religious, pro-dualist view of dualism (and frankly, I don't see why you would), you might try Charles Siegel's *A Skeptic's Faith: Why Scientific Materialism Cannot Be the Whole Truth*. Disavowal: Not only can it be, but it is. There are an extraordinary number of similarities between belief in the soul and in free will, as both the soul and free will rely on a kind of dualist nonsense, even while both are supported by many people who unthinkingly believe in both and feel that they'd be devastated if neither is true. I'm too close to the present book to assess how successful, if at all, I've been in critiquing the former, but I'm confident that in his magisterial *Determined*, Robert Sapolsky has demolished the latter. Unfortunately, dualists often discount science, preferring to bury their heads in the sands of, well, dualism. For a clear account of science and how it works, see Gordon Holman's *The Scientific Method*, suitably subtitled *Why Science Is a Crucial Process for Human Progress, Not Just Another Academic Subject or Belief*. To appreciate the foolishness of dualism it helps to have a basic grasp of neurobiology for which a solid introduction is *Principles of Neural Science*, by Nobelist Eric Kandel and three others; granted it's a textbook, but a really, really good one! And for a popularized accessible look at the neurobiology of consciousness, amid an avalanche of such books, even decades after its publication you can't do better than Francis Crick's *The Astonishing Hypothesis*. For a pithy intro to mysterianism, I suggest Colin McGinn's *Philosophical Provocations*. And for an exciting tour of what we don't yet know, and how the answers lie in science rather than superstition (i.e., supernaturalism, spiritualism, soul-embracing silliness, etc.), go balance delightedly on astrophysicist Lawrence Kraus's *The Edge of Knowledge: Unsolved Mysteries of the Cosmos*. Although I'm convinced that panpsychism doesn't deserve any more credence than does dualism, you'll find a serious account of this latest absurdity in Philip Goff's *Galileo's Error*, subtitled *Foundations for a New Science of Consciousness*, although it should have been "ways to avoid dealing with the hard problem of consciousness."

Chapter 7 "Purported Proofs and Practical Problems"

Several books that I highly recommended earlier—notably Michael Shermer's *Heavens on Earth* and Julien Musolino's *The Soul Fallacy*—are also pivotal in critiquing the notably nonsensical notion of near-death experiences. Social psychologists Carol Tavris and Eliot Aronson demystify why we stubbornly insist on this and other foolish notions, notably buttressed by confirmation bias, in *Mistakes Were Made (but not by me)*. Perhaps reflecting my own confirmation bias, I stubbornly refuse to recommend any of the many books that allege NDEs and how they "prove" the existence of the soul. Regrettably, I don't know any truly layperson-friendly accounts of the early stages of human embryonic development. I've been happy with Bruce Carlson's *Human Embryology and Developmental Biology*, and I defy anyone who reads this illustratively vivid, medically accurate account to identify at what point ensoulment takes place.

Chapter 8 "Soul-Free!"

In *Unweaving the Rainbow*, the redoubtable Richard Dawkins demolishes the Keatsian delusion that science precludes wonder. For Richard Feynman on the pleasure of finding things out, I suggest the essays of Richard Feynman, titled (what else?) *The Pleasure of Finding Things Out*. Michael Shermer's massive yet thoroughly readable opus, *The Moral Arc*, takes the reader through history, philosophy, and especially science to show how morality derives from science and certainly doesn't require religious dogma. Hanno Sauer's *The Invention of Good and Evil* provides, as the subtitle promises, *A Global History of Morality*, showing that cross-culturally, and regardless of great religious diversity, people's morality is substantially consistent. Steven Pinker's *The Better Angels of our Nature* celebrates the shift from saving souls to saving lives, even as two other masterpiece Pinker productions, *Enlightenment Now* and *Rationality* showcase the virtues and benefits of rational thinking over superstition, and truth over falsehood.

Index

Adams, Douglas 117
African Americans, soul tradition of 165–6
agnostic 187
Albigensian Crusade 165
Allen, Woody 33, 37
Ammit 57–8
amputees, does god hate 136–7
Apocalypse of Paul 61
apsychists (apsychism) 7
Aquinas, Thomas (Saint) 16
Aristotle 16, 59
Ark Encounter 192
Armstrong, Louis 68
atheism (soft and hard) 7
Auden, W. H. 187
Augustine of Hippo (Saint) 15, 36

Baba, Meyer 48
Bacon, Francis 44
balance sheet, for belief in the soul 168–9
Becker, Ernest 27–8
Bierce, Ambrose 193
"Big Gods" hypothesis 55
Bishop of Worcester, wife of the 126
Bisson, Terry 101–2
Blanc, Mel 40
Bloom, Paul 93, 95, 160
Bloy, Leon 52
Bohr, Nils 110
Bosch, Hieronymus 65

Boyle, Robert 14, 110
Brahe, Tycho 182–3
brain
    damage to 34, 107
    limitations of 118–9
    stimulation of 115–6, 144
Browne, Thomas 28
Bruno, Giordano 80
Buddhism
    view of hell 58
    view of the soul 19–20
Bunyan, John 38
Burton, Robert 71

Calivn, John 16, 38
Camus, Albert 87, 168, 180–1
Canetti, Elias 33
categorical imperative 163
cause and effect 106, 113, 179–80
Chalmers, David 117
Cherokee, view of the soul 21
Christianity
    animal souls, doctrine of 15
    contemporary belief in heaven and hell 51
    diversity of soul doctrine within 14
    view of the soul 12–3
Churchland, Paul 95–6
Clarke, Arthur C. 124
cloning 151–2
Cogito, ergo sum 116
Cohen, Leonard 85

"combination problem"   130–1
Conan Doyle, Arthur   135
confirmation bias   44–5, 138
Conrad, Joseph   6
Copernican Revolution   81, 85, 120, 185
Corinthians, Book of   40
Council of Trent   63
Counter-Reformation   63
Crick, Francis   116–7

Damasio, Antonio   118
Darwin, Charles   82, 159
Darwinian Revolution   81, 120–1, 185
Dawkins, Richard   125, 158, 170
death of the soul?   170–1
DeLay, Tom   176
delusion   8
Democritus   13
Dennett, Daniel   107
Descartes, Rene   15, 98–9, 112, 114, 117, 160, 178–9
Dhammapada   29
Dickinson, Emily   167
diclofenac   189
Diderot, Denis   112
Don Quixote   79
Donne, John   32
Doors, The   196
Drollinger, Ralph   50
Du Bois, W. E. B.   166
Dumbo's feather   175
Dunning-Kruger Effect   75
Durkheim, Emile   125

Ecclesiastes   5, 41
Edwards, Jonathan   69
Egyptians, ancient
    view of hell   57
    view of the soul   18
Einsteinian revolution   120
"élan vitale"   170
Eliot, George   8, 75
Eliot, T. S.   4
Elisabeth, Princess of Bohemia   112, 114
ensoulment   147–53, 179

Epicurus   13, 42
Ethnocentric views of heaven   37
euthanasia   179
"Every Sperm is Sacred"   196
Evolution, challenge to the soul via   106, 176–8

Falwell, Jerry   50
Faust   39, 184
Feuerbach, Ludwig   43
Feynman, Richard   157–8
first-person fallacy   96
free will   105
Freud, Sigmund
    Civilization and its Discontents   169
    The Future of an Illusion   26–7, 42, 70
funerary rituals   33

Gage, Phineas   107
Galileo   67–8, 82, 156–7, 182–3
Gandhi   18
Genesis, Book of   107
Giegerich, Wolfgang   103
Gilgamesh   27, 168
God of the Gaps   124–5, 128, 164
Goff, Philip   130
Gollum   86
Gould, Stephen Jay   122
Greeks, ancient
    view of hell   56–7
    view of the soul   18
Greenblat, Stephen   61

Hameroff, Stuart   119
hard problem of consciousness   121, 123
Hardy, Thomas   137–8
harrowing of hell   62–3
Harvey, William   14, 110
Hays, Warren   5
Hegel, Georg F.   74
Hell Houses   70
Heller, Joseph   126
Henley, William Ernest   73, 91
Hill, Joe   54
Hindu, view of the soul   18–9

Hitchens, Christopher   37
HM   116
Hobbes, Thomas   13, 25
Holbach, Baron d',   53
Hume, David   135, 138–9
Humphrey, Nicholas   122, 126
Huss, Jan   80
Huxley, Aldous   145
Huxley, Thomas   187

identical (monozygotic) twins   152–3
indulgences, sale of   63
Inferno (Dante)   51, 64–7
Inuit, view of the soul   20
"Invictus,"   73
Islam
    view of hell   61
    view of the soul   12–3, 17
It's a Wonderful Life   74–5

Jains, view of the soul   18
Job, Book of   153
John, Book of   30, 40, 184
Johnson, Samuel   32, 128
Joyce, James   70
Judaism
    view of hell   48, 59
    view of the soul   11–2
Jung, Carl   8

Kant, Immanuel   109–10, 163
Karamazov, Ivan (moral claim)   161
karma   18, 46, 59–60
Keats, John   156–9
Kepler, Johannes   110, 121
Kermode, Frank   171
King, Martin Luther Jr.   186
Kipling, Rudyard   178
Koestler, Arthur   174

Laplace, Pierre-Simon   155
Larkin, Philip   32
Leibniz, Gottfried   49, 100–2, 112, 117, 129
Lewontin, Richard   122

Lilla, Mark   97
limbo   147
Locke, John   14, 182
loss aversion   175
Lucretius   13, 42
Luke, Boof of   61
Luther, Martin   16, 63

Maat, feather of   57
MacDougall, Duncan   133–4
Maimonides, Moses   11
make-believe   90–1
Malraux, Andre   88
Mambrino, Golden Helmet of   79
Mandela, Nelson   191
Mann, Thomas   27
Margalit, Avishai   127
Mark, Book of   61
Marx, Groucho   25
Marx, Karl   53–4, 171
Matthew, Book of   59
Men in Black   111–2
Meslier, Jean   192
Millay, Edna St. Vincent   32
Milton, John   142, 156
miracles   135–9
"missing links"   111
Mohammed   66
Monod, Jacques   180
Montaigne, Michel de   79
Moore, Marianne   5
morality, natural sources of   162–4
Morgan, Augustus de   112
motivated perception   78–9
Mumford, Lewis   183
Musolino, Julien   34, 96, 133–4, 146, 174–5, 181
mysterianism   119

Napoleon   74
near-death experiences (NDEs)   140–6
negative capability   158–9, 169
Nesse, Randy   68
Newton, Isaac   14, 110
Nietzsche, Friedrich   26, 125

Nighttime prayer   42
Norenzayan, Ara   55
"not even wrong"   109

Occam's Razor   10
Odysseus   180
Oliver, Mary   167–8
opiate of the people   171
Orchestrated Objective Reduction theory (Orch OR)   119
Orwell, George *(1984)*   40
Overton Window   9, 14

Palace of Culture and Science   119
panpsychism   128–31
Parkinson's Disease   136
Pascal, Blaise   86–7, 139–40, 180
Pascal's Wager   176–7
Paul, Saint   126
Pauli, Wolfgang   109
Pauli Exclusion Principle   193
Penfield, Wilder   116
Penrose, Roger   119
Philips, Emo   95
phlogiston   111
pineal gland   112
Pink Floyd   52
Pinker, Steven   167–8
Placebo   43–4
Plato   15–6, 59, 97, 185
Pope Benedict   15
Pope John Paul II   82, 99, 135–6, 173
Pope Paul VI   15
Pope Pius IX   147
"Preacher and the Slave, The"   54
Proximate causation   121
psychedelic drugs and near-death experiences   144–5
purgatory   38, 64

resurrection   135
retribution, biblical   49
Revelations, Book of   40, 41
Robertson, Pat   49–50

Ruggieri, Count   67
Ruskin, John   126
Russell, Bertrand
    China Teapot assertion   103–4
    impossibility of surviving death   35, 181
    pervasiveness of self-importance   76–7
    religion as source of cruelty   165
Ryle, Gilbert   100

Sachs, Oliver   115, 145
Sagan, Carl   68, 104, 107, 134–5
Santayana, George   30–1
Sapolsky, Robert   105–6
Sartre, Jean-Paul   16, 105
Sauer, Hanno   163
science, paradox in the US   171–3
Scott, Walter   158
Secret, The   43
Shelley, Percy Bysshe   124–5
Shermer, Michael   30, 36–7, 83–4, 115–6, 138, 143–4
Shinto, view of the soul   19
Ship of Theseus   94
Sikh, view of the soul   19
Sinners in the Hands of an Angry God   69
Sioux, view of the soul   21
smoke-alarm principle   68–9
Socrates   4, 59, 123
spandrel   122
spontaneous abortions   151
"spooky action at a distance"   114
Stele, (containing Kuttamuwa's sou)   21, 22
Stevens, Wallace   90
Stewart, Potter   23
stupefacients   5–6
Sun Also Rises, The   83

Tennyson, Alfred   108
Tertullian   62
theophany   85
Thoreau, Henry David   128

Thucydides   45
Tibetan sky burials   29
truth, importance of   181–6
tulpas   104–5
Twain, Mark   36
type 1 and type
   2 errors   176–7
type 3 error   197
Tyson, Neil deGrasse   170

Ugolino, Count   67
ultimate causation   121–2
Unamuno, Miguel de   26
Underground Man   183

Voltaire   49, 55–6

weight of the soul (supposed)   133–4
Wells, H. G.   161
Whitehead, Alfred North   15, 129, 150
Wittgenstein's beetle   142–3

xenotransplantation   94

Yeats, W. B.   31, 32

Zeno's arrow   117
zombies   159–62

About the Author

David P. Barash is an evolutionary biologist, an emeritus professor of psychology at the University of Washington, where he taught for forty-three years, and a fellow of the American Association for the Advancement of Science. He has written, co-authored, and edited more than forty books dealing with the biology of animal and human behavior and has also written and lectured extensively on "human nature" (notably atheistic naturalism), along with antiwar and particularly antinuclear topics. David has published several dozen pieces for the *Chronicle of Higher Education* and the *LA Times*, along with seven *NY Times* op-eds, and maintains a popular blog on *Psychology Today*. David lives in Goleta, California, with his wife, four cats, three dogs, and a horse. His favorite sports are hiking and birding.